PRISONER OF
PEACE

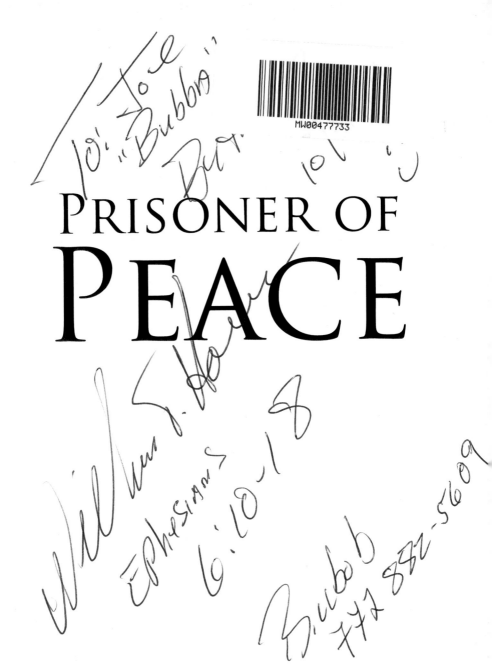

The photo on the cover is of my fighter pilot friend Lt. Col. James "Red" Clevenger standing behind his F-16. Just as he and my other fighter pilot-type friends stood behind their country for so many years, they also stood behind me in my hour of need. My intention now is to honor him and the others through him.

Lt. Col. William T. Hanson

LT. COL. WILLIAM T. HANSON

PRISONER OF
PEACE

A Story of the Abuse of Power
and Humble Justice

TATE PUBLISHING
AND ENTERPRISES, LLC

Published by Tate Publishing & Enterprises, LLC
127 E. Trade Center Terrace | Mustang, Oklahoma 73064 USA
1.888.361.9473 | www.tatepublishing.com

Tate Publishing is committed to excellence in the publishing industry. The company reflects the philosophy established by the founders, based on Psalm 68:11,
"The Lord gave the word and great was the company of those who published it."

Book design copyright © 2013 by Tate Publishing, LLC. All rights reserved.
Cover design by Lauro Talibong
Interior design by Mary Jean Archival

Published in the United States of America

ISBN: 978-1-62510-042-9
1. Biography & Autobiography / Personal Memoirs
2. Biography & Autobiography / Military
12.12.19

"Tell all the truth but tell it slant, success in circuit lies, Too bright for our infirm delight, The truth's superb surprise; As lightning to the children eased, with explanation kind, the truth must dazzle gradually, or every man be blind" (*Tell All The Truth*, Emily Dickenson).

ACKNOWLEDGEMENTS

I want to thank the Tate Publishing Company, and most especially Amber Lossen and Meghan Gregg, my editors, for their tireless efforts in making this book possible and hopefully professional. Additionally, I am deeply indebted to Professor Jay S. Hoar of the University of Maine, Farmington, for his mentoring and personal assistance in keeping my syntax, etc. in tact. He did, in fact, make two trips to South Florida from his home in Temple, Maine at his own expense, to help guide me along. I will be eternally grateful to my fellow author and dear friend, Joan P. Hopp, for her untiring help during the final stages of this book. And finally, I want to express my thanks and admiration to the folks at *Network Links, Inc.* in Port St. Lucie FL, especially Ryan and Jeff, who bailed me out on numerous occasions by keeping me from punching the wrong keys at the wrong time and possibly losing many years of work. They even made the odd house call and transferred all my work to another laptop, which they made, when my old one crashed and burned.

THE DAY WE WERE BAPTIZED

April 6, 1941
Words and music by Wm. T. Hanson
Copyright 2011

Lord, hear your people, the sheep of your flock
The day we were baptized Your spirit unlocked
A heart for the hurting, and eyes for the poor
Hands made for healing and oh so much more
The day we were baptized, we became more like You...
Washed clean by the water, Your spirit renew

chorus

To see the sheep still wounded, to see those still in pain
Give us the faith of Elijah to bring healing rain
Give us a heart for the hurting, and ears for their cries
Give us the faith of Elijah and the courage to try

16 bar instrumental

The day we were baptized we became more like You
Washed clean by the water, Your spirit renew...

repeat chorus

The day we were baptized, we became more like You
Washed clean by the water, Your spirit renew

FRONTISPIECE

I, William T. Hanson, do solemnly swear (or affirm) that I will support and defend the Constitution of the United States against all enemies, foreign and domestic, that I will bear true faith and allegiance to the same, that I take this obligation freely, without any mental reservation or purpose of evasion, and that I will well and faithfully discharge the duties of the office on which I am about to enter. So help me God.

I gave that oath to the American people, not some general bent on displaying his power or to some senator or congressman aligned with whatever cause.

DEDICATION

I dedicate this book to my fellow soldiers, especially Major General Andrew Pringle, Jr., Colonel Harold W. Kowalski, Jr., Lt. Col. Joe Anthony Buttram, Lt. Col. James "Red" Clevenger, Lt. Col. Laurel James Edwards, 1ST. LT. Anthony T. Kern, and finally, Lt. Col. Charles "Chuck" Quinn(Deceased). These soldiers (airmen) were expert at what they did, had impeccable character, and demonstrated loyalty, trust and love. I thank you for your service to our country. I was fortunate to have you by my side. Both in and out of combat you are what makes this country worth living in and fighting for. It has been said that "One can show no greater love than to lay down one's life for a friend." You were all willing to do that over the years. You were also willing to sacrifice your careers, and in many cases did, by coming to my defense against some mighty powerful people. Thank you seems so inadequate. My hope and prayer is that I can become worthy of your loyalty, trust and love. You are truly the salt of the earth. Thank you.

CONTENTS

FOREWORD

Our premise and, yes, our promise is that the reader will bear witness to a star-studded drama, a representative American tragedy that features both scoundrels and wholesome citizens, whether military or civilian. We have before us a work of creative nonfiction, a jet-age version of David and Goliath, courage in the face of intimidation and rank accusations, bullying tactics from face-savers. This is the suspenseful story of Lieutenant Colonel William "Tim" Hanson and how he overcame "superiors" bent upon handing him a general court-martial in January 1985.

Tim grew up in the modest rural town of Dixfield, Maine, a clean cut, athletically inclined youth, hungry for learning. He veered toward the old liberal arts, graduating from the University of Maine, Orono, in 1963. He joined the US Air Force and eventually went through flight training in time to execute many Vietnam combat missions, including the search and rescue of fellow fliers. His later flying career took him to Riyadh, Saudi Arabia, after training to fly the KC-135 Stratotanker.

During a normal air assignment December 9, 1983, Hanson turned over the controls of the KC-135 shortly after takeoff to the assigned crew. Not long after the scheduled refueling of the E-3A AWACS (Airborne Warning And Control System) , Hanson assumed control of the KC-135 as the AWACS carelessly, unnecessarily careened into the KC-135, rendering useless the two engines on the right side. They were 125 miles away from Riyadh. Had Hanson not acted instantly and intently, twelve lives and a multimillion dollar aircraft would surely have been lost. Fast thinking, original forestallings, prayer, non-by-the-book answers, he uniquely brought to bear. It was as if everything Hanson had learned in his flying career was brought to bear in his successful recovery of this badly damaged KC-135, including some procedures not in the flying manual and perhaps even some divine inspiration, namely, prayer. But the Commander (CO) of the AWACS, a full colonel, out-ranked Lieutenant Colonel Hanson, "and there's the rub."

Sheer intuition led him to discover, to his dismay, his vulnerability. At length, he was served with a general (*at least* a double meaning) court-martial, enough to make any mortal "shake in his mukluks"; truthfully though, Hanson surely did so. His Catholic faith made him courageous to his bone marrow. Consequently, he boldly helped assemble his defense team for the inevitable trial, which would have been totally unnecessary had the tower tape not mysteriously disappeared before his actual trial. Instead, gross, ploying, and petty charges—failing to sign a form, insufficiently observing the chain of command, allowing non-pilots to ride in the copilot's seat brought forth by the prosecution seemingly justified a verdict of guilty, thus entailing a sentencing (heavy fines) upon the accused, a shameful denouement!

Ever with a song in his heart and a baritone-like singing voice, Hanson's lyrics and marvelous guitar accompaniment are now gathered into his sixteen-song recording "Dream Corral." One senses an audible recurring theme of "Man of LaMancha," for readers will rejoice in Hanson's impossible dream—assurance that his USAF career (nearly twenty-three years) and subsequent military pension would be preserved. With what emotive depths does a USAF jet fly-boy walk and touch The Wall in D.C. to honor his very own buddies?

Blessed with "enoughness," USAF (RET) Wm. T. Hanson has been, and remains, a solid Amer-"I-can," what my father called "a counter"—a taxpayer, worker, voter, veteran, neighbor, musician. Lesser men would've had a complete breakdown.

Through all, he has been a hangfire from the "the great generation." Let's see what you think.

—Jay S. Hoar
March 2012

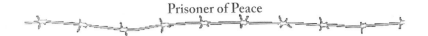

The first truth is that the liberty of a democracy is not safe if the people tolerate the growth of private power to a point where it becomes stronger than their democratic state itself. That, in its essence, is fascism—ownership of government by an individual, by a group, or by any other controlling private power.

—Franklin D. Roosevelt

CHAPTER 1

I began my flying career as an airborne weapons controller aboard the Super Constellation EC-121 out of McClellan AFB in Sacramento, California. The EC-121 was the forerunner to the modern day E3-A AWACS. I had gone there from a remote radar site on the tip of Newfoundland in Saint Anthony. There wasn't much call for these remote radar sites in the mid-sixties.

Not long after I arrived in California, we were deployed to Vietnam. While in Vietnam, our mission was to fly out over the Gulf of Tonkin and provide radar support to the fighter pilots in North Vietnam. Only occasionally did we ever spot any North Vietnamese migs. A Mig is a Russian-built fighter plane provided to the North Vietnames. Most of the fighter pilots had no great affection for our mission because we would get on the radio and broadcast what were called border violations. If one of our fighter pilots was getting too close to, let's say China, we would broadcast that information. Naturally enough, those fighter pilots would just as soon not have the enemy know where they were going to avoid surface to air missiles.

One F-105 colonel once told one of our crews to get our EC-121 off his base before he ripped all the radar out and put in seats to take his fighter pilots on Rest and Recuperation (R&R) flights. I did manage to log more than 490 hours over North Vietnam, albeit out over the water, before I returned to the United States to go to pilot training in Texas. Once my aircrew found out I was going to pilot training, they did give me some seat time. I was making the takeoff one morning going north out of Da Nang.

The pilot, an instructor pilot and captain, told me to step on the rudder to keep the nose aligned along the center line of the runway. Apparently I wasn't applying enough rudder so he shouted at me to put in more rudder, and I did, much to the chagrin of the rest of the crew in the back. I guess stuff came flying out of the bunks. In a word, the crew were some pissed off and they let the captain know it.

The relevant point I want to make is that by the captain allowing me in the seat he would have been court-martialed had they used the standards levied against me, but we'll get to that in a little while. As you will soon discover, I make a point that most of the charges brought against me were how we did business for the first twenty years of my career. I was promoted up through the ranks to Lieutenant Colonel precisely because *I thought outside the box*—not always by the book if you will. How ironically fitting, I suppose, that I would begin my flying career with the AWACS and end it the same way. "Live by the AWACS, die by the AWACS" so to speak.

I did go to Vietnam again in 1972. First, I was the commander of a Cessna O2-B squadron at Da Nang Air Base in South Vietnam, the 9th Special Operations Squadron (SOS). Our job in the O2 was to drop leaflets and play scary music to the Vietnamese in hopes that they would give up. That never happened.

I used to put in Merle Haggard tapes and play country music to our army guys at the various gun sites. They loved it. While commander, I did have a Vietnamese captain working with me as an interpreter. He spoke French. I'd swear that at night, he'd switch uniforms and put on his black pajamas and become a member of the VC, but we'll never know.

I did manage to convince the Pentagon to get rid of the O2-Bs and send them back to the United States along with the crews. They agreed to sending them back without me. They said I knew too much about the area to be sent home early. Instead, they sent me to Thailand where I worked out of a super secret

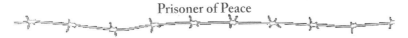

bunker building called Task Force Alpha (TFA) . My job was to control air strikes over North Vietnam and Laos.

We, the United States Air Force, had planted electronic sensors throughout portions of North Vietnam and Laos. When these sensors were dropped from an F-4, they had fins that would open up on impact and start giving off navigation information. They could also pick up voices from microphones installed in the sensors. I used the navigation information later on in my tour to help set up a successful rescue mission of some downed pilots. You'll hear much more about that during my trial from A1-E/F-16 pilot "Red" Clevenger.

Another of my more memorable moments occurred in March 1972. I was working with an AC-130 gunship which was truck hunting near Muang Phine, Laos. Spectre 13 was their call sign. 14 members of the 16th SOS were instantly killed when the airplane was struck by an SA-2 surface to air missile.

I went to the officer's club when I got off work and played Don Mclean's "American Pie" repeatedly until they kicked me out of the club for depressing everyone. I must admit that his song did help me maintain my sanity more or less. I told Don Mclean that story many years after when I met him in a grocery store in Castine, Maine, where he had a house. He actually wept from what I said.

The next mission I remember most is when another AC-130 gunship Spectre 22 was shot down, but this time, all crew members successfully bailed out and were rescued the very next morning . I was working that flight as well. There was one more mission that also involved me personally, but we'll get to that one later on.

I was one of the few student pilots going through pilot training with some combat experience under my belt. In other words, when I arrived at pilot training, I could already walk and chew gum—a must for a student pilot. As a student, all I wanted to do was fly. I became pretty good at it too. I think having played all the sports in high school and college aided me immensely, especially hockey. So, let's get to it.

Once upon a time—no, wait a second. That sort of beginning is reserved for fairy tales. All fighter pilot stories begin TINS. This Is No S. . . (Well, never mind. You get the idea). This is no joke , there I was at twenty-five thousand feet, two engines out on one side of my KC-135, a gaping hole in my right wing, 125 miles from my intended landing base with fuel fast running out and me scared nearly to death, with twelve people to look after and a twenty-five-million-dollar plane on my hands.

Did I mention it was in Saudi Arabia on December 9, 1983? This is no fairy tale. It's all true, or as true as I can possibly make it. I was scared. It was me and my twenty-one-year flying experience. And since I was so close to Israel, I didn't think it would be too much to ask if Jesus might hop on board to help me. I know he promised to come back the same way he left, but hey, Saudi Arabia is pretty close to home.

As the commander of the special refueling KC-135 operation in Riyadh, Saudi Arabia, our mission was to provide refueling support for the American E-3A AWACS patrolling the Saudi oil fields. We had been doing this since around 1980. There were two schools of thought as to why we were there in the Kingdom. One said that we were actually providing a security function for the Saudis. The other view said we were there with troops in case we needed to have more troops in the future. These views were expressed to me by an Air Force major who worked in the American Military Mission elsewhere in Riyadh. I was of the first school, rightly or wrongly.

On December 9, 1983, we had a routine refueling mission scheduled with one small change. We had a special request from the Navy to take some VIPs on the flight, along with an American Army flight surgeon who was working in a Saudi hospital. The Navy wanted to see what we were up to. Since we had so many VIPs on board, I decided to go along on the mission and make the takeoff.

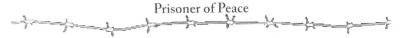

The rest of the crew were young folks and a little pissed off that I was going along, but no matter, that's what command is all about in my view. We finally took off around 3:00 p.m. and headed northeast towards the Kuwait-Iraq border to meet up with the AWACS. As I said, I made the takeoff which was mostly uneventful.

The KC-135 normally used water injection during most takeoffs to increase the thrust. I decided to dump the water prior to takeoff since the temperature was somewhat cooler on this particular day. That decision gave us a somewhat longer takeoff roll. I held the nose down a little bit longer to ensure enough speed for a safe liftoff. I must say that it did get the attention of one of our Navy VIPs, Captain Dick Martin, who was in the jump seat between the pilot and copilot's seats. Captain Martin had been the commander of the Navy's first nuclear powered aircraft carrier and no stranger to hairy situations.

Once we were safely airborne, I turned the aircraft over to the normal crew and began briefing our dignitaries on how we went about our day to day operations. Navy Captain Martin said they wanted to see how the Navy might go about getting some of that Saudi money the Air Force was sucking up.

The mission was routine through the refueling portion, if you discount the excessive takeoff roll. I had invited the VIPs to watch the refueling operation from the boom operator's pod in the very back of the aircraft. They were duly impressed. After the refueling, some of our passengers wanted to take some pictures of the AWACS out of the right side of our aircraft. The pilot of the AWACS pulled up along the right side of our airplane for a short photo shoot. Normally, the AWACS pilot would descend a thousand feet below the refueling altitude and go about his business. We would return to the base having accomplished our mission.

On this day the AWACS pilot, wanting to be obliging, decided that he would be a Thunderbird and pulled up on our right wing in close formation. Our flying crew consisted of a new first lieutenant copilot, an Air Force Academy captain, the pilot, a navigator, and the boom operator. The KC-135 was on autopilot. I have no idea about the AWACS, but I can only assume it was being flown manually. The AWACS got out a little bit ahead of the tanker and tried to get back into position. The KC-135 crew weren't paying that much attention to the AWACS (a mild understatement in hind sight). And before you could say, "Oh MAN, I think we're screwed," the AWACS's left wing smashed into our right wing, knocking out both engines on the right side and punching a giant hole in our right wing.

This was when I immediately took over flying the badly damaged tanker and making, quite literally, the flight of my life! They say that flying is hours and hours of boredom interrupted by seconds of stark terror. In my case, the next forty-five minutes were terrifying, but I still had to fly the aircraft and get somewhat inventive. I got on the radio and declared an emergency and began, in test pilot fashion, telling the tower back at Riyadh exactly what I was doing. It was a sound decision in case we didn't make it back and it was somewhat therapeutic. The forty-five minutes of stark terror was followed up with thirteen months of investigations and a subsequent court-martial at Blytheville Air Force Base, Arkansas, in January, 1985. What I was about to go through would make me into a *Prisoner of Peace.*

THE BEGINNING

I was always closer to my mother Madeline "Maddy" Hanson than my father Ray "Casey" Hanson. I was the youngest of four children. My sister Peggy was the oldest, followed by my brother Harry. Then came Geraldine, "Jazz," who died at the tender age of thirty-three leaving six kids. Ironically perhaps, she died on an Air Force Base in North Dakota.

Although born in Rumford, Maine, at the Rumford Community Hospital, I spent my formative years in a small, rural Maine town some six miles east of Rumford, namely Dixfield, Maine. The population of Dixfield was, and still is to my knowledge, about 2,500. Dixfield was a small mill town where everyone knew everyone. For the most part, all families looked out for each other. We had only one high school, which offered a diverse curriculum—shop, general studies, and college classical. If you chose the latter, which I did, you were required to take Latin, French, chemistry, algebra, etc. If you played sports, you probably played all of them—baseball, hockey, skiing, and football. They have since replaced hockey with basketball. I played on all the sports teams, and my favorite was hockey. They have since changed the name of our school from the Dixfield Dixies to the Dirigo Cougars. *Dirigo* means "I lead."

My mother received the Last Rites of the Catholic Church the day I was born. The priest administering the sacrament was Father William Timothy O'Mahony, thus my name, William Timothy Hanson. My mother survived my birth.

Mother taught us kids that to be a Hanson meant three things. It meant that you were hard working, you had a great sense of humor and above all, you were honest. These are the same traits generally ascribed to most native-born Mainers. My Hanson traits would be sorely tested from the end of 1983 through 1985, and perhaps beyond. I was never one to confide much to either of my parents. I did, however, call my parents in the summer of 1984 and tried to explain in some detail what I was going through with the Air Force and the Department of Defense. For whatever reason, my father was more understanding than my mother. She took the position that if the government was going through all this trouble and expense to take me to court, I must have done something wrong—not an uncommon (no matter how wrong-headed) assumption.

After having talked with my father at length I asked him for his advice. "What do you think I should do, Dad?" I asked him.

"Do you think I should just quit and walk away? I'm not afraid of these people, Dad. They are just making me tired."

"Aw, Tim," he said with the greatest compassion I had ever heard in his voice. "You may just as well get what you can." I told him what General Davis, the commander of the Strategic Air Command, had to say to the troops in England in early February of 1984: "I can guarantee you all here that Hanson will never see one thin dime of his retirement."

My father was no stranger to powerful people, especially men. When he first went to work for the Diamond Match Company across the river from Dixfield in West Peru, Maine, he became the first union president in the mill. Subsequently, he was promoted to foreman of the wood yard. He was also the baseball manager of the local men's league team in Dixfield—the Dixfield Dixies.

The team enjoyed a good reputation throughout New England. The pro teams often sent scouts to our games. I was the bat boy for the team for many years. There were two brothers who played for my father, although they didn't play often, and certainly not often enough to suit their father, who just happened to be one of the mill managers where my father worked. Another of my father's bosses was the actual mill manager, or superintendent as they called him.

As coincidence would have it, one day in the mid-fifties my father was called into the front office and accused of stealing eighteen-foot logs. The superintendent just happened to be out of town that afternoon. After a short discussion my father's temper got the best of him, and he said without mincing his words, "Well, screw it, if you believe I've been stealing logs, then, fire me." They did.

The next day the superintendent's son-in-law got my father's job. My father later admitted that he let his temper get the best of him. He said he came home and told my mother what had happened. She was also a working woman. In fact, she worked in the same dry-goods store for forty-six years. My father said

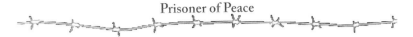

he gave the mill managers too few options. "Kinda like Patrick Henry," he said. "Or maybe New Hampshire." He said he cried for a few hours and then went out to find and land another job, which he did. "I had a family to support," he said.

When I got up enough nerve, I asked him if he had actually stolen those eighteen-foot logs. "Yes," he said somewhat sarcastically. "And I brought them home and used them on our electric stove." Once again, my mother's theory that to be a Hanson meant (and still does mean) you were honest, hard working, and have a great sense of humor.

I took my father's advice and decided to stand up against the senators, congressmen, and generals. My father proved that there was life after the Diamond Match Company. Perhaps there's life after the Air Force as well? Oh, by the way, my father did not receive one thin dime for retirement. Perhaps some of the higher-ups in the government had relatives at the Diamond Match Company? "Give me liberty or give me death." In other words, "Live free or die." Or perhaps, "Just screw it. Fire me." It's all about options in the long run, eh?

CHAPTER 2

Mayday! Mayday! Mayday! That was my first call on the UHF radio (243.0) Guard channel. My distress call was monitored in Israel, Saudi Arabia, Kuwait, and Iraq. More on how I found that out later.

We were at twenty-five thousand feet about 125 miles from our takeoff base back at Riyadh, Saudi Arabia. The cockpit instrument panel looked like something you might have seen at an arcade. The red fire lights for the right side engines were flashing, the RPM gauges were spinning, the hydraulic overheat lights down by my right leg were illuminated, the oil pressure gauges for the two right engines were rolling back towards zero, and the fuel quantity indicators were falling fast. We had only five parachutes on board and there were twelve of us.

I ordered the boom operator to give the chutes to our passengers. The navigator, a former ranger, was incredulous that he wasn't getting one of the chutes. We had the chutes to begin with only because the Strategic Air Command (SAC) (the Major Air Command to which our KC-135s belonged) didn't have any other place to store the chutes. At least, that's what I was told.

Each KC-135 in the command had five chutes according to that story. You could say that the entire crew were committed to recovering the plane rather than riding it into the Saudi sand, this latter choice a distinct possibility in my mind. I turned the aircraft southwest back towards Riyadh and began a shallow descent. And since the hydraulic overheat lights were on, I had to decide, and fast: (1) whether or not the landing gear would come down, and (2) if it did, would we be able to retract it again?

I reached up and put the landing gear handle down. To my amazement, the gear came down as advertised. The remaining two engines on the left side were beginning to overheat like crazy, especially the left outboard engine. I had to try and retract the landing gear. It came back up. This eased the wear and tear on the remaining two engines. I slowed our rate of descent next to nothing.

All the while I was conferring with the Riyadh control tower telling them every little thing I was doing with the aircraft. All of my transmissions were being recorded. I told the tower how many souls we had on board. In the event that we did have to crash land, the recording would disclose exactly what happened. A Saudi tower controller was acknowledging all my calls. We did not have a cockpit recorder as the AWACS did.

It was now about forty thirty in the afternoon. The weather was clear. The copilot brought me the KC-135 Dash-1 operational flight manual. I told him in not very polite language that there was little in the manual to help with what we were going through. What I actually said was, well, never mind. Let's just say it wasn't very kind. I had my hands full of airplane trying to invent some procedures to save our pink asses, especially mine.

I knew the Dash-1 procedures pretty thoroughly as to what equipment we had or didn't have available. I instructed the pilot in the left seat, the Air Force Academy graduate, to monitor any incoming radio calls, except for the Riyadh tower calls. I would handle all tower radio traffic. As you may well imagine, I was on the edge of panic while doing my level best to remain calm and fly the badly damaged tanker.

We were taught from the get-go in the flying business to (1) stop, (2) think, (3) analyze the situation, and (4) take the proper action, and if time permits, (5) have a short smoke. No time for smoking now. As you will come to discover much later, some of the crew had quite a different story to tell about the aircraft recovery, except for the copilot, a truly honorable young man—

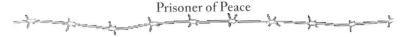

not so with some of the rest of the crew. But I get too far ahead of myself.

Obviously, we all made it back. Once I had the field in sight (landing to the south; we took off to the north), I briefed the pilot in the left seat on exactly what I wanted him to do. I told the tower controller that I wanted a foam truck along with the fire trucks and ambulances. The Saudi controller said he understood that I wanted a *phone* truck. "No," I said. "I want a *foam* truck. "Roger," he said. "Understand you want a phone truck."

A British pilot monitoring our channel pretty much cleared everything up as only a Brit can do. He came up on our frequency and said using the phonetic alphabet, "Listen here, he wants a *foxtrot, Uniform, Charlie, kilo, India. November. golf. foxtrot. Oscar. alpha. Mike.* A bloody *foam* truck." I guess the Brit's enunciation was better than mine because the Saudi controller was quick on the uptake as he immediately acknowledged the Brit, "Roger. Roger. Roger. I understand. A *foam* truck. All the rescue equipment would be in place as requested."

CHAPTER 3

I had instructed the navigator to start cranking down the flaps to about twenty degrees. His adrenaline must have been pumping through his veins because before I knew it, the flaps were nearly all the way down. I told the navigator to get the flaps back up or else we wouldn't have enough power on the remaining two engines on the left side to get us to the runway. He complied and started the flaps back up to around twenty degrees. The two good engines were cooking pretty good by now, anyway. I told the pilot in the left seat exactly what I wanted him to do as soon as we touched down. I told him I wanted him to panic stop the aircraft since I didn't have any breaks on the right side, having shut down the right side hydraulic system that was overheating. The pilot would still have good breaks. He said he understood and would do as I had instructed.

As I lined up for the final approach, I brought the two left engines to idle and flew the badly damaged KC-135 like it was a shuttle. I had always instructed my students that once they had their aim point on the runway picked out, if they didn't change it, that's where the aircraft would hit the runway. I aimed for the very front end of the south runway.

Since our hydraulics were out for the most part, I had only outboard spoilers left to aid in slowing us down. I began to slowly pump the spoilers as we descended toward the runway. Had I been able to see how badly damaged the right wing was I probably wouldn't have used the spoilers at all for fear the wing would snap off. Quite frankly, I'm glad I couldn't see the wing damage from the right seat. Sometimes it's better not to know everything, eh?

In the KC-135 we don't normally burn the forward body fuel down too far since it helps keep the aircraft somewhat nose heavy and helps prevent the plane from tipping on its tail. Out of necessity, we burned most—if not all—of the forward body fuel. "*Now!*" I shouted to the pilot in the left seat, "*Stop this aircraft!*" He did as directed.

The KC-135 is about the same size as a Boeing 707. Actually, the KC-135 model number is a Boeing 717. Amazingly the airplane came to a stop in just under 2,500 feet. Hot brakes can catch fire within fifteen minutes from application. That was another of my concerns. My thinking led me to hope that by *panic stopping* the airplane, the nose gear might collapse and thus prevent the aircraft from tipping on its tale. Neither happened—no nose gear collapse, no tipping on its tale. I ordered an immediate evacuation from the aircraft. By that time, the huge green Saudi fire truck was speeding toward us. The regular copilot was nearly creamed by the fire truck in his haste to get clear of the airplane.

Once everyone was safely out of the airplane, I told the fire chief to put some foam on the brakes and then on the two right engines where JP-4 was still streaming from the engines onto the runway underneath the plane. They did as I asked. The other concern was to get some ballast in the front of the aircraft to keep it from tipping on its tail. A US Air Force maintenance officer, a Major, I think, came up to me and said he would take it from here. Somebody brought a slab of granite for ballast and began cutting it with a concrete power saw. The sparks were spewing all over the place. I shouted for them to stop and have the granite hoisted into the aircraft through the cargo door. They reluctantly agreed and did it.

Having had a look around the outside of the aircraft, we found the damage was far worse than could be seen from inside to the cockpit. A piece of the AWACS's left wing was still stuck into the right wing of our airplane .

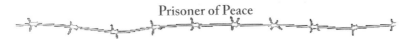

When we first had the midair collision, I got on the radio and asked the AWACS pilot if he was all right. "Roger that," he assured me. "We're going back on station." Someone in the AWACS must have eventually looked out one of the few windows in the E-3A only to discover they were missing a full eight feet of their left wing, right at the rivet line. One of the AWACS crew members came up to me after we landed and said he was so sorry they had run into us.

CHAPTER 4

It is important throughout this story to keep in mind that there were two competing major air commands involved in this Elf One mission, the project name assigned to this flying mission in Saudi Arabia. The E-3A AWACS came under the operational control of the four-star general commander of the Tactical Air Command (TAC), General Creech. The KC-135s came under the operational control of the four-star general Commander of the Strategic Air Command (SAC), General Davis. I was in charge of the KC-135 operation as its detachment commander in Riyadh, Saudi Arabia. Another Air Force colonel was in charge of the E-3A AWACS operation. My immediate supervisor was a full colonel stationed at RAF Fairford in England. His boss was a one star general in Germany.

From there the chain of command eventually made its way to General Davis at SAC headquarters in Omaha, Nebraska. The AWACS chain of command went through Germany to Florida and ultimately to TAC headquarters at Langley Air Force Base in Virginia. To my knowledge, neither of the major air commanders had ever set foot in Saudi Arabia. Our one star general in Germany had only visited Riyadh once, and that was for about two hours, where he reportedly spent most of his time downtown shopping. In Vietnam we used to say that, "When the going gets tough, the tough go shopping."

There was a sizeable American Military Mission located elsewhere in the city, but not far from our base. The American Mission consisted mostly of Air Force personnel who worked jointly with the Royal Saudi Air Force (RSAF). The commander of the RSAF was also a member of the Royal Family, namely

Prince General Fahd, with the same last name as the king. I had been successful in doing a favor for the prince. He had been trying for a couple years to get the United States to allow his F-15 pilots to practice air refueling off our KC-135s after we refueled the AWACS—our primary mission. I sent a teletype message to the Pentagon explaining all the reasons, both militarily and politically, why this would be a good idea.

The following Monday, I received a tersely-worded approval message informing me that I was never to send messages to the Pentagon on weekends. When the prince asked me how I did this, I said, "I simply asked them." He just laughed and shook his head. "If it was that easy, I wonder why no one has done it before now," he said. I had no answer for him, but I could see that he was genuinely pleased with what I had done. He would return the favor later on in my tour.

When the crews weren't flying, they would mostly hang out at the hotel provided by the king. Most crew members shared rooms. Some of us were fortunate enough to have our own single rooms and a car. The hotel was just below first class, but not bad. The food was very good and available 24/7. The fruits were especially delicious and plentiful, and you could have as much as you wanted. There was no alcohol allowed in the kingdom, in principle at least. If you were blessed with transportation, you could get about anything you wanted to drink. Most of the services at the hotel were provided by either South Koreans or Filipinos. The standing joke was "If the Saudis go to war, guess who gets the contract?"

All personnel assigned to the American Military Mission were entitled to diplomatic cargo. That meant that your cargo coming into the kingdom was not subject to search. Most mission personnel had well stocked bars.

There was one other practice that provided some fun for those who could get around the city. Most countries working in the Kingdom had their own compounds—the Brits, South Africans,

Americans, etc. Each compound had their own competitions to see who could make the best whiskey, beer, and/or wine. We would visit these compounds on a somewhat regular basis. I had one distinct advantage as the commander of a flying unit. I could offer people rides on our tankers in exchange for inviting our crews to their wine tasting parties.

The Royal Saudi Air Force Academy (RSAFA) was collocated on the base from which we flew. They had just built a billion dollar recreation facility that had everything one could imagine. Because of efforts of myself and a few others, the commander of the RSAFA allowed us access to the facility. Most of us took advantage of their first-class bowling alleys. There was even a mosque within the palatial building.

Not all Saudis were bin Ladens. I had several Saudi friends in the Saudi Air Force with whom I took tea on a daily basis. I even took some of them on flight missions, including the RSAFA commander. His biggest request was that we try, whenever possible, to take off to the north to cut down on the awful noise a KC-135 makes during takeoff when using water injection. Apparently, his mother was in a nursing home off the south end of the runway, and she hated the noise.

On the day of the midair collision, December 9, 1983, I accommodated the general and dumped the water just prior to takeoff. I also made the takeoff to the north. That no doubt accounted for the unusually long takeoff roll. The landing was as short as the takeoff was long.

CHAPTER 5

After the damaged tanker was turned over to maintenance, we all headed back to the operations building. The AWACS had not yet landed. Having a somewhat suspicious nature, I jokingly said that they must be still up there erasing their in-flight recorder. Our information was all on the Saudi tower taper for the time being. A short and somewhat rotund individual dressed in a white Saudi garment was walking straight for me as I walked slowly off the runway. It was none other than Prince General Fahd. He actually put his arm around my shoulder and said, "My pilots said that was one of the best landings they had ever seen. Great bit of flying, Colonel, well done." He lit up a Marlboro and walked with me to the edge of the runway. I told him that, "When you are out of fuel and scared to death, you have only one shot and it's got to be right." He said, "I have no doubt you'll be a general when this is all over." I looked at him and laughingly said, "Yeah, right! Don't forget what country you're dealing with, General." And as it turned out, he was half right at least.

He asked me if I thought we could get the damaged tanker off the runway prior to the evening launch. I said we'd do our level best. He said, "Well, if you can't, then we'll push it off the runway and buy you another one." He was only half joking. He had his priorities right. He wanted the oil fields protected at all costs and could afford to do whatever needed to be done.

The AWACS finally landed on the east-west runway without further incident about forty-five minutes later. As you may well imagine, the phones and teletypes were buzzing by now between and among the various air commands, consulates, the Pentagon, and the White House. I instructed the crew to simply "Tell it like it is, period!"

I asked each crew member to fill out an accident report on their own without collusion with each other and turn it in to me. I did likewise. Whether or not the crew colluded, I'll have no way of knowing.

An American Air Force full colonel from the military mission showed up practically out of nowhere to begin the accident investigation. Within hours, he was suddenly taken off the investigation and replaced by an AWACS major. Rumor had it that the full colonel was actually in the employ of the CIA while still wearing the Air Force uniform.

When they (whoever the *they* were) appointed the AWACS major to conduct the interim accident investigation, I became annoyed and a little paranoid to tell you the truth. There are times when a healthy paranoia is justified. This turned out to be one of those times. The AWACS major was hardly a disinterested third party.

As the evening progressed, things began to calm down somewhat. To my utter astonishment and surprise, one of my old flying buddies from the United States appeared on the scene and invited my entire crew to his villa at the military mission compound. Colonel Jim Edwards and I had flown together back in 1968 or 1969 in Texas. He was now flying the F-15 and was an advisor to the Saudi Air Force, who also had F-15s. He took us to his apartment to meet his lovely wife and gave us some "green sandwiches" or whatever else we wanted. A "green sandwich" is the codename for a Heinekin beer in Saudi parlance. Everyone except the boom operator sergeant came over. I don't know if it was because he was black, enlisted, or what, but he returned to the hotel where things were getting interesting as well.

CHAPTER 6

Colonel Edwards and I went through instructor pilot training together back in 1968. I don't recall if we served in Vietnam at the same time. He went on to be a fighter pilot, and I went on to be an instructor pilot. Colonel Edwards appeared at my court-martial later on where he provided some very enlightening information to the court concerning some of the more ridiculous charges levied against me.

The crew enjoyed Colonel Edward and his wife's hospitality for a few hours. We were all still pretty hyper after our near-death experience. The crew were worried about what might happen to them as the investigation proceeded. I repeatedly assured them to "tell the truth and not to worry; simply tell it like it is." It was true then and it's still true today—the truth does set you free, but sometimes at a price. Someone once said that all evil in the world began with a lie. It would become a ghastly awakening to me that anyone could swear to God to tell the truth, then, blatantly tell bold faced lies under oath; but then again, given all my worldly travels, I was still quite naive concerning certain truths in this world.

As you will discover later on, several members of the crew had a vastly different recollection of the aircraft recovery, with the notable exception of the co-pilot, Lt. Kern. After we'd had our fill of libations, Colonel Edwards arranged for our transportation back to our hotel. My isolation within the Kingdom of Saudi Arabia was taking place, and without my knowledge, consent or desire.

During my prisoner of war training we were taught that one of the ways the North Vietnamese were successful in breaking down American prisoners was to simply keep them isolated. We are, by and large, quite a gregarious group. It appears that many of my higher-ups were employing the tactics of the North Vietnamese against one of their own, but to what purpose? That is a question that still haunts me to this day, some 26 years later.

I was called by my superior, a colonel in England, and informed that I would be relieved of command while the investigation was being conducted. That was understandable and proper. He said that I was to surrender my staff car, a late model Chevy Impala. He said I was not to go near the office. They say the reason there were so many GM cars in Saudi and no Fords was because they made Fords in Israel. I don't know about the veracity of that statement, but it's interesting nonetheless.

I complied with most of the colonel's orders, except the one of not going near my office. It's a good thing I did go because who knows what those guys were up to? When I arrived the next morning, there were hoards of guys going through documents looking for God knows what! They were stocking the shelves with all sorts of Air Force flight manuals not previously on hand there. Fortunately for me they were documenting everything they were doing. If their intention was to set me up as the scapegoat, they weren't being very bright about it.

An investigation team was on their way to Riyadh from all points around the compass: a general from TAC, a lieutenant colonel from SAC, an aircraft engineer from the Boeing Aircraft Company, and several more individuals from across the country. One of them was a safety officer from the Air Force Flight Safety Office in California.

This was supposed to be an accident investigation, but what it turned into was something quite different. We had a saying in Saudi Arabia that went like this: "When the going gets tough, the tough go shopping." Hey, I was a member of the 1958 Dixfield Dixies State Champion Hockey Team. I knew what it meant to take on the best and go into the corner to get the puck.

Many times, the opposition were much larger than we were, but in hockey and as in life itself, size ain't everything. If it were, we'd simply mail in the teams' weights. Whoever weighed the most would be declared the winner. When you go into the corner to get the puck, you know you might get creamed, but you do what you've been trained to do to try and win the game. To paraphrase Saint Paul, "No sense in playing, if you don't intend to win." This too was a game, but a deadly serious one. I was beginning to feel like my commissioning oath was being seriously tested. You know, the part about upholding the Constitution against all enemies, foreign and domestic.

Nobody in the Elf One operation was talking to me . My car was gone. I felt entirely alone in this Saudi wasteland. One of my Saudi Air Force friends at the hotel called me aside and said he had some news for me. "These keys are for you," he said. "Anything you want is available to you. If you want whiskey, women, food or whatever, you've only to ask me, and I'll see that you have it." When I asked my Saudi friend what this was all about, he said that Prince General Fahd told him to look after me. My friend said with a big broad smile that since the prince general was his commander and a member of the royal family, he thought he ought to do as he was told.

He handed me the keys to a brand new, white Chevy Impala parked in the hotel parking lot. "How is it you know the Prince?" he asked me. I explained in some detail and then left in my new car to the American Military Mission across town and got pleasantly smashed while meeting many high-ranking dignitaries of the American mission. The one person I met who had a major influence on the rest of my stay in Saudi Arabia and beyond was a Doctor Kaye Eckman, a Ph.D. in psychology and, ironically, the wife of the full colonel who initially started the accident investigation and left. She would become a moving force in my court-martial.

CHAPTER 7

They were having a Christmas party at the mission in a few days, and I was invited. In the meantime, the kind doctor of psychology took me aside and said, "Here, Colonel Hanson, these are for you to take as necessary. Watch your alcohol consumption if you decide to take any." She had cut up some Valium capsules into three parts. She said it was obvious that I was still keyed up from the midair collision.

"Who wouldn't be?" she said. "We know a lot more about what is going on over there than you may realize. I can't go into any details at the moment, but I promise to keep you posted as things develop. Now go back to your hotel and get some much needed rest, if you can. You did one hell of a job bringing that tanker back. Everyone over here knows that. You may not know it, but this 'little' international incident has already made its way to the White House. What you may not know, however, is what is going on in the bowels of the White House. Saudi Arabia is also involved." She, of course, was speaking of Iran Contra. "Now please go home, take a couple of those Valium and get some sleep. Good night, Colonel. See you at the Christmas party."

Thanks to the bourbon and coke and the magic bullets, I actually managed to get a few hours sleep. The next morning, having been isolated from my crews and the crews of the AWACS, I drove out to the base. What I discovered was even more upsetting. There were officers and enlisted running around my former office still putting regulations and manuals where before none existed. One of my strengths, or perhaps weaknesses, depending on how you look at it, is that I have pretty much a photographic memory;

maybe it's a phonographic memory because I remember pretty much everything I hear.

The Air Force Accident Investigation Team was arriving in Riyadh. The team was headed up by an Air Force Brigadier General—a one star. He was short and had somewhat of a Napoleon attitude about him. He was from Boston and belonged to TAC. SAC sent a lieutenant colonel from SAC headquarters in Omaha, Nebraska. It was no coincidence that he was the first detachment commander when our KC-135 operation began in Riyadh.

Boeing sent their technical expert. The Air Force also sent a member of their Safety Inspection Team from Norton AFB in California to take notes. An accident investigation is supposed to be a nonjudgmental, fact finding group, and most of the time they do a great job; most of the time.

An aircraft accident investigation is supposed to examine as many facts as possible and come up with ways to prevent a similar accident from happening again. That was my mindset as I approached the board when it was my turn to appear before them. A few preliminary observations are in order here before I tell you how it went with me.

The board president was a short and somewhat feisty brigadier general from Massachusetts—sort of a Napoleon-esque figure. The remainder of the board consisted of a lieutenant colonel from SAC headquarters. Not so coincidentally he had been the first KC-135 Detachment Commander deployed to Riyadh, Saudi Arabia, and held the very same job I had at present. I had a little problem with this lieutenant colonel being on the board in that he reported directly to the four star SAC commander. I thought his loyalties and judgment might be skewed.

There was an aircraft engineer from the Boeing Company. They made both the AWACS and the KC-135s. Boeing had a huge arms sale pending with Saudi Arabia. It was the largest foreign arms sales ever up to that time and not necessarily that

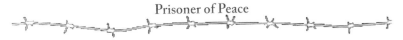

popular. Besides the Boeing rep, I believe there was an Air Force major . He was the recorder for the board.

An accident board is supposed to be fact finding and not fault finding. That, of course, is in a perfect world, and as we know perfectly well, nothing exists in a vacuum. Our military presence in Saudi Arabia at this time was politically charged and some military leaders are not immune from political pressure. One more piece of information should help complete the context for my appearing before the board. As I earlier mentioned, when our Napoleon-esque brigadier general arrived in the country, he, like everyone else coming into the kingdom, was required to surrender his passport to the customs authorities, to be returned on departure.

Our general was having none of this, at least not at first. His comments to the Saudi Customs officials went something like this, so I'm told, "No 'effing' raghead is going to take my passport. I just want to get in here and get this 'effing' accident investigation over and get the f—— outta here." And as I say, this was all relayed to me by my Royal Saudi Air Force Major back at the hotel over a cup of tea. I don't think he had a motivation to make it up.

Since it was the Christmas season, the entire accident board was invited to a cocktail party at the American Military Mission Compound. The party was hosted by a tall, beautiful woman, Doctor Kaye Eckman and her husband, Air Force fighter pilot Colonel Eckman, at their villa.

After the AWACS safely recovered, the interim accident investigation began. The first one to be in charge was none other than our party host Colonel Lucky Eckman. Don't ask me why he was heading up this investigation. He was nowhere in our chain of command, but he was a major player with the Saudi Royal Family, including the commanding general of the Royal Saudi Air Force, General and Prince Fahd. Colonel Eckman didn't stay on the job long. He mysteriously was gone as fast as he had shown up.

An AWACS major was put in charge of the initial investigation. I mean, c'mon, give me a break! You talk about the fox being in the hen house. So much for fair and impartial. I was getting just the tiniest bit paranoid, and understandably I think. The colonel was apparently gone back to his beautiful doctor wife.

At the cocktail party for the visiting investigation team, naturally enough, there was plenty of alcohol under the auspices of the diplomatic cargo rule—at least for the permanent party personnel at the American Military Mission. Other personnel from other countries had their own system for beating the booze problem. In fact, there was a sort of international competition to see who could made the best booze—wine, beer, etc.

According to the good doctor and party hostess, as the party progressed, our investigating general got more and more in his cups and made several attempts to, how shall we say, put the make on the good doctor. How do I know this you ask? She told me when I went to see her more or less professionally as my stress level mounted.

The morning following the aforementioned Christmas party, it was my turn to appear before the board. Naturally, I put on my Dress Blues and drove to the base. I still had not been relieved of my car yet. My stress level was still pretty high after having recovered that badly damaged KC-135, truly a memorable moment for me.

I entered the small, long, and narrow room where the board was assembled and saluted smartly as I said, "Lieutenant Colonel Hanson reporting as ordered, Sir."

"Sit down, Colonel, and tell me exactly what you said to the tower during the recovery of the tanker." I told him that I was pretty busy with my full attention on flying and recovering the aircraft, and I suggested that he might be better served by listening to the tower tape. The general stood up abruptly and

said if I didn't answer his questions the way he wanted me to, he would take me outside and teach me how to answer his questions properly. I told the general in that case I had nothing further to say to the board. I stood up, saluted smartly and left.

Somewhere out there in cyberspace, there is a copy of the Air Force Safety Magazine from February 1984 in which it tells you how not to conduct an accident investigation. I guess the general was trying to put the fear of God into me. And while I most assuredly fear God (and not always as much as I should), I sure as hell am not afraid of a brigadier general—or any general for that matter.

If that general thought he was going to scare me, he was dead wrong. He did however slightly piss me off. I was subsequently invited to that very villa for yet another Christmas party where I ran into some more flying buddies from the United States and Vietnam. The doctor told me that they had all ready heard about my run-in with the general. That's when she told me how the general tried coming on to her.

While it was true then and is true now, I was not afraid, but others were ducking for cover all around me. The word was getting around that the forces were aligning against me. I even made an off-handed remark that I probably should get a lawyer from Kansas City or somewhere. And before you could say F. Lee Bailey, the Air Force sent yet another colonel from England to the circus, along with a major lawyer. "For me,?" I asked. "No," the colonel said. "We heard you were getting a lawyer from Kansas City." "Oh, for Christ's sake," I said. "The only person I know in Kansas City is Roger Miller, and he's been dead for years."

Finally Doctor Eckman put me in touch with a military defense lawyer in another part of Saudi Arabia, an Air Force major. "Tell them nothing, Colonel Hanson," he advised. "They can't exploit your silence."

I am sure the investigation board listened to the tower tapes. A Dallas, Texas judge, and a former co-pilot of mine in the

KC-135, explained to me what sometimes happens to evidence in cases like mine. Henry M. Wade, Jr. said that often times evidence has a way of disappearing if it's not favorable to the prosecution. Whether or not that happened in my case, I have no way of knowing.

And now for the tower tapes. Mayday! Mayday! Mayday! Tower tapes? There are no tower tapes anymore. Someone, somewhere, either erased them or ordered them destroyed. Too bad for me and too bad for historical accuracy. You'll hear what the lead prosecuting attorney had to say about the tower tapes during the trial. See Judge Wade's comments above. Had the tower tape been made available to my defense team the trial in all likelihood would not have been necessary. The tower tape itself would have made for one hell of a TV documentary! Nearly all the charges against me were covered on the tape as I told the tower exactly what I was doing in the aircraft from moment to moment until we safely landed. I told them everything except how many rivets were in the wings. It was very much like what a test pilot does when testing an airplane. A short history of the recent arms sales to Saudi Arabia may help the reader understand the complexities with which I was dealing as I chose to go to trial against the United States Air Force in early 1985 stemming from a midair collision in Saudi Arabia between two United States Air Force aircraft on December 9, 1983. The two airplanes involved in the collision were a KC-135 Strato Tanker and an E-3A AWACS. Both these planes are built by the Boeing Aircraft Company.

The sale of the AWACS surveillance planes to Saudi Arabia by the United States administration of President Ronald Reagan was a controversial part of what was then the largest foreign arms sale in US history. The sale saw objections from a majority of the Americans, prominent US senators, the State of Israel, and the Israel Lobby. The sale included the five E-3 Sentry AWACS aircraft and eight KE-3 refueling aircraft, with spare parts and support, delivered between June 1986 and September 1987.

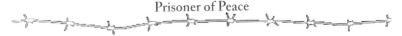

The United States currently has a fleet of thirty-three AWACS, the largest in the world. NATO possesses seventeen, the United Kingdom has seven, Saudi Arabia has five, and France has four. Some have described the inside of the AWACS as a movie theater, with its subdued lighting and blue carpet. There is a lack of windows compared to most planes this size. When asked, one colonel said, "We don't want them looking out the window. We want them looking at what's in front of them."

The arms sale proposal was not received warmly on Capitol Hill. The sale was harshly rejected by Israel and disapproved by a majority of Americans. Several U.S. senators felt that this was the most dangerous arms sales ever. It was the largest arms sale ever, up to this time in our military history. These same senators saw this sale as a kind of blackmail for oil. Those in favor of the sale said it was designed to promote stability in the region. Israel saw the sale as an action that would take away it's most strategic military advantage, namely surprise attacks because of the AWACS' ability to monitor operations from such a stand-off position. In late April, 1982 at a Senate Armed Services Committee hearing the late Massachusetts Senator Edward Kennedy said "This is one of the most dangerous arms sales ever," as he opposed the sale. At that same hearing Senator Donald Riegle said we were being asked to submit to a kind of blackmail, the price gouging of oil.

President Reagan and his people said the sale was designed to promote stability in the region. The opposing senators and congressmen said it was designed to secure US oil resources. Senator Bob Packwood, a Republican member of Reagan's party said flatly that "They [the Saudis] have displayed a hostility that must be interpreted as their deliberate intentions to promote continued instability in the Middle East." Packwood questioned the choice of Saudi Arabia as an arbiter of peace saying, "Let's think about which nations have been seriously committed to negotiating peace in the Middle East and which have not shared that commitment." With the recently ended American hostage crisis fresh in mind, Americans were reluctant to sell military equipment to anyone. A 1981 poll showed that 52 percent of those surveyed opposed arms sales to any country, and only 19 percent wanted the United States to sell AWACS to Saudi Arabia.

Israel felt that its security was directly threatened and was most strongly opposed to the AWACS deal. Prime Minister Menacghem Begin expressed "profound regret and opposition" to the Saudi AWACS proposal. Experts said that the AWACS could track every move of the Israeli Air Force, denying it the chance to launch a surprise first strike, the basis of the Israeli defense doctrine.

Many in Israel felt betrayed by the United States. Reagan had made a campaign promise to enhance Israel's security. Many felt this sale would further destabilize the region, a region whose stability was supposed to be a strategic priority of the Reagan foreign policy. The Reagan Administration actively sought to diminish Israel's voice over the deal. In public speeches, administration officials admonished Israel for getting involved in a US foreign policy matter. Secretary of State Alexander Haig said that the President must be "Free of restraints of overriding external vetoes," and went on to say that were the AWACS deal blocked by Israeli influence, there would be "serious implications on all American policies in the Middle East." "I'll just leave it there," Reagan himself declared. "It's not the business of other nations to make American foreign policy."

In August 1981, the administration delayed indefinitely the delivery of military aircraft to Israel, a move that Israel interpreted as pressure to approve of the AWACS sale.

In order to gain support for the deal in congress and in the country, the administration lobbied strongly on behalf of it. The administration continually insisted that the deal would benefit US interests in the Middle East. The administration also gave promises of the AWACS planes' importance in securing peace.

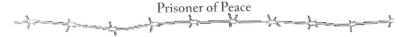
Alexander Haig told Congress that if the AWACS sale was blocked, our security, the security of Israel, and peace itself might be endangered. President Reagan said that by contributing to the stability of the area, it improves Israel's security. Henry Kissinger was enlisted by the administration to sell the deal. He said, "It is essential for the peace process in the Middle East." Congress approved the AWACS sale, and as part of the then largest arms export ever, the planes were a symbolic commitment to the US-Saudi relationship.

You may be asking about the relevance to my case. It was somewhat ironic that two of the major players in this drama were both from Maine. I was one of them; the other was a United States Senator, namely William S. Cohen. When it became obvious that the Air Force was intent on court-martialing me, I contacted Senator Cohen's office in Washington, D.C. I was not pleased with my senator's response and I said in effect, "I will get out of the Air Force and come home and run against him." Of course, I would have had to wait six years since Senator Cohen was just re-elected. As fate would have it, Senator Cohen had received large sums of money from the Boeing Aircraft Company toward his reelection bid (some say more than fifty thousand dollars). Boeing got the contract for this huge arms sale and Senator Cohen voted "Yeah." The final irony in this instant circumstance is that Senator William Cohen is Jewish.

CHAPTER 8

My Saudi friend at the hotel told me that a lady sergeant upstairs wanted me to stop by on my way to my room. He said she had some important information for me. "Good luck, Colonel Hanson, and may Allah be with you." I believe he was sincere with his best wishes.

Rather than going to her room, I called her from my room. You know, avoid even the perception of wrongdoing. She told me that she had overheard yet another conversation between the Elf One commander and a general in Germany. The general told the Elf One commander that he was sending a colonel down to Riyadh to have what he called a "sneak peek" at the operation. The Elf One commander was told to keep the colonel's visit quiet. The colonel would be arriving the next morning according to the sergeant. When I asked her why she was telling me this stuff, she said that not everyone around here was against me.

"You'd have to have blinders on not to see how you are being railroaded. The colonel will be arriving at the hotel in a few hours," she said. "He won't be hard to pick out, since you already know practically everyone here. Good night, Colonel Hanson, and Godspeed."

I got up early next morning, like I had a choice. Adrenaline does funny things to the body, and boy, would I find that out over the next thirteen months. I began wandering around the halls of the hotel and whom, to my surprise, did I run into on the second floor of the hotel but our "sneak peek" colonel from Germany. I walked up, introduced myself, and asked him what he was doing in Riyadh?

"How in the hell did you know I was here? My visit was supposed to be unannounced," he said. He asked me to meet him at my former office at eight o'clock that morning. I said I would be there. When I arrived there was another man with him, an Air Force major. He said that the major was a lawyer from the General's staff in Germany." We would like to ask you a few questions concerning the midair and the ground operations here at Riyadh," the colonel said. "Would it be alright if the major recorded your answers?" I said, "I guess I'd best be contacting my attorney in Kansas City before answering any of your questions." He said I was free to go, and I left. The attorney-in-Kansas business, of course, was my attempt to show off my Maine sense of humor in a time of stress. What I, of course, meant was that if the government has an attorney, shouldn't I have one as well? Lo and behold, they took it seriously, as I would discover later when I was ordered to Germany to meet this famous or infamous general.

This was turning out to be a much bigger hockey game than it ever should have been. I flew out of Riyadh the next morning on a Lufthansa flight to Rhein Mein Air Base in Germany. The "sneak peek" colonel told me that the general's staff car would be there to pick me up.

My seatmate on the flight was the Boeing Tech Rep who had been part of the Accident Investigation Team. He said I did one hell of a job bringing that airplane in. "You nearly *cooked* the remaining two engines on the left side," he said. "But I don't see how you had any other options. That investigating general is quite a piece of work, dontcha think? I can't say I've ever been on an accident investigation quite like this one. It's going to cost in excess of five hundred thousand dollars to fix that beauty, but I know we can do it."

"Guess they'll just have to take it out of my pay," I said with a hint of sarcasm. "You know what it says in the Bible," he said. "They will make you pay every penny, although I don't think He [Jesus] was talking necessarily about money (Matthew 5:25–26, KJ)." He was right.

Once the flight was outside the international limit, the Saudis on the flight threw off their Arabian garb and put on their decadent Western clothes, lit up their cigarettes, and ordered their favorite drinks. Some Saudis are like some in the rest of the world. You know, MINO —Muslim in name only.

We arrived in Germany in the early morning hours, and I looked around for the general's staff car driver—nowhere to be found. Having been stationed in Germany before and speaking the language, I hitchhiked a ride with a German truck driver on his way to Ramstein Air Base, the home of the general. I was surprised when the German truck driver told me he was going to pull into one of the many roadside kiosks on the Autobahn for a quick beer. He asked if I wanted to join him? I wholeheartedly agreed. I was so bloody tired by now that one German beer would all but put me under.

You can say what you will about Germans, but they do make great beer. Their Mercedes' and BMWs' ain't all that bad either. One time, I was riding on a train coming back to Munich from Rome. I asked a German from Berlin what the best beer in Germany was. "Oh, that's easy," he said. "The best beer in Germany is… free beer. Same in the States, eh?" He walked away laughing.

The driver dropped me off at Ramstein Air Base, and I made my way to the BOQ (Bachelor Officers' Quarters). I got a room and called the general's office to tell them I had arrived. I also called a military lawyer at the Area Defense Counsel's Office explaining why I was there. He said he'd already had a call from Saudi Arabia. He said he agreed with the major lawyer in Saudi that I should tell the general nothing. The general thanked me for coming to Ramstein when I told him I had nothing to say. And, who to my continued astonishment should come on the phone but our "sneak peek" colonel who said, "Well, Colonel Hanson, I guess you hold the cards now. You are free to return to the States. We'll make all the arrangements. We'll send a car around for you." I wondered to myself if it would be the same car that should have picked me up at Rhein Mein.

I told the colonel not to bother. I told him I would take the bus back to Rhein Mein and ride with the troops, which I did. Back at the hotel at Rhein Mein, I met up with some of the AWACS crew who had been on the midair flight. One of the officers from Elf One actually came to my room that evening and brought me a beer. He had been the assistant commander of Elf One in Riyadh and was interested in only one thing: saving his sorry ass, and at my expense. He said that if only I would cooperate in this investigation, everything would go away. I told him that he must be living with Dorothy somewhere in Kansas. He got pissed off and left in a huff. Once again, my Maine attempt at humor failed me. Or did it?

The next morning, December 22, 1983, my charter flight to the States was scheduled to take off about midmorning. We were flying back to New York City via a military charter on a DC-8. They pack you in like a can of Maine sardines to get as many people on board as possible. I can't blame the civilian airlines for wanting to maximize their profits. After all, that's what they are in the business for in the first place.

I settled into my seat near the front of the aircraft and had a few drinks while en route to New York. The flight was pretty much uneventful, but long. Whenever you are flying West, you invariably encounter a head wind.

A few drinks and many hours later we landed in New York. I had to catch a shuttle bus to Philadelphia for my flight to North Carolina and, then, on to Memphis. The South was experiencing one of their worst ice storms in recent history.

The flight from Philly to North Carolina was a piece of cake. The flight from North Carolina to Memphis was quite a different story. We boarded the plane in North Carolina. It was around seven in the evening. I was wearing my blue dress uniform and my flight jacket with my insignia and wings in plain sight for

all to see. I asked the stewardess if the pilot in command was planning on deicing the aircraft prior to takeoff. Given my experiences over the past few weeks I was more than a little bit upset. A civilian airliner had recently crashed into the Potomac River where severe wing icing was the most probable cause.

The stewardess returned after apparently having a discussion with the pilot and informed me that the pilot knew what he was doing by not deicing the plane. I said that they perhaps should let me off the plane. She was getting visibly upset with me and the surrounding passengers' sudden interest in my concerns about deicing. It wasn't long before the cabin crew were trying to quell my concerns by bringing me liquor at no charge. It's sort of funny how airline passengers get interested in their safety when someone who knows a thing or two about flying voices their concerns, particularly when the weather's bad.

We did manage to finally get airborne by using most of the runway. We were on our way to Memphis. Upon landing in Memphis, while deplaning, I had a few choice words for the pilot who was standing in the cockpit doorway about his failure to deice the plane. You may remember that it was about this time that another plane, which was not deiced, ended up in the Potomac River, killing most on board. My fears were not without some merit and the pilot knew it. He told me that the deicing equipment was broken back in North Carolina. The profit motive won out over passenger safety in this case.

CHAPTER 9

It was late in the evening when we landed in Memphis. Memphis was suffering under the same pervasive ice storm as the rest of the southeast. The airport was nearly deserted, except for a few cab drivers. I hailed one down and said, "Blytheville, Arkansas, please." He drove out of the airport and asked if I had the money to pay for such a trip. I told him that I would pay when we arrived at my home in Steele, Missouri (just north of Blytheville). He said he needed at least half the fare before going on. I told him to drive me back to the hotel at the airport—the Hilton or Sheraton, I can't remember which.

When I reached into my pocket to pay for the short ride, all I had on me was $7.50 in cash, and no credit cards. I gave him what I had and went to check in at the hotel. I used the hotel phone to call home and got my wife's credit card number. She was most obliging. She was somewhat surprised to hear my voice and that I was in Memphis. We both agreed that it was simply too dangerous for her to drive to Memphis that night.

I used her credit card to check in, get a beer, and go to my room. My wife said she would pick me up in the morning. I went to my room, drank the lone beer, and took my last Valium. I was asleep in no time. It was a fitful sleep to be sure. I was still keyed up from everything that had happened to me over the past few weeks.

My wife arrived the next morning, and we headed home to our horse ranch in Steele, Missouri. I asked my wife to drive by the base so I could check-in before going home. Oddly enough, no one at the base knew what to do or what to say to me. You can be sure they all had heard about the midair collision in Saudi Arabia.

My sources told me that the base newspaper was going to print a story making me out to be some kind of hero for the way I recovered the damaged KC-135, but much higher powers directed the base newspaper to scrub the story. I finally tracked down the vice commander of the 97th Bomb Wing (a full colonel) and told him I was going home. He was a nice enough guy, or so I thought. He told me to go home, rest up some, and return to the base when I was ready. I did just that. I still had not talked with anyone in authority about the accident. Apparently, there were some nervous people all up and down the chain of command worried about what I might have to say concerning the whole ordeal.

My step-daughter said that she learned about my near death experience from one of her teachers at school. My wife only knew what I had told her by phone from Saudi. I was so frigged up when I called her; I actually wished her a happy anniversary when it was in fact her birthday.

It will be important later on to recall that my wife was a very good looking woman of Basque descent with dark skin and jet black, curly hair . Some might even say her hair was kinky. There would be many more congressmen and senators involved. Even a CBS *Sixty Minutes* crew came to my civilian attorney's Livermore Falls, Maine, office to check things out after I had had a lengthy discussion with CBS's David Martin (who is still with CBS, 2012).

CHAPTER 10

I took a few days off from work. When I did finally return to the base, I had no job, nor did I have a boss to answer to. It was as if I was suddenly persona non grata at my own base. The vice commander (who would eventually be promoted to wing commander) asked me to occupy a desk in the office adjacent to his. He calmly and somewhat slyly, in my view, asked me to write down everything that had happened while I was in Saudi. As we are fond of saying in Maine, "I was born at night, but not last night."

I did as he asked, but only included generalities. I described how lax security was at our hotel. I said that it was a wonder that none of us had been killed up till now. I said we had been successful in helping the Saudis get a water desalination plant up and running, one they had been trying to fix for a couple years. I explained how I got a friend of mine from South Africa, an expert in desalination, to come to the base and help us. For his help, I gave him a ride on one of our KC-135. That's how we did business over there, a sort of quid pro quo system. That would subsequently become a criminal offense during my trial. I went on in that vein for several pages and handed in my report.

The colonel was disappointed that I hadn't talked about the accident or its aftermath. He did, however, tell me that the four-star at Offutt Air Force Base, Nebraska (SAC headquarters), had ordered my flight pay halted. The local finance office complied with the four-star general's orders. When I asked if that was legal, the vice commander's assistant, another full colonel, said, "The general can do about whatever he wants." *"If that's how it's going to be,"* I said, *"I'll be checking in with the local Area Defense Council."*

The vice commander said it would not be necessary, that his assistant had spoken out of turn and unwisely. Just to be on the safe side, I said I would walk down to the Area Defense Council, which I did.

The man in charge of the local area was a young captain not long out of law school. I explained to him what was going on with me. He said he would make some inquiries, and I was to stay in touch, and by all means, to keep my mouth shut. He was particularly interested and perplexed by the SAC general's order to stop my flight pay. He used words like *jingoistic, overreaching power*, and a few others that I'd have to go home and look up. I don't remember if he actually used the word *fascistic*, but I think he did. I suggested to the vice commander that since I didn't really have anything to do, I might just as well take a week or so off, which I did. A young pilot friend of mine suggested I take his Corvette and head down to the Air War College at Maxwell AFB in Montgomery, Alabama, to visit our mutual friend and former squadron commander in the KC-135 unit at Blytheville. Our former commander was being promoted to full colonel and being groomed for a wing commander's job in Fort Worth, Texas.

Maxwell AFB was also the headquarters for all Area Defense Council lawyers, to whom my local captain lawyer back in Arkansas reported. Lieutenant Colonel Bob Reed was in his office at Maxwell, although I didn't know him at that time. He had the reputation throughout the entire Air Force of being the best and most effective defense lawyer in the Air Force. He would be joining my legal team in the coming months, along with a civilian lawyer from Livermore Falls, Maine, Dave Sanders, and naturally, the captain back in Arkansas.

I did manage to hook up with our former squadron commander. We shared a few beers, and he got to listen to me rant and rave about the past few weeks. He said that whatever and wherever I needed him, he would be there for me. You must keep in mind that our former squadron commander was being promoted to full colonel and taking over as a wing commander, a general officer position, and as such would be answerable to the same four-star who was hell bent on doing me in. One of my flying buddies had just returned from Fairford Air Base in England. He told me that a very high ranking officer had held a meeting with all personnel on the base in which my accident was addressed. There were certain promises made by this general according to my friend. He had made a guarantee about my retirement. The proof of that last statement will be made plain in a speech that four-star made on February 1, 1984, in England while briefing some troops headed for Riyadh, Saudi Arabia. What the four-star didn't know was that a very close friend of mine was at that briefing and relayed to me nearly verbatim what the general promised everyone in the room. In short, the general promised all the crew members at that briefing that, "Hanson will never see one thin dime of his retirement. I can promise you that."

That was a full eleven months before my court-martial. I thought undue command influence was supposed to be a crime, but I'm not a lawyer. But I do know the difference between bullshit and barbed wire, as we like to say in Maine.

CHAPTER 11

I guess we've all had an "agony in the garden experience." We can all, to some extent, know how He must have felt having taken on all our sins upon Himself. He could even tell when someone touched the hem of His garment. He must have had something akin to shingles over His entire body. He was, after all, the perfect man. Everything worked. All His brain cells were firing on all cylinders. I came close to that feeling, at least for a while after my trial.

When the judge made his final comments before sentencing me, he could not have known that I was, in his words, "In the fetal position because of what I had done while in Saudi Arabia or Vietnam." I was proud, and still am, of my service in Vietnam and in Saudi Arabia, especially proud of bringing that KC-135 back in one piece—more or less—and in helping save twelve lives, especially mine. We all know when we have done something particularly well and that is the only real reward—the knowledge that we did it. I didn't need any medals for doing a good job, but a simple thank you, especially from the rest of the crew would have been nice .

My remorse came from waiting twenty-five years for my examination of conscience, versus doing it daily, and then moving on. The Mormons have a great saying that "no success in life can ever compensate for a failure in the home." And while I achieved a measure of success in the Air Force, both in and out of combat, I was pretty much a failure on the home front, both as a father and as a husband. I was, in a sense, married to the Air Force. I got to examine my conscience over the 13 months before my trial. That examination covered nearly 25 years. I highly recommend a daily examination and then moving on. The sins of 25 years can be nearly more than one can bear. Someone once said that if we look too deeply into the abyss, we will find it looking back. I think it was Franz Kafka, but I'm not sure. Thank the Lord that we have(had)someone who bore all of our sins to Calvary and through His mercy and grace make it possible for us to start all over again. I came close to making the same mistake as Judas in thinking that I was not worthy of forgiveness. Having said all that, I was a personal failure in many regards, but not as a soldier. I have my enemies to thank for putting me onto the One who made my mistakes (sins) as white as snow. Yes, one of the greatest lessons I learned throughout this harrowing ordeal, is to make peace with ourselves on a daily basis. I agree with Franz Kafka, however, there is such a thing as State sponsored self-destruction, and I nearly bought into it. We all have to live with the results of our bad choices, but they don't have to keep us from picking up the pieces and making a positive difference in the world. Otherwise, Jesus Christ died for nothing.

My life was forever changed on April 5, 1985, when I sought out a Catholic priest at a local church in Blytheville, Arkansas. We Catholics, even us bad ones, call it confession. Others call it something else. I want to confirm in the strongest possible terms that it works no matter what you call it! Some religions pooh pooh the idea of confessions, especially as we Catholics practice it because they, the various religions and sects, see us Catholics as being able to do whatever we wish, over and over again, then simply going to confession. Well, hockey fans, that is not how it works. I agree with those who see us in that light. Taking full responsibility for our actions is no easy matter. A few days after my meeting with the priest on that Good Friday, back in 1985, people all over Blyheville, Arkansas were remarking on my obvious transformation. My physical appearance was different. Some even commented on my joyfulness. I seemed almost child-like, playful if you will. A few days after Easter, 1985, as I was preparing to go to bed, I said to the Lord: if I was to die tonight then I was ready. When I awoke the next morning, my whole body was rigid with arms and legs stretched out. I can not to this day tell you exactly what happened, but I know that something of some magnitude took place in my body during the night. I never cared all that much for our horses. I mostly left them alone and they didn't bother me either. But on this morning as I went into the corral all the horses came over to me and gently sought out my patting them. It was as if all fear had left my body. For lack of a better description all I can say is that I was experiencing that peace that passeth all understanding as the Scriptures describe it. Because of Christ's crucifixion and subsequent resurrection I was given this unmerited gift of grace and mercy. My only unanswered question was what was this new peaceful warrior supposed to do in this old warrior's body? Somewhere in Scripture it talks about reconciling the double-minded into a new creation. "A double-minded man is unstable in all his ways. KJ James 1:8. And that's where I was at. Some called it Post Traumatic Stress Syndrome (PTSD) ; some said it was a form of Bi-Polarity, and some simply thought I had gone nuts. One of my many college degrees was in Psychology. I knew that something was wrong, but I didn't quite know what to do about it. Shakespeare says somewhere that "I can more easily teach 20 people what to do as to take my own advice." I had a friend in Maine who was raised a Catholic and then decided to do his own thing. He said he was going to count on a death bed conversion. He died several years ago. Whether or not he was successful the Lord only knows. I, for one, am not willing to take such a grave risk. Are you? And yes, in a very real sense, I was, to coin a phrase *born again*. My problem was I was a brand new creation in a badly beat up body. You could say it made me a little bit crazy, and some did say that. It sounds so trite and common place to say it, but *Thank you, Jesus.*

A STARRY CROSS

I was nailed to a Starry Cross many years ago
Like so many soldiers I have come to know
Now I can't speak for all soldiers, sailors, airmen, and marines
I can only tell you what I've felt and seen

When I signed on to serve my country like so many others,
I was young and green
I was luckier than most
I got to be a wheel

But sometimes the bigger wheels
Used us smaller wheels like hydrants
And as big dogs will
Used us to clean their spleens

And as luck would have it, I was hauled into court
I was nailed to a cross of shiny stars
All because two planes ran into each other
While guarding the oil fields oh so many miles away

And when the trial was over so was my career
They took me back to my basic DNA
As criminal trials are designed to do
They with the shiny stars also paid a price
They were asked to leave the service a few months after me
I was left as a little boy in a combat veteran's body
The experts said I was left with "bipolarity"

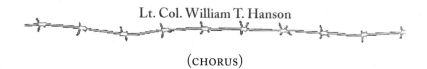

(CHORUS)

Even after all these years with many an up and down
The one thing I know for sure
It's still real hard to find a middle ground

God sometimes uses the weak to confound the mighty
And such was the case with me
When I came down from that starry cross,
I was left with my pension and my bipolarity

My best medicine is a God-fearin' woman and a
Good ol' Blue Grass song

CHAPTER 12

Sometime in late spring or early summer of 1984 while in the pro shop of our small golf course at Blytheville AFB in Blytheville, Arkansas, an Air Force full colonel came up to me, wrapped one arm around my shoulder, and said, "Sometimes, Colonel Hanson, things (or people—I'm not sure if he said *things* or *people*) are diabolical."

I have been wondering about his comment for more than twenty-five years. Was he telling me that I was up against an evil system or up against someone evil? Given his rank and position in the military food chain, he must have known something. Was he saying that someone in my chain of command was actually evil, and if so, who?

Was it Colonel Croker? Was it Lieutenant General Bill Campbell? Was it General Bennie Davis? Was it General Creech? Was it Casper Weinberger? Who? In all my tours in Vietnam and the Middle East, I can't say I ever considered my enemies evil. I always thought of them as soldiers, only on a different side. Of whom might this colonel been speaking? And if he was right, then, my situation may have been even more sinister than I first thought. Perhaps we'll discover who or what the colonel was speaking about as we begin.

The story is true and as accurate as I can possibly make it. The players are real—alive or dead, as the case may be. I know at least one of them is still alive (or was at the time of this writing).

Abraham Lincoln was supposed to have said that were he given eight hours to cut down a tree, he would spend the first six hours sharpening his ax. I have spent the better part of the last

twenty-six years sharpening my pen to write this incredible story. So let's see if the pen is actually mightier than the sword.

One last thought: if the colonel mentioned above was right in saying that I was in fact up against diabolical forces, how does one combat evil? Some writers have said that God permits evil so that a greater good can come from it. You, of course, dear readers, will be the judges of whether or not a greater good has emerged. And having said that, let's get our story airborne.

A Letter to General Bennie Davis

> I remember the first time I met you. You were only a one star then at Randolph AFB, Texas, where I went through undergraduate pilot training. I had just finished my last solo flight in the supersonic T-38 and was preparing to become an instructor pilot at Randolph. You met my aircraft as I was climbing out of the cockpit on the ramp because some folks on the base thought my flight looked dangerous on takeoff in that I never came out of afterburner as I left the area. It wasn't dangerous nor was it illegal, but, it looked dangerous is how I believe you put it. You informed me that they were going to change my assignment to the much slower T-37 trainer and send me to Laredo, Texas. I'm pretty sure the they you referred to was. . .you. That wouldn't be the last time that you ordered people to either do something for or against me. You did tell me that if I were still alive in three years you would give me a job, and true to your word, you did. I had to refuse because I was headed back to Vietnam for another combat tour. The next time I ran across you, you had your second star and were now the commander of the Air Force Military Personnel Center at Randolph. By that time I was flying the T-39 Sabre Liner, a VIP-type plane. I was assigned as your personal pilot.
>
> The flight I remember most was the day I flew you to Washington, D.C. I think you were in Washington to be questioned by members of congress about dropping bombs in Cambodia, *illegally* as it was alleged, but found not to be

true. I have included a short piece about your boss at the time, one General Lavelle. General Lavelle lost two stars and retired in disgrace. Only recently did the senate of the United States discover by listening to the Nixon tapes that he, the president, had ordered the bombing in Cambodia.

What stands out in my mind is the flight back to Randolph AFB from Andrews. The weather back at Randolph was about as bad as it could be with near zero visibility and ceiling. You asked me if I could get you back and I said I would do my best, but we'd only get one shot. The tower advised me that the base was *technically* closed but given the nature of my passenger (two stars), they would allow one try to get the aircraft on the ground. I flew what was one of my better flights even though we had to be towed to parking by a tug. My next significant flight would come years later in Saudi Arabia, and wouldn't you know? You were involved in that one also; but by then, you had four stars.

You did ask me after the flight from Washington, D.C., to Randolph what you could do for me. You gave me a pat on the back, and I said, only half-jokingly, "Just make sure I make major." The very next morning, you called my boss, Lieutenant Colonel Cooney, and asked him for my service number. My boss, being a somewhat nervous type, automatically assumed I did something to piss you off because he came running out of his office and asked me what I had done to make you mad. "Nothing, to my knowledge," I assured him. After a day or so you called me and asked me if I could keep a secret. I said I could and you said, "Well, you made major, but keep it under your hat. One hell of a good job flying the other night. Thanks." You weren't nearly so generous with your compliments concerning my recovery of the badly damaged KC-135 in Saudi Arabia on December 9, 1983. Saving one life was okay, but saving twelve lives and a twenty-four-million-dollar aircraft was quite another matter.

It would be years before I had occasion to communicate with you again, General Davis. You had four stars now and were the Commander of the Strategic Air Command (SAC) in Omaha, Nebraska. I was in Munich, Germany, as the director of procurement for the Army and Air Force Exchange Service (AAFES). I think it was late 1979 or early 1980. I had been grounded on Christmas Eve 1973 from a bout with bleeding ulcers. I remember sending you a short note about my upcoming meeting with the Flight Standards Evaluation Board at Ramstein AFB to see if I could be returned to flying status. You sent me a post card saying, "Sometimes you just have to tell people what to do." You said I would, in fact, be returned to flying status.

General Davis, that would be the last time I'd hear from you, even if only indirectly After the midair in Saudi Arabia on December 9, 1983, and prior to my court-martial, I guess you *just felt compelled to tell people what to do* one last time. No, no, that's not quite right. You also ordered my flight pay stopped way back in early 1984 before I'd met any boards. They did stop it for a short while, but later gave it all back when they found out that even four-star generals have to follow certain rules and legal procedures.

One last question, General Davis: Did you tell a group of pilots on February 1, 1984, while in Fairford, England, that "I will guarantee you all here today one thing, Lieutenant Colonel Hanson will never receive one dime of his retirement pay?" Sir, did you tell them to do that too? Why? General Lavelle was scapegoated and lost two stars. Apparently he's getting his stars back, but little good it will do him, eh? He's been dead for thirty-one years now. It's not difficult to imagine how a four star general in charge of the most powerful nuclear arsenal in the world might think to himself that he could do just about whatever he wanted to. He was, after all, constitutionally in line to be president of the United States.]

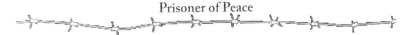

A Letter to Lt. Gen. William Campbell, Commander Eighth Air Force

Dear General Campbell,

I have never met you, but I do have your endorsements on some of my Officer Effectiveness Reports (OERs) recommending that I be promoted to full colonel. As the Commander of the Eighth Air Force in Bossier City, Louisiana, you approved my being assigned as the detachment commander of the KC-135 tanker operation in Riyadh, Saudi Arabia in 1983 when, on December 9, 1983, we had the midair collision with the E3-A AWACS. The AWACS was under the command of General Creech, commander of the Tactical Air Command (TAC). You were also the one who ordered my court-martial against the advice of your own legal counsel. Why was that, Sir?

I talked to you briefly several years ago by phone from your home in Florida.

When I asked you if you really did have that beautiful VC-137 aircraft assigned to you destroyed in Cairo, Egypt, I got no answer. Some people on your immediate staff speculated to me that you thought I was going to go public and tell how the citizens of Bossier City had paid to have your beautiful VC-137 outfitted to the nines, so to speak. That can't possibly be true, can it, General? General Campbell, are you the diabolical one the colonel spoke to me about back at the golf course at Blytheville AFB in Arkansas while I awaited my court-martial?

A Letter to Stephen B. Croker
Colonel USAF, Commander 97TH Bomb Wing
Blytheville AFB, Arkansas

Dear Colonel Croker,

I know you are now a retired three star general working for USAA in San Antonio, Texas, my insurance company. Hell's bells, General, you're still getting into my pocket book. Wasn't my court-martial enough for you? I refer to you as Colonel Croker just to keep things in context. Please forgive my literary license.

We knew each other pretty darned well back in 1983 when you were the vice commander and subsequent wing commander of the now-defunct 97th Bomb Wing at Blytheville AFB in Arkansas. I vividly remember how we used to enjoy sitting around discussing the latest book we'd just read.

I recall being *one of your favorites* until all hell broke loose following the midair collision on December 9, 1983. By then, I think you had replaced your fellow Air Force Academy classmate as the wing commander of the 97th Bomb Wing, but I might have my dates mixed up. When I returned from Saudi Arabia, I was, to say the least, somewhat messed up physically and emotionally. And since I no longer had a job, you made me your *special assistant* doing not much of anything, unless you consider coming into an office adjacent to yours and sitting there as being something. I should point out to the readers that neither of these gentlemen ever responded to my letters.

I do remember your asking me to write an in-depth report of what happened in Saudi Arabia on the fateful day. My lawyer advised me to say nothing about the accident and all the subsequent investigations. I gave you a general synopsis of my observations of the goings-on in and around Riyadh. I do remember telling you how lax I thought security was over there. And, Colonel, if I'm not mistaken, you made a special trip over there for the Air

Force Chief of Staff based in part on what I told you, did you not?

Then came April 1984 when you called me into your private office. You had the base lawyer with you, but no lawyer for me. I could tell it was serious because you were seated erect behind your big mahogany desk, when, normally, you'd either be standing beside or sitting on the front edge of your desk. I also remember calling you later that day from my horse ranch on the Arkansas-Missouri border in Steele, Missouri, and telling you, "This is not an effing joke." You did say to me, one of the last times you'd ever talk to me, "You have more power, Colonel Hanson, than you might realize." I never did get that, entirely.

Most of what follows is conjecture on my part, except for my final Officer Effectiveness Report (OER) you wrote on me. You can read what the judge had to say about that report in his concluding remarks to the court. Just three more points, Colonel (Okay, General), and I'm finished—for now.

Do you remember the softball game between the officers and the enlisted men sometime in the spring of 1984 when, in a critical part of the game, a base hit would probably have won the game? You took the bat from me and went to the plate yourself. Do you recall how the enlisted men reacted? They all turned their backs on you for a brief second because you took the bat from me.

Do you remember the pool party at the Officer's Club right after my name was splashed across the front page of the local Blytheville newspaper? I hadn't shown my face around the club much for obvious reasons. I don't know what possessed me to go that night, but I do remember one of my friends and fellow pilots, Rich Busa, coming up to me and giving me a big bear hug and a kiss on the cheek— very Italian I thought. I've always fondly remembered it as a sort of *anti-Judas* kiss. Do you remember how pissed off that made you, Colonel?

And finally, Colonel Croker, do you remember going to the nuclear alert facility on the day I was to be sentenced and telling everyone there to go to the small, second floor court house across the base so they could see firsthand what happens when someone decides to buck the system? This is not, I repeat, not mere conjecture on my part, nor a figment of my imagination. You in fact did do it and I can still prove it to this very day. Do you remember that, Colonel Croker? Fortunately for me or out of respect or whatever, not one officer or enlisted man showed up.

Colonel Croker, weren't you the diabolical person I was dealing with, the one described to me by one of your full colonel deputies earlier at the golf course? Or perhaps you were diabolical in another sense? Maybe, you were only playing the devil for the higher-ups, and deep down were a decent guy? Maybe not? Only you know that, right? You were right about one thing, Colonel. When you told everyone on the base that "Hanson was good, but he was also lucky." I was and I am, but I was not deserving of either a court-martial or that career-ending OER you wrote. So which were you, Colonel, the devil or just the devil in disguise?

NO BILL

According to my civilian defense attorney, David Sanders, from Livermore Falls, Maine, a military Article 32 hearing is somewhat different from a civilian grand jury procedure. "If a civilian grand jury finds insufficient grounds to proceed to a trial, it's called a *no bill*. The military can decide to ignore the recommendations of the Article 32 presiding grand jury officer and press on to a court-martial," Mr. Sanders explained. That is what Lieutenant General William Campbell, the commander of the Eighth Air Force at Barksdale AFB in Bossier City, Louisiana, decided to do. He was the convening authority in this case.

CHAPTER 13

The Waiting Game. During the summer and fall of 1984, not much was going on while I waited for a firm trial date, at least on the surface. Although I can't prove it, nor would the government ever admit it, I swear that someone had broken into our ranch-style home on the outskirts of Blytheville, Arkansas in Steele, Missouri. I don't know what they may have been looking for, but my papers and files had been moved on more than one occasion. My wife said she never messed with my documents. She knew I was trying to chronicle what was going on in my life on a daily basis—more to keep my sanity than anything else. Besides, it was good therapy.

I remember reading something written by I. B. Singer wherein he said that the reason Job put up with all of God's *tricks* in his life was because "it was all part of the big game; we all play chess with Fate as a partner." And so it was with me. Had it not been me in the game, one would think it to be all a great farce.

I did have the opportunity to fly aboard one of our local KC-135s from Blytheville to a base in California to attend the wedding of my former copilot, the aircraft commander on this flight. When he was still a lieutenant, we served a short tour in Riyadh, Saudi Arabia, in 1981. He was subsequently promoted to captain and upgraded to aircraft commander in the KC-135.

Before we were allowed to depart on our Saudi tour, I had to do some fancy paperwork involving the lieutenant. I had to figure out a way to make the lieutenant a non-Jew. I wrote a special Officer Effectiveness Report making him a deacon in the Methodist Church. You see, Jews were not allowed in Saudi Arabia. How did we arrive at Methodist? I think we flipped a coin. Heads was Baptist, tails was Methodist. All concerned thought I pulled off a creative religious transformation. We served our Saudi tour without further incident—no passport problems, nothing. In fact, we were dubbed Batman and Robin.

Back to 1984 when Captain Wolborski asked me to join in his wedding party in Reno, Nevada. Our present wing commander, Colonel Steve Croker, was nervous about allowing me on the flight with Captain Wolborski, who had been a very loyal copilot and friend. The colonel even made me promise not to intervene with the crew on the flight to and from California. I don't know who was more paranoid, the United States Air Force or me.

As I have said elsewhere in this story, the books I needed to be reading to help me cope somehow *fell* into my lap. Call it divine intervention, coincidence, or serendipity. All I know is that they appeared right on time. The book I read on my flight to the wedding was Nicholas Proffitt's *Gardens of Stone*. It became a best seller and was made into a movie of the same name. I was so moved by the book, which had me laughing and crying on each turn of the page that I actually called the author to tell him how much I enjoyed his book. He thanked me, and we talked at some length about my present predicament.

At one point, I said our conversation was probably being monitored. He agreed that it probably was. I asked him to write my story. He said, "Colonel Hanson, you have to write your own story, but you can use my agent. But," he concluded, "you have to know one thing about literary agents. No matter how good the story might be, agents are only interested in one thing. *Can they sell it?*" I would talk with Mr. Proffitt years later.

MISSILE SECRETS: A BRIEF STEP BACK

Fast forward to January 1985. According to Franz Kafka in his book *The Trial*, the major function of the defense is to find *a friend on the court*. Sometime in 1981, while Major General Pringle was the chief of staff, SAC, commanded by General Bennie Davis, an

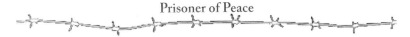
Air Force lieutenant, was alledged to have given missile secrets to the Russians. General Pringle was assigned to handle the case. This, of course, is only a rough synopsis of the case, but the case still makes Kafka's point.

One thing led to another, and a deal was made to not prosecute the lieutenant if he cooperated and told what he knew. Somewhere up the chain of command this decision was going to be reversed. Perhaps it was Secretary of Defense Casper Weinberger, maybe General Davis, hell's bells, it may have been President Reagan himself.

As you may well imagine, things became very heated. One thing led to another, and before you could say "You're fired," General Pringle was summarily fired in one day after more than thirty-three years of dedicated service. A young Air Force major and lawyer (Major Barton L. Spillman) was put on the case by somebody in Washington, D.C., to try and reverse General Pringle's decision. This attorney and General Pringle were obviously at odds, which is pretty much an understatement. Please keep in mind that the judge at my court-martial was none other than now-Lieutenant Colonel Barton L. Spillman.

The fight was on against General Pringle with Major Spillman leading the way. And voila, one F. Lee Bailey arrives on the scene in his private jet representing the lieutenant. Bailey explained to all present that a deal is a deal. To my knowledge, the lieutenant walked. As I said, Major General Pringle was forced to retire in one day. In effect, he was fired. Casper Weinberger, General Bennie Davis, and Major Spillman were all instrumental in one way or another in General Pringle's early demise. He and his lovely wife Ann (also a seasoned aviator) left for Freeland, Washington, on Whitby Island. In the moving process I'm told that two moving vans carrying most of their belongings caught on fire and burned up much of their stuff. Apparently, all accidental.

General Pringle is one of my key witnesses. He flew into Memphis, Tennessee, the day before he was scheduled to testify

on my behalf and was subsequently picked up by a staff car from Blytheville AFB. General Pringle had once been the Director of Operations at Blytheville AFB and still had many civilian friends in and around the town of Blytheville, Arkansas.

One such friend was a civilian attorney who hosted a cocktail party at his home in honor of General Pringle. Another guest at the party was none other than my trial judge Lieutenant Colonel Barton L. Spillman. Somehow, General Pringle and Lt. Col. Spillman got over their previous differences.

Of necessity, I must include some of the direct trial transcript testimony. I will only be including the direct testimony of the ones I feel are significant. Truth be told, my dear readers, most of the charges against me don't amount to a hill of beans. Most of the charges leveled against me, we had been doing for years and are probably still being done. The one charge of significance is the one in which I was supposed to have somehow coerced the boom operator into changing the Form F (the weight and balance form). That would have been *Conduct Unbecoming*.

CHAPTER 14

A General's Promise:
General Bennie Davis (a four star) was the commander in Chief of the Strategic Air Command (SAC) located at Offutt Air Force Base in Omaha, Nebraska, during this period (December, 1983–June, 1985). On or about February 3 , General Davis was on a visit to RAF Fairford Air Base outside London. The flying unit at Fairford was under his command as was the detachment at Riyadh, Saudi Arabia. In between General Davis and the Saudi detachment was a one-star general located at Ramstein AFB in Germany, and under the general in Germany was a full colonel at RAF Fairford. The Fairford colonel was directly in charge of the detachment commander at Riyadh, Saudi Arabia, namely yours truly at that time.

I had been a part of, or seen, too many investigations not to suspect that something about this one was out of whack. I was not the most cooperative witness during the myriad investigations that followed the midair. In a word, I was being set up to be the scapegoat for this entire mess, and I had had enough of that sort of thing, given my past history in Vietnam.

Something very similar had happened back in Vietnam when I had taken it upon myself to set up a rescue mission to get some of our downed crew members out of the North one night. I was working the night mission in a secure computer bunker on the border of Thailand and Laos at a place called NKP (Na Kom Phenom). We had some very sophisticated computer-sensor equipment with which to track the enemy.

The weather was bad the night in question, so I called one of my flying buddies in Saigon at 7th Air Force Headquarters. He was in charge of the FRAG section and could order aircraft from around the surrounding countries to fly air strikes. Captain Jock

Patterson agreed with my plan to launch four F-4's loaded with laser guided bombs to drop on one of the sensors located adjacent to a Surface to Air Missile site (SAM) that was shooting down our planes. There were several downed crew members in the area, but the weather was so bad that our rescue aircraft teams couldn't get to the crew members. The sensors by this SAM site gave off navigation information. My idea was to have the F-4s drop their laser-guided bombs directly on the sensor itself since we knew the exact location of the sensor. Captain Patterson agreed, and we did it. The next morning the A-1Es went in and rescued all the downed crew members.

So what's the connection to General Davis and the midair collision in Saudi Arabia you may be asking? My boss in Thailand was an Air Force full colonel. When he came to work the next morning, he called me into his office and said he was going to take legal action against me for dropping bombs in North Vietnam without higher headquarters approval. You may recall, in the seventies that, oftentimes, we were supposed to get White House approval to bomb certain targets. Later on in this story, you will see how General Davis himself along with his boss, General LaVelle, were brought before congress for similar actions in Cambodia.

At any rate, my colonel was preparing the necessary paperwork to have me punished. A major in the A-1E rescue squadron who had been in on the rescue the previous morning heard about my dilemma and came rushing to my aid. We called the major the Six-Million-Dollar Man. Major Jim Harding, I think that was his name. He was on his third or fourth tour in Vietnam, perhaps more. He had medals on his chest, up over his shoulder, and down to his backsides. He told the colonel to go ahead with his legal paperwork, and they (the A-1E pilots) would put me in for a Silver Star.

"Now won't that make you look like the real dope," Major Harding said. No further action was taken. The difference in this case is that a group of seasoned combat pilots came to the aid of one of their own. And as you will see later, they did it again.

CHAPTER 15

Lt. Col. James "Red" Clevenger by his F-16, a fighter pilot's fighter pilot. I used this as the cover photo to honor "Red" and, through him, the others who stood behind me in my hour of need.

The actual AWACS just prior to impact.

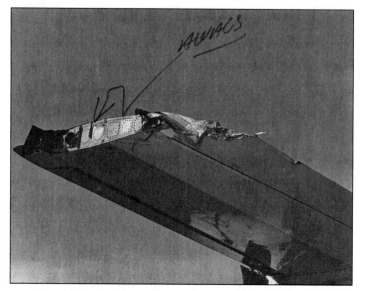

The AWACS left wing after impact missing eight feet

KC-135 right wing on the ramp at Riyadh after landing.

KC-135 Right wing after landing, on ramp at Riyadh, Saudi Arabia.
Note right wing fuel tank area

KC-135 Right wing

93

KC-135 # 3 engine. The first thing I saw when I
looked out the copilot's right window.

Part of the AWACS wing still stuck in the
right wing on KC-135 after landing

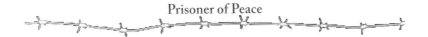

As I said previously, I returned to the States on or about December 22, 1983 as a persona non grata with pretty much nothing to do, except stew in my own adrenalin juices. One might say I was on a more or less permanent adrenalin high, much I imagine, like our Prisoners of War were, except that I was still a Prisoner of Peace. The aircraft recovery was scary enough as the photos show, but it was to get much worse.

CHAPTER 16

I went back to work once my vacation was over. It would be more accurate to say I went back to the base, but with no job or duties whatsoever. It was January 1984. I truly had nothing to do; accordingly, I started playing golf in the mornings at our nine-hole course. Sometimes I would be invited to play at the local private country club with some civilian friends. The country club was an all-white one with black folks doing much of the maintenance When I wasn't home or playing golf, I hung out at the local VFW bar just outside the base.

It was a small place with a horseshoe bar, pool table, and little else if you don't count the back room where it was rumored that some card games took place. Several of the town's influential businessmen frequented the bar. We would play pool, sometimes for healthy amounts of money, and generally talk about whatever was going on. I can remember playing a well-to-do rancher for—believe it or not—his ranch. He, of course, was well into the Who-Shot-John by then and had no recollection of the bet on the pool game. It was just as well from my point of view because I had no interest in his ranch. Many of the spectators wanted me to at least press the point of the bet for no other reason than to teach him a lesson. He got to keep his ranch, with one proviso: that he would never play pool against me again. He agreed.

It was an odd group who gathered at the VFW most days. The conversation eventually got around to my situation. The local manager asked me what the Air Force was charging me with. I told him that was a very good question. I had just saved a twenty-five million dollar plane and twelve lives, including my own.

I had been reading a lot of books by that time, sometimes two a day. I quoted Socrates when I told the manager that I couldn't, for the life of me, figure out why I was being fed hemlock. Socrates had apparently asked his accusers for what good deed he was being punished. As the weeks turned into months, I obviously was becoming more irritated, paranoid really. I began to be wary of everyone, especially strangers. There were a couple of guys who hung out more or less regularly at the local VFW. They just sat in the corner, drank beer and watched the pool games. Numerous rumors circulated around the area as to who they were and what they did. I asked my VFW manager friend if the two guys in the corner really did kill people for the government. He said they did, but I was not to worry. "They only kill bad people," he said. "And you ain't a bad guy." He said he wished he was younger so he could still drink and really get into my case. He asked me how I was coping with all the pressure. I told him I was writing a novel about the whole thing as it was transpiring as a therapeutic technique. He mentioned how that was a stroke of ingenuity. "Will I die in your book?" he laughed.

Not much was going on for me at the base, so I stayed home and became immersed in literature. I have very often found the answers to my problems by having the right book fall into my lap at the appropriate time. I began with Plato and went from there. As I said, when I came to that part where Socrates was sentenced to drink hemlock, I was pretty sure I was in big trouble. And of course, there's Jesus, but we'll get to him later.

I guess you could say the SAC four-star general was the head of the military Sanhedrin and not about to relinquish his power. He was, after all, in the chain of command to be the next president of the United States should things get that bad. What is it that would have a young hockey player from the sticks of Dixfield, Maine, thinking he could take on the all powerful Department of Defense, including the Strategic Air Command and all their nukes?

When I returned home one evening, there was a green check from the United States Treasury in my rural mail box, and without a stamp or postmark. Someone had obviously had hand-

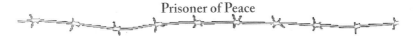

delivered it from the base. It was my entire back flight pay that the four-star had ordered stopped. Three and four-star generals *are* powerful, but they're not gods.

When I wasn't playing golf or drinking beer at the VFW, I would go home, feed our Arabian horses, have a martini, and listen religiously to the evening news on NPR. I was still devouring books and searching for answers. Of Kipling's *Six Honest Working Men* (Who, What, Why, Where, How, and When), I was mostly asking *Why?* I think I must have gone through over three hundred books. And yes, the Big Book played a key role in my survival. I can hear some of you saying, "Oh, here we go, another finding God while in his foxhole." It ain't exactly that simple, but we'll get to all that later on. If my newfound friend, King David is right, He never leaves. It's we who go away from time to time.

Nothing much happened in January 1984. I got my handicap down to a six. There is something to be said for practice. As I said, our ranch was on the outskirts of Blytheville, Arkansas, just off I-35 in Steele, Missouri. There was an all night gas station a few hundred yards down the road from our ranch just off the highway. One night, while I was still in Saudi Arabia, someone robbed the gas station and decided to hide out in our hayloft in the barn. A neighbor saw them (or him) go into the barn and called the county sheriff. The land around our home was pancake flat— cotton and soybean country. One could see practically forever. Anyway, the sheriff, a friend of the family, came and arrested the robber and took him away.

I used to throw a big weekend party every Memorial Day weekend. We erected a big tent in the driveway, cooked a pig, played poker, and drank copious amounts of beer. Lots of people from the base showed up over the course of the weekend, including many civilians from around the area. In fact, one of my flying buddies, who had his own plane, provided the opening ceremonies' flyby. We even had a band. It was quite fun really.

One such guest was the arresting county sheriff. He called me aside and said that, if it ever happened again, I was to shoot the culprit, drag him inside, and he would take care of the rest. I do believe he was serious. They do things a little differently sometimes in the deep south, kind of reminiscent of the two guys in the corner of the VFW. As I say, January 1984 was pretty much a time for golf, beer, martinis, NPR radio, and feeding the horses. My wife was a traveling salesperson who covered Arkansas, Tennessee, and Mississippi. Needless to say, we didn't see that much of each other. To coin a phrase, she pretty much did her thing, and I mine.

There was plenty going on behind the scenes concerning the accident in Saudi Arabia, but I wouldn't find out about that until February when I was ordered to be in Michigan's Upper Peninsula, for what the Air Force calls a Collateral Board Investigation. What that means is that the Air Force is going to assign blame for the accident. My high powered and intelligent lawyer from Maxwell AFB in Montgomery, Alabama, one Lieutenant Colonel Bob Reed came to the scene, much to the chagrin of the Air Force power brokers. He made a call to the investigating officer, a full colonel F-15 pilot from Langley Air Force Base in Virginia, home of the Tactical Air Command (to whom the AWACS belongs) and, coincidentally, an Air Force Academy Graduate and classmate of my present wing commander in Blytheville, Arkansas. Colonel Reed told the F-15 pilot investigating officer that we'd have nothing to say. "Well, come on up anyway," the investigator said. We did. You could have fed a lot of starving people for the amount of money they were spending just to teach me a lesson.

The SAC Commander, the four-star, had recently written an open letter that appeared in our local base newspaper. In that article, he said, partly in response to my attitude about feeding the poor, that, "The milk of human kindness was flowing too freely through our veins." I assume by *our*, he meant the United States. A phrase making its way around the country those days was *compassion fatigue*.

CHAPTER 17

My senior military lawyer and I flew from Memphis to Chicago and then on to K. I. Sawyer Air Force Base in Michigan. We remained overnight and then went to the hearing at which time my attorney, Lieutenant Colonel Reed advised the investigating officer, the F-15 pilot, that, "My client, Lieutenant Colonel Hanson, has nothing to say at this time." "Okay," the colonel said, "you are free to go. Thanks for coming." What a waste of time and money.

We reversed our course and returned to Blytheville AFB in Arkansas. But, before we got back, the F-15 pilot had already flown his F-15 to my base, ostensibly to refuel. Blytheville is somewhat out of the way if one is flying to Virginia (and it's a SAC base, not a TAC base, to which the investigating officer was assigned). The F-15 pilot and my wing commander were classmates at the Air Force Academy in Colorado Springs, Colorado. It's purely conjecture on my part, but I assume that he had been directed to touch base with my wing commander to see if he could put some additional pressure on me to cooperate and settle this matter more quietly.

As you may recall, the Iran Contra business was brewing in the bowels of the White House as Marine Lieutenant Colonel Oliver North and his team were doing whatever it was to raise money to conduct the war in Nicaragua. There was further conjecture that the Iranians had been persuaded to delay release of the hostages from our Iranian Embassy until after President Reagan was sworn in, thereby making President Carter look even more incompetent than he might otherwise have been. The Saudis were also rumored to be providing money for the Iran

Contra operations. Couple this with the facts that the midair collision took place in Saudi Arabia and the pending arms sales to the Saudis and it's perhaps understandable why the powers that were simply wanted this international incident to simply go away.

Not long after the F-15 pilot investigating officer made his refueling stop in Arkansas, my present wing commander, his Academy classmate, was fired—well, in the Air Force, we don't say *fired*; we say he was transferred. His assistant, the vice commander, and also an Air Force Academy graduate and perhaps his classmate as well, was elevated to the wing commander's position, all but assuring his promotion to general. The wheels kept on turning behind the scenes, and I kept on playing golf.

I took the paperwork and headed for the local Area Defense Counsel's office just down the street from the wing commander's office. On the way out of the wing commander's office, I asked why my lawyer was not allowed to be present. The new wing commander's assistant (another academy graduate) stopped me and said, "Colonel Hanson, the Constitution doesn't apply in this case. General Campbell's calling the shots now." General Campbell, of whom he spoke, was the Eighth Air Force Commander stationed at Barksdale AFB in Louisiana. He was a three-star and on his way up the promotion ladder. My wing commander was answerable to Lieutenant General Campbell. Ironically enough, General Campbell had endorsed my last officer efficiency report (OER) and had approved my assignment to Saudi Arabia as the detachment commander there. Not only that, he had recommended that I be promoted to full colonel during the next promotion cycle.

My Article 32 hearing was approaching. Civilians call it a grand jury hearing. I felt that I needed more legal assistance. I asked for and was granted permission to fly to Maine to try and secure some more legal horsepower to augment my military team. I contacted my cousin, one Billy Rowe, who had a legal office in

Livermore Falls, Maine. I explained my dilemma to my cousin. He said, "What you need is a smart New York Jew to help you watch over the military. I have just such a partner working with me, Dave Sanders. I'll cut out my share of the fee and have him work for you." In what might be typical lawyer parlance, when I asked my cousin how much it would cost, he said, "Well, how much you got?"

We settled on five thousand dollars to get the legal ball rolling. I went back to Arkansas and informed my other two Air Force lawyers that a civilian attorney would be joining the team. When they asked me why, I only half-jokingly said that he would be there to watch them and assist where he could. I went on to explain to Colonel Reed that he himself was still the lead counsel. The Article 32 hearing was scheduled for some time in April as I recall. The other side, that is to say, the Department of Defense (DOD) assigned a lawyer from Lowry AFB in Denver, Colorado, to be the Article 32 hearing officer. I knew this man from my having been the chief of procurement at Lowry AFB back in my career in the mid-seventies. Many of our procurement contracts had to be reviewed for legal sufficiency prior to being awarded. He and I had worked together on numerous contracts.

Lieutenant General Campbell assigned one of his lawyers, a major, to represent the prosecution. The prosecution called a minimum number of witnesses. We called none. The one Air Force witness who generated the majority of concern was the boom operator sergeant on the midair collision in question. I affectionately referred to him as Sergeant Othello. He was quite Shakespearean in his own way. My civilian attorney put the young sergeant through his paces under oath for what seemed to be forever. It was obvious to everyone in the room that the sergeant was both lying and confused. The key issue at hand was whether or not I had compelled the sergeant to change the weight and balance form (Form F) to reflect fewer passengers on board the KC-135 during the midair collision on December 9, 1983, than were actually on the plane. Had the Saudi tower tape been available to us, the issue would have been resolved in an instant. I think the tower tapes back then were acetate and cost about eight bucks. It's my understanding that neither side wants to reveal their theory of the case during the preliminary hearing phase.

The prosecution called a few witnesses, including a couple of the KC-135 crew members on the flight in question. Some of the crew members testifying against me were rumored to have been given assurances at the highest levels that if they stuck to their stories, they would be okay. I was not without friends throughout all this. They passed on bits and pieces of information they thought I should know.

The Article 32 hearing was held in the Base Headquarters building, an old WWII building converted to office buildings. The Base Headquarters was separate from Wing Headquarters. Base Headquarters personnel were responsible for maintaining the day-to-day facilities , sort of the public works division of the base. Whereas the Wing Headquarters was responsible for carrying out the primary mission of SAC, putting hot nuclear iron on our enemies should the occasion ever arise. The motto of SAC was "*Peace* is Our Profession." On all SAC aircraft you can see, or could see, the Clenched Iron Fist holding an Olive Branch.

Once the Article 32 hearing was completed, after only a few hours of hearing testimony, the presiding officer recommended a possible Article 15 (non-judicial punishment) against me. Lieutenant General Campbell's lawyer, the major from Barksdale AFB, saw no reason to go forward. Lieutenant General Campbell, not much liking his lawyer's opinion, ordered that a general court-martial be held. I actually contacted General Campbell at his retirement home in Florida a few years back and asked him why he did this. He said that lots of people were watching over his shoulder, and he had to protect his backside. Cover Your Butt (CYA) we call it. He went on to say that he thought I was guilty.

When I asked him just what it was I was guilty of—saving twelve lives and a $25 million dollar aircraft—he hung up.

According to our Constitution, we are entitled to a fair and speedy trial. That was not going to happen in my case. But you'll recall the colonel's comments a few pages back, that the Constitution doesn't apply in this case—just venting a little bit, that's all. The trial kept being put off for this or that reason, not the least of which was that the assigned attorney on the general's staff had personal family problems at home. He probably did.

Truth be told, I don't think he wanted any part in this witch hunt. I went back to my golf. My civilian attorney returned to Maine. Colonel Reed went back to Alabama while I and the defense counsel captain stayed in Blytheville, Arkansas. My wife kept on with her sales throughout the region. My local defense counsel captain would stop off at the ranch from time to time. He thought my writing was a great idea. I told the captain that I was not one bit afraid of all these generals all the way up the chain of command. I said, "All they do is make me tired."

"Yes," he said, "and that has them worried. If the White House, DOD, SAC, and TAC can't bring you under their thumbs, what will the average GI think? You have, at the very least, two four-star generals and one three-star mighty pissed off, not to mention several senators and congressmen. There's a lot more riding on this trial, Colonel Hanson, than you might think. Were I you, I would be in touch with my senators and congressmen from Maine."

"Yup, been there, done that. Least I got one Jew on my side..."

"How's that again?"

"Oh, you know, Mister Sanders, the New York Jew."

"Gotcha."

When it became obvious that Senator Cohen was not going to intercede for me, I put in a call to David Martin of CBS News. He listened intently and said he'd get back to me. It wasn't long before my civilian lawyer in Maine called me to tell me I was about to get my fifteen minutes of fame. He said a *Sixty Minutes* crew was in his office as he spoke. God knows why, but *Sixty Minutes* suddenly called off their journalistic investigation. I had always been a big fan of the *Sixty Minutes* show. I don't know to this day why they backed off the case. Maybe it just wasn't newsworthy? It sure as hell was to me.

Throughout the Air Force, my case was called an *open-and-shut case*, or, if you prefer, a *slam dunk*. Everyone around me went back to their business as usual. Well, everyone except me. I had no business as usual, except to continue to dwell on my own problems. It's sort of peculiar in a way because, once my friends and associates found out I was actually going to be court-martialed, they began reminding me of instances of wrong doing throughout the Air Force. I guess they thought I could use this information in my own particular case, which, of course, I couldn't, nor would I.

As you may recall from an earlier chapter, a technical sergeant from Barksdale AFB in Louisiana sent me a note about how Lieutenant General Campbell (the very general who insisted on my court-martial against his own lawyer's advice) had his own VC-137 flown to Cairo, Egypt, and set on fire at the far end of the runway. Apparently the general got word that I found out how the local citizens had his airplane interior outfitted to the nines. As I recall, they blamed the fire on a malfunctioning APU (Auxiliary Power Unit) in the rear of the airplane. Nonetheless, the aircraft was completely destroyed. It's difficult to imagine that a three-star general would go to such bizarre extremes just to protect his career by destroying such a beautiful, not to mention, expensive machine. As I said, this was all relayed to me by a sergeant. Additionally, I can't imagine the command structure or senators and congressmen permitting such behavior. All of this just because some snotty-nosed hockey player from the sticks in Maine was giving them a bad time, so to speak. Hockey is a great game. It's fast. It's tough. It's graceful. Justice in a hockey game

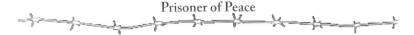

is generally meted out immediately on the ice and in front of all the fans. Such was not the case here .

Although the trial date had not yet been set, the prospective juror list was sent out. I had either flown with, or otherwise been stationed with, many on the list. I discussed the list with my attorneys, and I decided that I would go with the judge alone. "I know most of these guys," I said. "They would convict their own mother if it meant another possible promotion. I know a Nazi when I see one." I wasn't being entirely facetious either. Even back in the mid-eighties we were in danger of becoming a jingoistic fascistic country. That's what I envisioned myself up against. This wasn't the first time that military leaders went after one of their own.

CHAPTER 18

In the summer of 1932 in Washington, D.C., a group of World War I veterans came to the nation's capital to seek some financial relief from the government during the Great Depression. A soldier's bonus was authorized by the Adjusted Compensation Act of 1924, but not due until 1945. If the men could get cash now, they would receive about five hundred dollars each. They were called the bonus marchers, but called themselves the Bonus Expeditionary Army or BEF. The BEF had hoped for help from congress, but in vain as it turns out. They then turned for help to President Hoover, but he refused to see a BEF delegation because, in the words of William Manchester in his book *The Glory and the Dream*, "He was just too busy." Some saw them as a threat to the country, but, as Manchester points out, "They had a depressing effect on business, and," he says, "that was the true extent of their threat to the country."

General Douglas MacArthur was the army chief of staff. Major Eisenhower was his aide. Just across the Potomac River at Fort Myer, Major George S. Patton Jr. was playing polo. These were dog days for professional soldiers according to Manchester. By midsummer, President Hoover had reached the end of his patience with the BEF and their wives and children. The President was determined to evict the ragged squatters even if he had to call out the army, which is exactly what he did.

Manchester further explains that there was a general hardening throughout the land of the attitude of the well fed toward the ill fed. Some of the men who moved among them (the Bonus Expeditionary Force (BEF)) included General Glassford, General Billy Mitchell, and Marine Corps General Smedley

Butler, twice winner of the Medal of Honor, liked them. The BEF didn't know what it was all about. They had no work, they were hungry, their families were hungry, and they wanted to be paid. Will Rogers said the BEF held "the record for being the best behaved on any hungry men assembled anywhere in the world." One general was to have said, "Why worry about the delays in the process of law in the settlement of their individual cases? Why not just ship them off to some sparsely inhabited Hawaiian island not suitable for growing sugar. There they could stew in their own filth."

Finally MacArthur goes into action. MacArthur said they were going to break the backs of the BEF. He called Eisenhower and Patton into action as well. MacArthur was going to use tanks as well. The BEF mistakenly thought the awesome display of military power was a parade in their honor as they applauded. Patton's cavalry charged into the unsuspecting BEF where thousands were indiscriminately ridden down. For MacArthur there was no substitute for victory. President Hoover sent a message to MacArthur forbidding him to actually cross the river into the largest encampment of veterans on open ground beyond the bridge. MacArthur said he was just too busy doing his job to be interfered with by some civilian. He disobeyed the president, and not for the last time as Manchester points out.

And finally, the route was on. There were hundreds of casualties and two babies were dead from gas. Numerous more well-to-do Washingtonians in yachts cruised close to look at the show as Major George S. Patton Jr. lead his cavalrymen in a final destructive charge. Among the ragged bonus marchers routed by their sabers was Joseph T. Angelino who, on September 26, 1918, had won the Distinguished Service Cross in the Argonne Forest for saving the life of a young officer named George S. Patton Jr.

Such is the nature of the abuse of power by some of our generals in history, both ancient and modern. How's it go? "What you do to the least of them, you do to me?" Something like that,

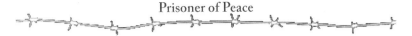

eh? I used to have a leadership technique that I borrowed from the Scriptures. I'll share it with you now.

When I was the Operations Officer of our KC-135 flying squadron at Blytheville AFB in Blytheville, Arkansas, I found it necessary from time to time to call in a junior officer or an enlisted man for what I called, only half-jokingly, a "Come to Jesus" meeting. One short example ought to suffice. One of our enlisted boom operators exhibited many traits of a *dope smoker*—small earring, hair parted down the middle, using the slang of the era (early eighties), etc. I asked him to step into my office, sat him down, and had a short dialogue with him, a monologue really. I said, "Sergeant Brown, I'm not saying this is the case, but you exhibit all the outward signs of someone using drugs. If this is the case, I will have you out of the Air Force in a heartbeat. That's all I have to say to you. You might want to consider a grooming change. You are dismissed, and peace be with you." He saluted smartly and left. He was a quick study. The very next day his appearance was in keeping with normal Air Force grooming standards.

I always felt the direct approach was the most honest and effective leadership style. You know, "Tell the truth but tell it slant, success in circuit lies," as the poet said. Most times, telling the truth in a gentle but straight forward manner works. Sometimes a little story or parable works. When it was my turn to "come to Jesus," I had no such leaders in my immediate chain of command willing to employ my leadership style. In my imagination I ended up going to the man himself. I did most of the talking. He interjected a word now and again.

"Well, Jesus," I said. "Looks like I'm up against it now. I'm gonna meet Pontius Pilate tomorrow, and it doesn't look too good. From what I've heard and seen around the base and in town they intend to crucify me on a star-laden cross." Jesus interrupted me as He said, "Looks to me like you're doing a much better job of it than they ever could. But," he said, "it isn't over till the fat lady sings."

"You guys had that saying back then as well?" I asked Him.

"Oh, it was something like that," he said. "Actually, we liked to say 'Man proposes, but God disposes.'" He went on to say that I had some of best lawyers that money could buy, both my own and the taxpayers' money.

"Yes," I said to him, "But given what they did to You, what chance do I have?" "Hell's bells," I said, "I was even contemplating suicide for a while there."

"I know," he said. "Who do you think had your wife hide the gun in your night stand? It'll all be over soon," he said. "Then, we can move on to something different. Think of it this way," he said getting up to leave me on the porch swing on my front lawn. "At least you know some things you don't want to do in your next life. Then he said something quite strange. "Listen here, you hockey puck, you're exactly where I need you to be. Just think of it as another hockey game like when you won the State of Maine High School Hockey Championship back in 1959 with the Dixfield Dixies." "Yeah," I said, "It's like the Dixfield Dixies going up against the Boston Bruins." "And above all," He said, " don't worry, I'll be with you every step of the way. Besides, " He concluded, "my father in heaven loves it when someone with a broken heart calls upon him. Sometimes when we are at our weakest, is when we do the most good for ourselves and others. They can't kill you twice, ya know."

"And what about all that stuff of *Father, forgive them for they know not what they do?* Was that just tongue in cheek or did You really mean it? Am I supposed to do that too?" I asked him. "Oh no, that's a little too much forgiveness for you right now. Maybe later on. You're getting just a little taste of what it means to be me. Now you know about the Sword of Damocles. Like me, you'll rise again in time," he said. He was gone before I could ask him why he never got a lawyer. Then, I thought I heard his voice on

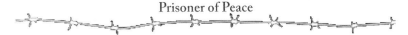

the wind saying, "We didn't have no F. Lee Bailey's back then. All the really good lawyers were on the other side." And to think that folks think Jesus Christ has no sense of humor, even if his English ain't all that good. "Anything else I can do for you before I go? I have miles to go before I sleep." Now He's throwing Robert Frost at me, but I guess one could do worse than be a "swinger of birches." I said I had just one more question, projecting into the future. "How come it only took you three days to rise again, and it took me twenty-seven years?" With loving humor he said, "In my Father's Air Force, there's only one commander-in-chief, and you aren't him. Just like you told the sergeant earlier, *Go in peace to love and serve the Lord*," he concluded, *"And each other*. Shalom."

And as it says in a new Bluegrass song.

Yes, this is my song.

JAIL AND JESUS

You don't have to be in jail to find Jesus
You don't have to be in some muddy foxhole
You don't have to be fightin' in some foreign land
You can find Jesus just sitting quietly in
a lawn swing on your own land

CHAPTER 19

There is only one charge in this trial that is significant. The rest don't amount to a hill of beans, as we say in Maine. We will get to that significant charge directly. First, a word or two about the lesser charges. I say *lesser* because for more than twenty years in my Air Force career that's how we operated on a daily basis, more or less, especially when operational necessity dictated. In my case, these everyday procedures were suddenly deemed crimes. I guess the Air Force felt it necessary to heap charge upon charge to ensure their victory in court. It's probably the same in civilian court as well. I mean, if you have enough charges, some have to stick, right? And, as I said elsewhere in this book, all sides involved in the Grand Jury hearing recommended that no further action be taken, with one major exception.

Lieutenant General William Campbell, the commander of 8th Air Force stationed at Barksdale AFB in Boosier City, Louisiana, ordered the prosecution to proceed to a general court-martial. Otherwise, in civilian legalese there would have been a no bill finding and that would have been that. Let's get right to the one significant charge.

The important charge carried with it the very damning phrase *Behavior Unbecoming An Officer and A Gentleman*. It's a serious charge, and it should be. I was supposed to have coerced an enlisted man, the boom operator, to change the Form F, the weight and balance sheet which shows the amount of fuel on board, it's distribution , number of passengers, etc. to reflect fewer people on board than were actually there, or *souls on board* as we most often referred to them. The only thing is I didn't do it, but we'll get to that subsequently.

A few weeks before my trial was to begin, somebody from the prosecution side of the house sent a junior officer out to my house to ask me what I really wanted. The answer was easy. What I *really* wanted was for the Air Force to stop acting so foolish and spending all that money to show me how powerful they were. Hell's bells, hockey fans, I already knew how important they were. Aren't we all created a "little lower than the angels?" And as I said elsewhere, I wasn't afraid of them. They just made me awfully tired.

The prosecution wanted to offer me a deal, as they called it, as long as they could keep the charge involving Sergeant Bolling. My civilian attorney, Dave Sanders from Livermore Falls, Maine, said, "You can do whatever you want, but you didn't do it. You're the one who has to live with yourself after this is over." I nearly went for the so-called deal until Mister Sanders said that. To be perfectly frank I was simply worn out from all the pressure. As Franz Kafka so clearly points out in his book *The Trial*, "There's nothing quite like State Sponsored self-destruction. Logic is doubtless unshakable." Kafka concludes, "But it cannot withstand a man who wants to go on living." I wonder if that's what Jesus meant while in the garden when he said, "Father, if possible take this burden from me... but not my but your will be done?" I'm paraphrasing, of course . I was in my own little garden of Gethsemane wondering what God's will for me was. Was he going to use a weak man as me to confound the mighty generals? Perhaps it's odd that I am writing this during the Lenten season, albeit some twenty-seven years later, or perhaps not.

The next few pages are the guts of the trial from the prosecutor's point of view, and it's not insignificant for my defense either. I want to make one more point, perhaps two, and then we'll get to the crucifixion. I discovered, what may very well be a review for most of you, but it was a revelation to me. It's fairly easy to remain focused and composed when the prosecution is trying to tear you limb from limb. It's quite another matter to hold up when so many men and women come forward to show their unwavering love for you. As I'm sure most of you already know, there is absolutely no defense against unconditional love.

My good friend and mentor, Professor Jay S. Hoar from the University of Maine–Farmington (author of at least twelve books on the Civil War) recently flew to South Florida to help me with my grammar and punctuation and to encourage me to stick with the book until finished. "You do the work and leave the results to the Lawd." That's how they talk in Maine. Anyway, when I told the professor that I thought the lead attorney for the prosecution, one Major Oxley from Washington, D.C., although quite effective, was somewhat of a prick, the professor was quick to point out that the prick index in our nation's capital is quite high. "Both in the Pentagon and in congress," he said.

STRATEGIC ABBREVIATIONS

ADO: Assistant Director of Operations
ADC: Area Defense Counsel
ATC: Air Training Command OR Assistant Trial Counsel
AWACS: Airborne Warning and Control System
COC: Combat Operations Center
DA: District Attorney
DC: Defense Counsel
DCM: Deputy Commander of Maintenance
DCO: Deputy Commander of Operations
DO: Director of Operations
MJ: Military Judge
OER: Officer Effectiveness Report
SAC: Strategic Air Command
SOF: Supervisor of Flying
TAC: Tactical Air Command
TC: Trial Counsel
TDY: Temporary Duty
UCMJ: Uniformed Code of Military Justice
VIP: Very Important Person

STRATEGICAL CODENAMES

Elf One: Saudi Arabia Operation
One-Star: Brigadier General
Two-Stars: Major General
Three-Stars: Lieutenant General
Four-Stars: General

CHAPTER 20

TRIAL TRANSCRIPT

I have included only those portions of the trial that I feel add any heat or light to the proceedings. My main goal here is to point out the difference in character of prosecution witnesses and the defense. Quite obviously, the defense witnesses were on my side, so to speak. But, almost to the man, they were all combat tested and old school. In this modern person's military, one can no longer lead by fear. Our troops are simply too well informed to be cowed by fear. If you don't want to sift through the large number of pages of trial testimony, may I suggest you at least read all of Sergeant Bolling's testimony and just the introduction of each of the rest of the witnesses.

Finally, allow me to say a thing or two about the differences between military and civilian doctors, especially psychologists and psychiatrists. Military doctors can share what you tell them if you should need their assistance. This was explained to me when the pressure was really starting to get to me. I went to the base hospital to see the local resident psychologist. Almost before I got started, he told me that whatever I said to him could be shared with the prosecution lawyers. I subsequently sought help in the private sector, of course, at my expense. You can read Doctor Hester's testimony in the latter portion of the trial if you wish.

My attorneys assure me that I have every right to use any and or all of this trial transcript in that absolutely no classified information is ever discussed. It is a completely public document.

SSGT CRAIG M. BOLLING

Called as a witness by the United States, was sworn, and testified as follows:

QUESTIONS BY TRIAL COUNSEL

Q: Please state your full name and rank.
A: Staff Sergeant Craig M. Bolling.
Q: To what organization are you assigned?
A: Forty-sixth Air Refueling Squadron.
Q: Where's the 46th Air Refueling Squadron located, Sergeant Boiling?
A: K. I. Sawyer Air Force Base, Michigan.
Q: You're a member of the United States Air Force?
A: Yes, Sir.
Q: What do you do in the United States Air Force, Sergeant Boiling?
A: I'm a boom operator on a 135.

DIRECT EXAMINATION

Q: Were you performing those duties as a boom operator on 9 December 1983?
A: Yes, I was, Sir.
Q: Beyond the operation of the boom during air refueling, do you have other responsibilities as a boom operator and a member of the crew?
A: Yes, Sir, I'm responsible for the weight and balance of the cargo or any type of passengers that we carry.
Q: Is there a paperwork matter that you have to accomplish...
A: Yes, Sir.
Q: ...associated with that?
United States Witness Boiling—Direct
A: Yes, Sir.

Q: The weight and balance document, is that characterized in some other form? Is that what is referred to as a Form F by chance?

A: Yes, Sir.

Q: Who's responsible to prepare that particular form as it relates to the weight and balance that you've just talked about?

A: I am.

TC: The exhibit, Your Honor. (Prosecution Exhibit #12 was retrieved from the military judge.)

I hand you what's been admitted into evidence as Prosecution Exhibit Twelve. Are you familiar with that?

A: Yes, Sir.

Q: To what flight does that document relate, Sergeant Bolling?

A: It relates to the December 9th flight out of Riyadh, Saudi Arabia, the flight which I was on.

Q: Who was on that crew?

A: Captain Robertson, Lieutenant Kern, Lieutenant Petsch, myself, and Lieutenant Hanson, I mean Lieutenant Colonel Hanson.

Q: Is Lieutenant Colonel Hanson in the courtroom today?

A: Yes, he is.

Q: Could you please point him out and call him by name?

A: He's sitting right there. (The witness pointed toward the accused.)

TC: The proper identification.

Q: At the bottom of Prosecution Exhibit 12, there's two signatures. Whose signature is the uppermost of those two?

A: That's my signature, Sir.

United States Witness Boiling—Direct

Q: On this 9 December flight, were there any passengers?

A: Yes, Sir.

Q: Do you recall how those passengers got on the aircraft?

A: They were—I don't recall how they got on the aircraft. I can say they were brought out to the aircraft.

Q: All together?

A: No.

Q: Would you please explain when you saw the first passenger or first group of passengers?

A: We saw the first group of passengers at SAC Ops and the next group of passengers we saw out on the flight line later on.

Q: Let's talk to the first group. How many were in the first group?

A: I can't remember exactly. I remember three being—three people being there.

Q: Can you describe them at all?

A: Two were civilian personnel and one was, I guess, an Army 0-6. He had on a tan uniform, so I distinguished him as being Army.

Q: Now when did they board the aircraft?

A: They boarded the aircraft when myself, and I don't know who else, went out to the aircraft to do our preflight.

Q: Did you have any responsibilities with regard to those three passengers, the two civilians and the—what was the other one I heard you describe?

A: As an Army 0-6.

Q: And the Army colonel. Did you have any responsibilities with regards to those three passengers?

A: I had to give them a briefing on their responsibilities and how they were to behave aboard the aircraft during the flight.

Q: Do you give that briefing to passengers frequently?

A: Yes, sir.

Q: How long does that briefing normally last?

A: Ten minutes.

Q: How long did it last as it pertains to these three passengers?

A: Ten minutes.

Q: After you completed that briefing, where did you go in the aircraft?

A: I was standing in the cargo section of the aircraft.

Q: And after you had done that, what happened to the aircraft?

A: Two other crewmembers boarded, and we prepared for takeoff.

Q: Did you in fact take off immediately?

A: No, we didn't.

Q: Where did you go?

A: We taxied to another part of the air base itself.

Q: Where were you located on the aircraft during that taxi?

A: During the taxi I was sitting in the boom operator's seat.

Q: Once you got to this other location somewhere on the strip or airport, what should I call it? What is it, airfield?

A: Airfield.

Q: What happened there?

A: We stopped, we opened up the hatch, and we loaded some more passengers.

Q: Uh huh. Now, do you recall who they were?

A: I can't be sure, but they were referred to as Navy personnel.

Q: I see, and how many do you remember boarding the aircraft?

A: I don't remember the exact number.

Q: Was it more than—it was plural, so it was two or more?

United States Witness Boiling—Direct

A: More than two.

Q: Less than how many?

A: Less than ten.

Q: But you don't remember exactly?

A: I don't remember the exact number.

Q: Okay. Now after these additional Navy personnel, or what had been told to you as being Navy personnel, boarded the aircraft, what did you do?

A: I got the new passengers, the Navy personnel, in the back and started briefing them, got them strapped in and was briefing them.

Q: How long was it between when those Navy personnel boarded the aircraft and the plane started taxiing and took off?

A: About two, maybe three minutes.

Q: How long does your briefing normally last for passengers on the aircraft?

A: Ten minutes.

Q: Where were you located when the aircraft took off?

A: I was sitting in the cargo compartment.

Q: Sergeant Bolling, as a boom operator, where are you required to be during the operations of the aircraft?

A: In the cargo in the cockpit area of the plane itself.

Q: Do you have a flight manual that addresses your duties and responsibilities as a boom operator?

A: Yes, I do, Sir.

Q: Do you refer to that as a flight manual, or what do you call it?

A: A flight manual, I would call it a flight manual.

TC: Government exhibits one and four, please, Your Honor.

Q: What does that manual say about where you're supposed to be during takeoff?

A: It says that I'm supposed to be sitting in the boom seat for takeoffs and landings to monitor, to help the crew monitor overhead gauges and electronic functions.

Q: Are there any other provisions that provide for alternative locations...

A: Yes.

Q: ...for the boom operator to be?

A: Yes.

Q: I provide you what has been admitted into evidence as Prosecution Exhibit 1. Are you familiar with the language contained thereon?

A: Yes, I am.

Q: What does that provide for an alternative boom operator position?

A: It provides for what is called a jump seat or an instructor pilot's seat that the boom operator can occupy during takeoffs and landings.

Q: During the takeoff of this 135 mission on 9 December, were you in either one of those locations?

A: No, I wasn't.

Q: Why not?

A: I didn't have time to get back to the seat and that was just it, I didn't have time to get back to the seat. Also, Captain Robertson was sitting in the boom operator's seat and there was, I don't know who it was, but another person was sitting in the instructor pilot's seat or jump seat.

Q: Now back to Prosecution Exhibit 12. I believe it's your testimony that you prepared this form in preparation for the flight, is that correct?

A: Yes.

Q: I note that in the central upper part of this form there is a block that has "COMPT" on it.

A: Yes, Sir.

Q: And beneath the letters "COMPT" there are some additional letters. First, what does COMPT stand for?

A: It stands for compartment.

Q: Now below that there are the letters *B, B,* and *J.*

A: Yes, Sir.

Q: What does *B* refer to?

A: *B* stands for the section of the compartment or the compartment itself.

Q: And which compartment is *B*? Where is that on the plane?

A: That would be referred to in civilian terms as the cockpit.

Q: And *J*, what does that refer to?

A: *J* is the cargo compartment itself, part of, a section of the cargo compartment.

Q: And where is that, toward the back of the plane?

A: Toward the back of the aircraft.

Q: Now to the right of the two letters "B" there are some numbers in the next immediate column.

A: Yes, Sir.

Q: To whom or to what do those numbers refer?

A: Okay, the first *B*, as it's written here, it's the standard crew which would have been myself, Lieutenant Kern, Lieutenant Petsch, and Captain Robertson.

Q: And the number 1, which follows the second *B*?

A: That would refer to Colonel Hanson.

Q: Now there is a number following the letter *J*. What type of individuals does that refer to?

A: That would refer to passengers or extra crewmembers that couldn't get in the cargo compartment itself, I mean the cockpit section itself.

Q: How many Form F's are prepared?

A: One. Well, as you refer to it, one is prepared and then there is a duplicate of it made.

Q: Is that accomplished with a duplicating machine or with a carbon or—

A: It's accomplished with a carbon.

Q: Do you recall whether that in fact took place with the preparation for this particular flight?

A: Yes.

Q: Okay. Now the form that you have as Prosecution Exhibit 12, is that the original or is that the carbon?

A: That's the original.

Q: When did you prepare that form?

A: This form was prepared at SAC Ops.

Q: Prior to boarding the aircraft?

A: Yes, prior to boarding the aircraft.

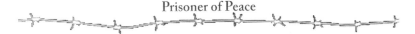

Q: After you completed it, did you sign it?

A: Yes, Sir.

Q: Who else's signature did you obtain?

A: Captain Robertson's signature.

Q: Now as pertains to this document, what you've testified to as being the original of the Form F, where would that form then have gone?

A: It should have gone and been filed with the rest of the mission paperwork.

Q: Where would that have been?

A: If it was a normal mission here in the states, it would have gone to a Base Operations type, Riyadh, I would say it would have gone to whoever takes the paperwork to Base Operations or whatever was being used as Base Operations.

Q: Okay. You don't know exactly where?

A: I don't know exactly where it went.

Q: How about this would, during the normal course of events, this form get on the aircraft?

A: No, this form wouldn't.

Q: Okay. Now let's talk about the copy, the carbon copy. After you've completed the original and the copy, what happens to the copy?

A: The copy goes to the aircraft.

Q: And accompanies you folks on your mission?

A: Right.

Q: Do you—you do not recall the exact number of passengers on the aircraft, total, is that correct?

A: No, I can't recall the exact number.

Q: Were there more passengers on the aircraft than you had listed, when you prepared the Form F, next to the letter *J*?

A: (No response)

Q: Were there actually more passengers on the aircraft than what you had originally reported on...

A: Yes, yes.

Q: ...the Form F next to the code *J*?

A: Yes.

Q: When did you realize that that was going to be the situation?

A: When we arrived at, I guess, the other part of the airfield and picked up the extra passengers.

Q: Well, what should you have done then?

A: I should have been able to annotate those folks to the Form F, the copy of it, not the original, but the copy.

Q: Which was located...

A: Which was located on the plane.

Q: Did you ever do so?

A: No, I didn't.

MJ: Just a second, Counsel. You said you should have been able to.

WIT: Yes.

MJ: Why didn't you?

WIT: I didn't have time to do it.

TC: Now that goes to the copy that's on board.

WIT: Right.

Q: This form would not have been on board.

A: No.

Q: What changes, if any, did you ever make to the number of passengers reflected next to the letter *J* on this piece of paper?

A: I didn't make any changes next to the letter *J* on this sheet of paper, no changes at all. Okay. What happened during the flight of this 135?

A: We took off and we had a midair, and we landed back at Riyadh.

Q: Midair collision?

A: Midair collision.

Q: And you came back to Riyadh.

A: And we came back to Riyadh.

Q: After you had landed, Sergeant Boiling, were there any conversations about this Form F that you're aware of?

A: There were some conversations, I don't think about this one, but there were some conversations about the Form F itself.

Q: More than one?

A: More than one.

Q: What was the first one?

A: I don't know the details of the conversation, I can just tell you the subject matter, and that was…

Q: Pardon me, let me make sure of that. What was the first conversation that you were a part of as relates to the Form F?

A: The subject matters was that…

CIV DC: I object, Your Honor. It's not responsive; it's hearsay.

TC: Let's try again. Who was…

MJ: Sustained. I'll let you rephrase.

TC: I'll withdraw the question.

MJ: I'll let you rephrase.

TC: Thank you.

Who was this conversation with?

WIT: Lieutenant Petsch.

TC: I believe, Your Honor, that already in evidence is the recollections of the person to whom this man is going to talk about as to what he said exactly. Therefore, this is not being offered as Lieutenant Petsch's statement for the purposes of evidence, only for the fact that it occurred. It's already in evidence by Lieutenant Petsch directly…

MJ: I agree.

TC: …as to what he said.

CIV DC: Your Honor, I have no objection to counsel asking this individual if he had a conversation with Lieutenant Petsch. I do have an objection as hearsay as to this individual reciting what Lieutenant Petsch may have said to him; it's clearly hearsay.

MJ: Is it being offered for the truth of what Lieutenant Petsch said or for the mere fact that it was said?

TC: The latter, Your Honor. Lieutenant Petsch has already testified directly as to what he said.

MJ: I agree.

TC: He said...

MJ: Overruled. It's not being offered for the truth, therefore, it's not hearsay.

TC: Now, Sergeant Boiling, concerning the conversation between you and Lieutenant Petsch, what do you recall about that conversation?

WIT: The subject matter of there had to be some changes made to the Form F.

Q: Who said that? Who said that to you?

A: Lieutenant Petsch mentioned it to me that changes had to be made.

Q: I see. Did he reference anyone else's name during the course of that conversation?

A: He referenced someone else's name. And who was that?

A: That was Lieutenant Colonel Hanson's name.

Q: And what did he say about Lieutenant Colonel Hanson and the Form F?

A: He said that, "Boom, someone," or something to that effect, "someone is going to come up to you and ask you to make some changes to the Form F." And I referenced to him, I said, "Who?" He said, "Lieutenant Colonel Hanson." I go, "Well, okay," and that was it.

CIV DC: Your Honor.

TC: Did he say anything more?

WIT: There was...

CIV DC: Your Honor, if I could be heard, I have a continuing objection. It would seem to me that if this is being entered not for the truth of the matter but only the fact that it was said, there is not sufficient information to tie up the testimony of Mister Petsch, or Lieutenant Petsch, and the sergeant. It would seem to me also that if it's to be entered for something other than the truth of the matter, there has to be a showing on the part of the government as to what it's being entered for.

TC: I will pursue that line of questioning no further, Your Honor.

MJ: Fine.

TC: After that conversation took place, do you recall where you were when that conversation took place?

WIT: We were on the flight line.

Q: Do you recall approximately how long after the flight that conversation between you and Lieutenant Petsch took place?

A: About twenty, thirty minutes after the flight, after we had departed the plane after it landed.

Q: Subsequent to that, did you have any further conversation with anyone referencing the subject of the Form F?

A: If you mean after the conversation with Lieutenant Petsch, yeah, one other conversation.

Q: And with whom was that conversation?

A: Lieutenant Colonel Hanson.

Q: And would you please tell the court how that came about?

A: He walked up to me and he just approached me with the idea, he said, "Boom, I'm going to need your help on the Form F." And I told him, "Sir, don't ask me to do that," and, "I can't do it." And he said, "Never mind, I'll take care of it."

Q: Now you attributed to him words to the effect, "Boom, I'm going to need your help on the Form F." Did he say anything else before you responded?

A: Well, he made reference to two individuals that weren't supposed to be on the plane.

Q: And after you said, "Don't ask", what did he say?

A: He said, "Well, never mind, I'll take care of it."

MJ: I have a question, counsel, if I may.

TC: Certainly, Your Honor.

MJ: During this conversation with the accused, did he reference the two individuals?

WIT: He referenced them as two individuals. He didn't name names or what they did or anything. He just said "two individuals".

MJ: Proceed.

TC: Sergeant Boiling, when you originally prepared the Form F, Prosecution Exhibit 12, to the best of your memory, what entry did you make following the code J?

WIT: It was three. It was three.

MJ: May I see that, please? (Prosecution Exhibit 12 was presented to the military judge, examined, and returned to trial counsel.) Thank you.

TC: After you prepared that form and signed it, what changes, if any, ever, did you make to the numbers associated with the letter *J*?

WIT: None, no changes at all.

Q: Ever?

A: Ever, not on this sheet of paper, not this one.

Q: All right. Now let's speak to the other one, which would have been the carbon, is that correct?

A: Yes.

Q: Where would that form have been located again?

A: On the plane. It would have been somewhere on the plane for me to find.

Q: Did you ever see that form after landing?

A: No.

Q: You testified that your entry following the letter "J" was a 3.

A: Yes.

Q: What would have been the number just following the 3?

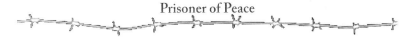

A: Six hundred.

Q: Please take a look at Prosecution Exhibit 12. What numbers appear on that form now?

A: Eight hundred and a four.

Q: You're telling me that you did not change the three to a four or the six hundred to an eight hundred?

A: Yes, I did not change the four—the three to a four—or the eight to a six—a six to eight hundred.

TC: Thank you.
(Prosecution Exhibits #1, #4 and #12 were returned to the military judge.)

Q: What's a passenger manifest, Sergeant Bolling?

A: A passenger manifest would be a document that would give you the names and social security numbers of individuals that were traveling as passengers. On the crew operating the 135 refueler, who would prepare the passenger manifest?

A: I could have prepared the passenger manifest.

Q: Have you prepared them in the past?

A: No, I haven't, but I could have on this particular flight.

Q: Did you prepare a passenger manifest for this flight?

A: No.

Q: To your knowledge, was there a passenger manifest?

A: I didn't see one, so I no, there wasn't one; I didn't see it.

Q: Well, now, how can you say that there wasn't one because you didn't see one?

A: I would—

Q: Would you have been required to do anything to that document?

A: I would have been required to look at it.

Q: Why?

A: Because that way I would have known what passengers and who they were.

Q: In your capacity as the boom operator?

A: I would have been responsible for being the person in charge of the passengers, loading, and unloading.

TC: Pass the witness, Your Honor.

MJ: Cross-examination?

CROSS EXAMINATION: QUESTIONS BY CIVILIAN DEFENSE COUNSEL

Q: Sergeant, you said you never saw a passenger manifest for that particular flight?

A: No, I didn't.

Q: Did you ask for it?

A: Yes.

Q: And who did you ask?

A: I asked Captain Robertson.

Q: And did he give it to you?

A: No.

Q: And did he tell you where it was?

A: He didn't tell me where it was, he just said it had been taken care of.

Q: Captain Robertson said that?

A: Yes.

Q: Now, do you remember a conversation that you and I had yesterday?

A: Yes.

Q: And do you remember me telling you, particularly with regard to statements and what exactly was contained in a particular statement, that all anybody was interested in is what your actual recollection was?

A: Yes.

Q: Okay, and that both the government in the case and the defense were really looking for you to tell the truth?

A: Yes.

Q: Okay, you remember me telling you that?

A: Yes.

Q: Then do you remember us having a conversation concerning this issue of the number of passengers on that flight on December 9?

A: The number, no, I don't recall the number of total passengers, if that's what you're saying.

Q: Do you recall telling me that you remember there being the three passengers, the two air traffic controllers and the one Army doctor, plus another individual that was walking back and forth?

A: Yes, I remember another individual walking back and forth.

Q: And that fourth individual, you indicated to me, you weren't sure whether he was going to be a passenger or not, isn't that correct?

A: Yes.

CIV DC: And did you not also indicate to me that, with regard to may I see the Form F, Your Honor?

MJ: Twelve?

CIV DC: Yeah.

(Prosecution Exhibit #12 was retrieved from the military judge.)

CIV DC: It's a very popular exhibit.

Q: The reference in *J* here to four, that you could not tell me at that time whether or not that's what you wrote down?

A: Yes, I remember saying that.

Q: Now you realize that you just testified to the fact that you didn't write four down there, that you wrote three.

A: Right.

Q: And now you've also indicated that yesterday you told me that it's quite possible that you wrote the four down there, referencing that other individual that was walking back and forth.

A: No, you asked me if it was possible that I wrote the number four down, that's what you said, if it was possible I could have written the number four down.

Q: And didn't you indicate to me that the reason you might have written the four was because of that other individual?

A: That's what I said, I might have written it down.

Q: And that's why it would be four—eight hundred?

135

A: Yeah, if I wrote it down.

Q: And that's in fact what you testified to at the AFR 110-14, isn't that the case?

A: I don't know, I would have to look at the testimony to see.

CIV DC: Excuse me, Your Honor.

(There was a delay while civilian defense counsel researched the testimony of the witness contained in the AFR 110-14 Report of Investigation. Additional delay occurred while the counsel for the accused conferred.)

MJ: Would you like a brief recess, counsel?

CIV DC: Well, Your Honor—yeah, if I could, just to gather my thoughts.

MJ: Fine.

CIV DC: I just want a clean copy of the 110-14.

MJ: We're in recess.

(The court-martial recessed at 1513 hours, 10 January 1985, and was called back to order at 1533 hours, 10 January 1985, with all parties present who were present when the court-martial recessed.)

CIV DC: Your Honor, I apologize...

MJ: Sergeant Bolling is still on the stand.

Sergeant Bolling, I'll remind you that you're still under oath.

WIT: Yes, sir.

CIV DC: Your Honor, I apologize for the delay. I have checked with the government and they have no problem with the authenticity of the transcript of the...

MJ: This is the accident investigation board?

CIV DC: The AFR 110-14.

MJ: All right.

CIV DC: Now, Sergeant Boiling, I would ask...

TC: Your Honor, I hope I have not misled the defense counsel...

MJ: Just a second now.

TC: I must object. I have no problem with the authenticity of the document, but I'm having trouble understanding for what purpose counsel intends to use it or, you know, show it. Is this coming into evidence or are we just going to show it to the witness, or what is planned here? CIV DC: It's coming into evidence.

TC: Under what...

CIV DC: A prior inconsistent statement under oath.

TC: Then I'm going to have to look closely, Your Honor. I have not yet noticed that, Your Honor.

MJ: Well, I'm going to have to hear the statement before I can rule.

TC: Yeah.

CIV DC: Sergeant Boiling, I ask that you review that page of your testimony and—

MJ: Now what page is this?

CIV DC: Your Honor, I'm sorry, it's U-II-14, Your Honor.

MJ: Eleven dash fourteen, point fourteen?

CIV DC: Eleven dash fourteen.

MJ: Fine.

CIV DC: Would Your Honor like a copy of the page?

MJ: Not yet, but I will want whatever is shown to the witness marked as an exhibit, so we'll mark this as Defense Exhibit B.

CIV DC: Your Honor, it's my intention to take two pages out of there.

MJ: The two pages you take out will be Defense Exhibit B. Are they consecutive pages, counsel?

CIV DC: No, Your Honor.

MJ: Would you inform the court reporter of the other page number so that he can get it in the record?

CIV DC: The other one is listed as attachment one to the testimony of Sergeant Boiling—Dash-Tab U-1

TC: It's my understanding, Your Honor, that that has been labeled as Defense Exhibit B for identification.

MJ: Yes.

TC: But not admitted into evidence at this point.

MJ: It hasn't been offered, nor has A.

TC: I understand, Your Honor, thank you.

MJ: I understand A may be offered, but it hasn't been at this point. Have you reviewed the documents now sufficiently, Sergeant Boiling?

WIT: Yes, sir.

MJ: You may resume your questioning, counsel.

CIV DC: Do you recollect those questions and those answers at that time while you were under oath?

WIT: Yes.

Q: Okay, and you recollect a Colonel Koehnke asking you, "Sergeant Boiling, you have testified that there have been changes made to that Form F. Were these changes made by you? If so, which ones?" Then an indication again that the witness looked at the Form F. Do you see where I'm reading from?

A: (No response)

MJ: Why don't you describe it for him on the page?

(Civilian defense counsel pointed to his reference for the witness.)

WIT: Yes, sir.

CIV DC: And the Form F that we're referring to, I believe, is attached as an exhibit to your testimony, that is, tab U-1 , is it not?

WIT: (No response)

Q: Look two pages further; that's what you've been looking at?

A: Yes, sir.

Q: Now, is that Form F that is copied there as Tab U-il identical to the government's exhibit number twelve in this case?

A: Yes.

Q: It's just a carbon copy of that, isn't it?

A: Yes.

Q: Is that the Form F that you looked at, at the time of the AFR-110-14?

A: Is that the one or is this the one?

Q: It's the—

A: I mean if this is—

Q: The same form, isn't it?

MJ: The witness has been referring to the Prosecution Exhibit 12 and, then, to the attachment to the accident investigation report.

CIV DC: It is this.

MJ: It is Prosecution Exhibit 12.

CIV DC: Is Prosecution Exhibit Number 12 what you were looking at the time that you testified in this matter?

WIT: I don't remember if that is the one that was the Form F handed to me.

Q: Okay. That's what marked here as an exhibit?

A: Yes.

Q: And they are identical, are they not?

A: They are identical.

Q: Now in response to Colonel Koehnke's question, after you looked at the Form F, what did you say?

A: I said, *J* compartment, four people, which shows...

Q: It says, "It reflects four people"...

A: It reflects four people that were at SAC Ops, that there were no other changes other than that, it doesn't show.

Q: It says, "In *J* compartment it reflects four people which was the people that were at SAC Ops."

A: Right.

Q: Is that your present recollection?

A: I remember three people being on the Form F; I remember a fourth person walking in and out.

Q: At the time you testified that the J compartment four people in the J compartment reflected the four people that were at SAC Ops, is that not the case?

A: Yeah, I guess, yeah.

Q: And you indicated that it shows no other changes other than that.

A: No, it doesn't show any other changes.

Q: Then the question is, and this is prior to the mission, your answer is, "This is prior to the mission. This is a copy prior to the mission before we took off. This shows no other changes after or during the mission." And then the next question, "At SAC Ops, previous testimony has identified that there was an Army full colonel, a doctor, two civilians and a fourth person would have been?" Your answer, "I can't remember who the fourth person was. At this time I am lost as to who the fourth person was. I can't—I don't even—all I remember was seeing the two civilians and an Army doctor, a flight surgeon, I guess. I can't remember who the fourth person was." It is your present recollection that you do remember a fourth person.

A: A fourth person walking in and out, yes.

Q: And then the next question is by a Lieutenant Colonel Kretsinger. The question is, "Was he in uniform or in civilian attire? He or she?" "Uniform. I am not sure. I can't—like I said, I can't I can remember uniforms but I can't remember—the two civilian guys stood out, uniforms they all blended in except for the Army guy's uniform."

And the next question, the final question on the page is by Lieutenant Colonel Grillo, "As I understand it then Sergeant Boiling, these are the corrections that you had made in anticipation of the numbers of passengers that you knew, at least at mission planning time, that would be aboard the airplane?" Answer, "The people that were at SAC Ops there, I knew that we were taking at that time, yes. These are the changes that show that."

Is that your testimony...

A: Yes.

Q: ...at that time?

A: That's my testimony at the time.

Q: Your testimony was the changes to 4 on the document were made by you to reflect the number of people at the Ops that you believed were aboard that plane as passengers. Is that not correct?

MJ: Do you understand the question?

WIT: No, I don't...

MJ: Counsel, please rephrase.

WIT: ...understand the question.

CIV DC: Your understanding of this testimony at the AFR 110-14 that you gave last March or whenever, last spring.

WIT: I don't remember when I gave it.

Q: But you were indicating to—or indicating at that time that you made the change on that form to four to reflect the number of people that you believed, while you were at Ops, were going to be taken as passengers on the plane. Is that not correct?

A: No, I didn't say that. I made the corrections to that number four.

Q: Isn't that what it says here? The last question, "I...

A: These people, the people that were at SAC Ops there, I knew that we were taking, and at the time these changes show that. That shows a change. I didn't make a change; that's what I'm telling you. I didn't make a change at SAC Ups. There as a fourth person there. I'm telling you there was a fourth person there, he walked in and out. I didn't make a change to show a fourth person.

Q: But there's a *four* on the—

A: There's a *four* on that; I didn't make the *four*.

Q: You did not make the *four*?

A: I did not make the *four*.

Q: And you made no changes.

A: I made no changes.

Q: You're positive you wrote down only *three*.

A: I'm positive I wrote down only *three*.

MJ: That's enough, counsel.

CIV DC: I would ask for admittance at this time. I would ask that this exhibit be marked and entered.

MJ: Let's mark it as Defense Exhibit B. Do you have a stamp?

REP: (Nodded affirmative) Pages U-11-14 and Attachment 1 to Testimony of SSgt Boiling—TAB U-li, were marked Defense Exhibit B for identification.

MJ: Any objection by the prosecution?

TC: No, Your Honor.

MJ: Defense Exhibit B is received.

CIV DC: Now, Sergeant Boiling, with regard to the actual numbers on the plane, you presently indicate—the number of passengers on the plane, you currently indicate that you—

MJ: No, counsel, just a second.

CIV DC: I'm sorry, Your Honor.

MJ: The reporter is working here.

(A brief delay while the reporter completed his exhibit log.)

REP: (Nodded affirmatively)

MJ: Okay.

CIV DC: Sergeant Boiling, with regard to your recollection of the actual numbers of passengers on the plane, it's your present recollection that you do not know how many passengers were on it.

WIT: No, I don't.

Q: Isn't it also a fair statement to indicate that previously you have given various numbers as to your recollection as to the number of passengers on the plane?

A: I guess it's fair to say.

Q: Specifically, in the same testimony at the AFR 110-14, did you not originally indicate that there were seven passengers, or eight passengers, and then change your testimony to seven?

Defense Exhibit B Offered/Admitted

A: I think I said seven or eight. I'm not sure if I said seven and then changed it.

(Civilian defense counsel placed a copy of the second volume of the AFR 110-14 accident investigation before the witness, opened to his testimony.)

Q: I want to show you—

MJ: Now counsel, if you're going to show the witness anything further, I want it marked. Would you please withdraw the record of the accident investigation?

CIV DC: Your Honor, do you want—

MJ: Are you showing him the same page that you showed him before?

CIV DC: No, Your Honor. What I intend to do is ask him refer to several different pages. I don't think that it's necessary at this point that it be entered. It may just be a question—

MJ: It doesn't have to be offered, but I want it marked if it's shown to the witness. Would you like to confer with counsel, Colonel Reed?

(A brief delay while the accused's counsel conferred.)

CIV DC: Mark these three pages.

MJ: Are you going to mark them *C, D,* and *E*?

REP: *C.*

MJ: Now the three pages have been marked *C, D,* and *E*?

CIV DC: Yes, Your Honor.

REP: Just *C,* three pages.

CIV DC: Oh, I'm sorry.

MJ: Three pages under *C,* fine.

TC: Might I ask counsel through the bench, Your Honor, what the numbers are?

MJ: That's what I was going to ask next. What are the numbers?

CIV DC: U-11-10, U-11-12, and U-11-13.

MJ: Proceed, counsel.

CIV DC: Thank you, Your Honor.

I'm showing you what's marked as defendant's exhibit C.

MJ: Well, let's take *ten* and make it C-I.

CIV DC: This will be thirteen, Your Honor.

MJ: That will be C-3.

CIV DC: C-3. Read this part up here.

WIT: "Sir, to the best of my recollection, I can say twelve total.

"Twelve total. Five crewmembers?

"Five crewmembers and seven passengers.

"Seven passengers, okay.

"Sir, I would like to change that. It wasn't seven passengers, it was eight, because I remember there was an odd parachute missing."

Does that refresh your recollection in terms of what your testimony was at that time?

A: Yes, sir.

You first indicated there were seven and then you changed your testimony to eight.

A: Seven to eight, yeah.

Q: Do you remember further testifying at the Article 32 hearing?

A: Yes.

Q: Do you remember first, initially testifying to the fact that there were five or six passengers on the plane?

A: No, I don't remember testifying it was five or six.

Q: What is your recollection in terms of how many you testified to?

United States Witness Bolling—Cross

A: I don't remember what I testified to at the Article 32.

Q: After you completed the Form F, what did you do with it?

A: I gave it to Captain Robertson for him to sign.

Q: Did you ever get it back from Captain Robertson?

A: No, I don't remember well, yeah, I got a copy of it back. don't remember getting the whole thing back, but I got a copy of it back.

Q: You got the copy back, but you never got the original back?

A: No, I didn't get the original back.

Q: So this you never got back.

A: No.

Q: You never saw that again.

MJ: "This" being Prosecution Exhibit 12.

CIV DC: I apologize, Your Honor. Yes, Prosecution Exhibit Number 12.

WIT: No, I never got that back. What did you do with the copy?

A: I took it on the plane with me.

Q: What did you do with it on the plane?

A: I can't remember what I did with it.

Q: Whose function is it to put the fuel figures on the Form F?

A: The copilot's.

Q: Okay, that would be Lieutenant Kern.

A: Right.

Q: Did you give it to him?

A: Possibly.

Q: I mean you—

A: I can't remember if I gave it to him directly or if I put it somewhere and he picked it up.

Q: When was the last time you remember seeing the copy?

A: When we got aboard the aircraft to make the fuel corrections.

Q: Did you see it after the fuel corrections were made?

A: No.

Q: No?

A: No.

Q: So the last time you saw it was before you gave it to somebody to make the fuel corrections.

A: Right.

Q: And you never saw it again.

A: Well, I had to do some adding to make sure all the numbers matched up and we weren't out of limits or anything like that.

Q: Was that after the fuel figures were added to it?

A: That was after the fuel corrections and stuff like that.

Q: So does that mean you got it back after the fuel figures were added?

A: Yeah.

Q: So now your testimony is that you got it back.

A: Okay, I got it back.

Q: Then what did you do with it?

A: I don't know. I don't remember what I did with it.

Q: And you never saw it again.

A: Never saw it again.

Q: Once you got off the plane, did you go back on the plane to look for it?

A: I went back on the plane, not specifically to look for it, but to get my personal gear.

Q: Uh huh, did you look for it at that time?

A: I don't think I looked for it; I really couldn't care.

Q: Did you ever show that Form F or any Form F with regard to the December 9 flight to Captain Johnsen?

A: No, I don't even remember talking to Captain Johnsen.

Q: After December 9th, you don't remember talking to him and you don't remember showing him—

A: I don't remember talking to—

Q: The Form F?

A: Captain Johnsen at all.

Q: And you don't remember showing him the Form F.

A: I don't remember talking to Captain Johnsen.

Q: The question is, do you remember showing him a Form F?

A: I don't remember showing him a Form F.

Q: After the Navy 0-6's were added to the plane, and they were strapped, I presume.

A: Right.

Q: And you were strapped in?

A: Yeah.

Q: And this was prior to takeoff?

A: Right.

Q: Did you indicate on your radio at that time to Colonel Hanson that the passengers were strapped in and you're ready?

A: I told someone in the cockpit. I can't say it was Colonel Hanson or who. I told somebody I was ready, that I was ready and I was strapped in.

Q: And you told them the passengers were ready.

A: The passengers were ready and they were strapped in.

Q: And this was prior to takeoff.

A: Yeah.

Q: How long between when Lieutenant Petsch addressed you and Colonel Hanson addressed you was it?

A: I don't know, I can't remember; maybe forty-five minutes, an hour, and hour and forty-five minutes, something like that.

Q: So there was quite a bit of difference in time between the two?

A: No, I wouldn't say there was quite a bit of difference. I was saying it was probably twenty, maybe thirty—okay, twenty, maybe thirty minutes.

Q: I thought you said it was between an hour and an hour and forty-five minutes.

A: No, twenty, maybe twenty to thirty minutes.

Q: So you're changing your testimony?

A: I'm just saying—

MJ: Counsel, let's—

TC: Your Honor—

MJ: Counsel, have a seat. Let's not argue with the witness.

CIV DC: Yes, Your Honor.

Where was the conversation with Lieutenant Petsch?

WIT: On the flight line.

Q: Where was the conversation with Colonel Hanson?

A: On the flight line.

Q: Are you aware of the fact that at the Article 32 you indicated that you could not remember where the conversations took place?

A: No, I don't remember that in the Article 32, where the conversation took place.

MJ: Counsel, at this point, the significance of that information is de minimus.

CIV DC: Does that mean I shouldn't bother?

MJ: That's right.

CIV DC: Now when Colonel Hanson approached you, if I understand your testimony correctly, you indicated he said, "Boom, I'm going to need your help on the Form F."

WIT: Right.

Q: That was the first thing he said to you?

A: Yeah.

Q: And at some point thereafter you said, "No, I'm not—I won't help you," or, "I won't do it," or whatever.

A: Yeah.

Q: And he said, "I'll take care of it, myself."

A: Right.

Q: Now on your direct testimony you also indicated that he made some reference to the fact of two people. You don't know which two people.

A: Right.

Q: Two people not belonging—

A: Two people not belonging, right.

Q: Do you once again recollect a conversation that we had on this very point yesterday?

A: Yes.

Q: And do you remember telling me that you could not remember one way or the other whether he actually said that or whether or not that or whether that was just your assumption?

148

A: No, I said I don't remember if I said—what my exact words were, but I said he could have mentioned two people; that's what I said, he could have mentioned two people.

Q: He could have mentioned two people.

A: Yeah.

Q: And you don't remember whether he did it or not.

A: He probably did…I don't know…he might have,…probably did…I don't know.

Q: You don't know.

A: No. If I had said—

MJ: That's sufficient, counsel.

CIV DC: Isn't it a fair statement that the only thing that you know for sure with regard to that conversation was that he said, "Boom, I need your help on the Form F," and you said, "No, I won't do it," and he said, "I'll take care of it, myself"?

WIT: I can say that he made the statement "two people".

Q: Are you certain of that?

TC: Your Honor, earlier in this proceeding, Mister Sanders reminded me that the question had been posed and answered before after I posed it twice. I have patiently sat here and listened to him ask questions of this witness repetitively, repetitively. I think the line has to be drawn and I object. He accepts the answers and moves on.

MJ: Overruled.

CIV DC: Are you positive?

WIT: That he made reference to two people?

Q: Yes.

A: Yes, he made reference to two people.

Q: And you're positive, and it's not just an assumption—

A: It's not an assumption…

Q: That he made.

A: That he made reference to—he made reference to two people.

MJ: Now you may move on, counsel.

CIV DC: Now you didn't have the Form F then, did you?

WIT: When, when he made reference to the two people?

Q: Right, when he talked to you about it.

A: When he no, I didn't have it.

Q: So you couldn't have corrected the form, anyway.

A: No.

Q: After you left the flight line, where did you go?

A: SAC Ops

Q: And what did you do at SAC Ops?

A: We were told to write out statements of what happened.

Q: Who told you to write out the statements?

A: I don't remember who told us to write out the statements.

Q: Who was there?

A: Lieutenant Kern, Lieutenant Petsch, Captain Robertson, myself. can't remember who else was there.

Q: Was Colonel Hanson there?

A: I don't know. I don't remember seeing him.

Q: You don't remember seeing him there?

A: No, I don't remember seeing him.

Q: Do you remember him indicating to you and to everyone else to "tell it like it is"?

A: I don't remember—I remember someone handing me a sheet of paper and saying, "Write a statement as to what happened." don't remember who it was.

(A brief delay while the accused's counsel conferred.)

Q: Just a couple more questions. Sergeant Boiling, it's your testimony, as I understand it, that once you entered the *three* on the Form F, you never made any changes.

A: I never made any changes.

Q: To any Form F.

A: I never made any changes to the original. It's possible—I never made any changes to the original Form F.

Q: Did you make any changes to any Form F for the December 9 flight?

A: No, not that I can remember, as far—no, I can't remember any changes.

Q: You certainly made no changes as a result of what Colonel Hanson might have said to you.

A: No.

Q: No, you didn't make any changes.

A: No, I didn't make any changes on what Colonel Hanson said to me.

Q: Do you remember testifying at the AFR 110-14?

A: (Nodded affirmatively)

Q: Do you remember being asked whether or not you made changes as a result of what Colonel Hanson might have said to you?

A: No, I don't remember being asked that.

Q: Do you remember being read your Fifth Ammendment rights?

A: Yes, I remember that.

Q: And that was on that issue, was it not?

A: Yes.

Q: And do you remember asking for counsel?

A: Yes.

Q: And based upon the recommendation of your counsel, isn't it true that you stood on your Fifth Amendment rights...

A: Yes.

Q: And did not answer that question?

A: Yes.

CIV DC: I have no further questions.

MJ: Redirect?

REDIRECT EXAMINATION: QUESTIONS
BY TRIAL COUNSEL

Q: Did you ever answer that question later, Sergeant Bolling?

A: I can't remember if I—probably, I don't know, I don't remember. I answered all the questions being asked to me, I guess. Somewhere along the line it came up.

Q: How many formal proceedings, Sergeant Rolling, do you recall that you have spoken to about the subjects that you are speaking to today?

A: Counting this one?

Q: Yes.

A: Three.

Q: Now the first one would have been...

A: The 110-14.

Q: And—

A: No, I take that back, it wouldn't have been; it would have been the—the was an investigation in Saudi Arabia, so that would make it four then.

Q: All right. The first one was there?

A: The first one was in Saudi Arabia.

Q: And the second one was what now?

A: The second one is the 110-14 one.

Q: That's the one that made up a part of the long piece of paper that became a defense exhibit?

A: Right.

Q: What was the next one?

A: The next one was the Article 32 board.

Q: Okay, and finally today.

A: Today.

Q: Counsel, on cross-examination, asked you if you answered that question at the 110-14. I ask you, did you answer that question at the Article 32?

A: Yes, I answered it at the Article 32.

Q: Have you ever had anybody read to you your legal rights before?

A: No, no one has ever read me my legal rights.

Q: Sergeant Boiling, in response to certain questions by defense counsel, you provided answers, "No, I don't remember or know." What do you mean when you say you don't remember?

A: I don't remember.

Q: It doesn't mean that the event occurred or didn't occur...

A: No, it means—

Q: .It just means that you don't remember.

A: I don't remember.

Q: Now could you have possibly talked to Captain Johnsen sometime after this midair collision?
United States Witness Boiling—Redirect

A: It's possible. I don't remember specifically talking to him, but it's possible.

Q: Is it also possible that you could have shown him the Form F or talked about the Form F with him?

A: It's possible.

Q: What day of the week is it?

A: Thursday.

Q: Could you testify with absolute certainty as to every individual that you spoke to last Thursday, only a week ago, one week ago? Can you tell me everybody that you talked to one week ago today?

A: No, there's no way I could tell you everybody I spoke to one week ago today.

Q: Sergeant Boiling, you have testified extensively about the two Form Fs, an original and a carbon copy you prepared. This is the original.

A: Right.

Q: Prosecution Exhibit 12.

A: Yes, sir.

Q: Now during the latter part of the cross-examination, you expressed some hesitancy concerning whether or not you may or may have not made any changes to the other copy of the Form F.

A: Right.

Q: Is your concern because you don't remember whether you did make changes after the fuel adjustment on the plane?

A: Yeah, that's more my concern. I don't—like I said, I don't remember making any changes.

Q: But as to the number that follows the letter "J".

CIV DC: I object, Your Honor, it's leading.

TC: Very well, Your Honor.

MJ: Sustained. You may rephrase.

TC: Thank you, Your Honor. (Prosecution Exhibit #12 was shown to the witness.)

I refer to the number following the letter *J*—

WIT: Uh huh.

Q: On Prosecution Exhibit Twelve, the number following the letter *J*. After you prepared the original and carbon copy of that form, did you or did you not ever change that number on the original, Prosecution Exhibit 12?

A: No, I didn't.

Q: Did you or did you not ever change that number on the carbon copy?

A: No, I didn't. (Prosecution Exhibit #12 was returned to the military judge.)

MJ: Here, I'll get them.

TC: Thank you, Your Honor; nothing further.

MJ: Recross?

CIV DC: No further questions of this witness.

MJ: Fine. Should I hold the witness subject to recall?

CIV DC: Yes, Your Honor.

MJ: Sergeant Bolling, do you know what that means?

WIT: I guess it means—I'm assuming it means that I can't leave the area.

MJ: You may leave the legal office building, but I'd like you to be on 15 minutes standby, giving the trial counsel a telephone number where he can reach you.

WIT: Yes, sir.

MJ: I'll further instruct you that you're not to discuss your testimony in the case with anyone other than the counsel in this room until the trial is over; particularly other witnesses, you cannot discuss it with them.

WIT: All right, sir.

MJ: Fine, you're excused, we thank you for your time today.

WIT: Okay, thank you.

United States Witness Bolling—Excused from the court-room

Major General Andrew Pringle Jr. US Air Force Military Biographies

Page 1 of 2

Major General Andrew Pringle Jr.
US Air Force Military Biographies, Annual, 2004
Major General Andrew Pringle Jr.
Retired Aug. 1, 1982.
Major General Andrew Pringle Jr. is the chief of staff, Headquarters Strategic Air Command, Offutt Air Force Base, Neb.

General Pringle was born in 1927, in Seattle and raised in Riverside, Calif. He has a bachelor of arts degree from Central Michigan University, Mount Pleasant.

General Pringle enrolled in the aviation cadet program and was commissioned a second lieutenant in June 1950. His initial assignment was to Castle Air Force Base, Calif., with the 93rd Bombardment Wing. From 1954 to 1960, he served with the 90th Strategic

Reconnaissance Wing, Forbes Air Force Base, Kan., and the 100th Bombardment Wing,

Pease Air Force Base, N.H. His next assignment was as a pilot evaluator with the 1st Combat

Evaluation Group, Barksdale Air Force Base, La.

In 1963 he transferred to Headquarters Eighth Air Force, Westover Air Force Base, Mass., where he served in various operations positions. He was then assigned to Headquarters SAC as a plans officer. In 1969 General Pringle returned to Westover Air Force Base's 99th Bombardment Wing. During this period he performed temporary duty at Andersen Air Force Base, Guam, for B-52 air operations in Southeast Asia. While with the 99th Bombardment Wing he commanded the 348th Bombardment Squadron, was assistant deputy chief of staff for operations and deputy commander of the 99th Combat Support Group.

He transferred to Blytheville Air Force Base, Ark., as the deputy commander for operations with the 97th Bombardment Wing in December 1971. He served a second temporary duty tour at Andersen Air Force Base in late 1972 during Operation Bullet Shot as the deputy commander for operations for the 72nd Strategic Wing (Provisional). In December 1972 General Pringle was assigned to Wright-Patterson Air Force Base, Ohio, where he commanded the 17th Bombardment Wing.

Major General Andrew Pringle Jr. I US Air Force Military Biographies

* * *

Page 2 of 2

In June 1974 General Pringle returned to Andersen Air Force Base to command the 43rd Strategic Wing. In June 1975 he become the inspector general for Air Training Command, Randolph Air Force Base, Texas, and then in

January 1977 assumed command of the Lowry Technical Training Center, Lowry Air Force Base, Col.

He returned to Andersen Air Force Base in April 1978 to command SAC's 3rd Air Division. In August 1979 he became deputy chief of staff for operations at SAC headquarters. He assumed his present position in August 1980. He is a command pilot with 9,000 hours in Strategic Air Command aircraft, including more than 440 combat hours in the B-52 Stratofortress. His military decorations and awards include the Legion of Merit with oak leaf cluster, Bronze Star Medal, Meritorious Service Medal, Air Medal with three oak leaf clusters, Air Force Outstanding Unit Award ribbon with "V" device and Good Conduct Medal.

He was promoted to major general July 1, 1978, with date of rank Sept. 1, 1974.

(Current as of September 1980)

MJ: Very well, proceed.

PRESENTATION OF DEFENSE CASE

ANDREW PRINGLE, JR. called as a witness by the defense, was sworn, and testified as follows:

Questions by Trial Counsel:

Q: Sir, would you please state your full name?

A: Andrew Pringle, Junior.

Q: I note that you're wearing civilian clothes, sir. Would you please explain what affiliation you have with the Air Force?

A: Well, I'm retired as of August 1st, 1982.

Q: And in what rank did you retire, sir?

A: Major general.

Q: And you are now a retired Air Force officer.

A: I am, yes.

TC: Thank you.

DIRECT EXAMINATION: QUESTIONS BY DEFENSE COUNSEL

Q: General Pringle, do you know the accused in this case?

A: Yes, I do.

Q: If he's present in the courtroom, would you please point to him and identify him by name?

A: Bill Hanson.

(The witness pointed toward the accused.)

PRESENTATION OF DEFENSE CASE

Defense Witness Pringle—Direct

DC: Let the record reflect the proper identification.

General Pringle, you indicated that you retired from the United States Air Force at the rank of major general, is that correct?

A: Yes.

Q: And when did you retire, sir?

A: One August '82.

Q: And from what position did you retire?

A: Chief of Staff of the Strategic Air Command.

Q: General Pringle, could *you* give us a summary of what your military service has been for the United States Air Force prior to your retirement?

A: I served a couple of years as an enlisted person, out, educated, back in thirty-two years commissioned. Primarily, my duty as an officer was in the operative end of the Air Force, flying operations and things of that sort, and it culminated in thirty-two years with the rank that you are aware of, and departed the service on the date that I've indicated, and having an association with an enormous amount of people and having commanded a lot of people one, two, three, four, five times.

Q: And have you had any combat service, sir?

A: Vietnam.

Q: You indicated that you knew Colonel Hanson. Could you indicate to the court how you came to know Colonel Hanson?

A: Yes. I became the commander of the Technical Training Center in, I think, in late '76 through early '78, and during that time Bill Hanson was the Center procurement officer, though he didn't work directly for me as the center director, he was assigned under the base resource commander, and during that period of time, during daily staff meetings, his immediate boss would be present daily, and at least three times a week at staff meetings Bill Hanson would be there, in the second row, backing up his boss, as is so typical in the military, where the captains and the majors know all the things and the colonels and the generals live by them, which is very normal, very typical, and during that period of time, the Air Force, it was still recovering from post-Vietnam and the economics within the Air Force were very difficult in that

Defense Witness Pringle—Direct

Congress wanted the military to continue to do more with less in dollars, and Base Procurement then became a primary management objective and a focal point for the commander to get the job done with the resources which the country was giving us.

In addition to that, there was a process where the military was experimenting with contracting out various functions within the military to civilians to perform that had traditionally been done by the military and this fell on the shoulders of the Procurement people. There was a very difficult situation at the time at Lowry wherein one of the contractors who was bidding challenged the Air Force, in particular Lowry, and specifically took on then Major Hanson, and the allegations were that they didn't get their contract because of all sorts of

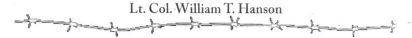

improper this and that. Well, that would obviously get the attention of a commander, so—

Q: What was your rank at that time, sir?

A: Brigadier general, and so I jumped into the middle of that, obviously, with both feet, and one of the things that I quickly learned about that young major was that he was aggressive, he was out front always, he was insisting on some things that a lot of people were saying were not so. I quickly checked with the staff of the Air Training Command and found that there was enormous support in the technical sense, and I can't describe all of the technicalities of it, but he went through this situation and, lo and behold, Major Hanson was exactly correct, and the allegations against him and about him and about the Air Force were totally wrong. I learned three things about that man as a result of that, and these are things that commanders learn about people all the time, and it was that there is a character that very was desirable for the Air Force, a man that had mission objective for the Air Force always number one, and he would even perhaps subject himself to a little unnecessary criticism because of the manner of his enthusiasm, and that was a good trait. His motives were always for the Air Force, always; he was not a self-motivated person, and finally, above all, he's probably the most honest human being I've ever known. Those three traits make good leaders, and that's what this United States Air Force needs. So I became a fan of his. Now at that time, I think he was a grounded aviator, and I don't even recall what he was grounded for, but he expressed a desire.

Q: Was it related to a physical disability?

A: I think a physical disability, yes, and he came to me and requested my support to help get back on flying status, which I did, but at that time he had some fairly good offers to stay in the Procurement end of the Air Force because he had done so well, and there were people who had pushed him to do that, but he wanted to go back and be an aviator and, being an aviator, myself, and understanding the Air Force mission and supported that, off he went. So that's my background with Bill. Now over the years since then, we've bumped into one another in our services, we've not served together since then, but because of the nature and the character of the person that I've described, I've watched him and followed him; that's our background.

Q: Based upon your experience and knowledge of Colonel Hanson, do you have an opinion as to his value to the United States Air Force?

A: To his what?

Q: His value to the United States Air Force.

A: Yes, I do. I could not imagine an organization like the military and the Air Force, whose primary mission it is to be called on, in the final analysis, to fly and fight to have people not like Bill Hanson; you'd lose the Goddamned war if you don't have that kind of guy, because he'll stick his nose out and he'll take things on and he'll make it happen, and that's the base, gut issue of that man.

DC: No further questions.

MJ: Cross-examination?

TC: Thank you, Your Honor.

CROSS-EXAMINATION

Questions by Trial Counsel: Good morning, sir.

A: Good morning.

Q: How was your trip to Blytheville?
Defense Witness Pringle—Direct/Cross

A: Fine.

Q: Sir, what was the point in time that you had your last association with Lieutenant Colonel Hanson in an official military capacity?

A: You mean when did we see one another or when did we serve together at the same station?

Q: What was the point in time that you had your last working relationship, military relationship, with Lieutenant Colonel Hanson?

A: Well, I think I would probably have to say it was at Lowry. However, I was very aware in my last duty assignment, which terminated in '82, of Bill's current situation of being assigned here, or some place else, I'm not really sure, but I would see him on and off in my capacity as the DO for SAC and the Chief of Staff, but then when I left the Air Force, I hadn't heard from Bill until I received a call here, I don't know, a month or so ago.

Q: You said during your testimony that you are an aviator. Am I to presume, sir, that you were a rated pilot during your active duty time?

A: Yes.

Q: Sir, you testified that you were on active duty in excess of thirty years?

A: Yes.

Q: Is it not true, sir, that during the course of that active duty you have had occasion to be associated with and know people who have acted in an uncharacteristic manner of the impression that you developed with them during your association?

A: Oh, well, I would have to say yes, but I can't think of any specific case.

TC: Thank you, Sir.

DC: Your Honor, we have no redirect; if Your Honor has any questions, we invite them now.

MJ: Well, I just wonder if we have—since we have General Pringle on the stand, would you like to develop evidence through him as to the accused's character, military character, which would be applicable to the merits. It would appear that he could lay the proper foundation, or you could.

162

DC: Thank you, Your Honor.

REDIRECT EXAMINATION

Questions by Defense Counsel:

Q: General Pringle, you did make some comments regarding your opinion of Colonel Hanson based upon his working with you.

A: Uh huh.

Q: And in that conjunction, I gather from your testimony that you did have frequent contact with him on several important issues.

A: Uh huh.

Q: Did you also have an opportunity to evaluate Colonel Hanson regarding his performance of his military character as an Air Force officer and those qualities that belong to that?

A: Oh, you bet I did.

Q: Could you share those with us, please?

A: Yes. I think the general statements which I have described about Bill's personality, his character, resulted in a professional performance in expectation of those who were about him and those who were fortunate enough to be his commander were that if you have a tough job to do and you wanted it done, Bill Hanson was one of the people that would quickly come to your mind. Now as we grow, or as you guys grow in the military and the longer you grow in it, then you assume more and more responsibilities in leadership and management. You rely on your people to get the job of the Air Force done. The character and the quality and the presentation and representation that we, as human beings, make wearing that uniform of that service all add to that great word "professionalism," getting things done for our country, and Bill Hanson has been extraordinarily good at that.

Q: And how did he perform his duties at Lowry as you knew them?

A: In a very professional manner that you'd be proud to take with you wherever you went, and I think if you'd go back in some of my performance reports, I might have said things like that about his character and qualities.

DC: I have nothing further, Your Honor.

MJ: Well, there's one other area. I was told during a recess yesterday that your client may take the stand.

DC: That's right, Your Honor. The sequence of things have gotten a little out of...

MJ: Well, I realize that, but if General Pringle has any opinion as to your client's character for truthfulness, that would be relevant at this point.

TC: I beg your pardon, Your Honor.

MJ: Major Oxley?

TC: I think that's being presumptious until such time as the individual's reputation for truthfulness is attacked. It seems to me to be inappropriate to go into such a matter.

MJ: Well, in view of General Pringle's scheduled and his inability to remain today, if the defense would like to go into this, I will allow it. If the accused does testify and his character is not attacked, I will disregard. Can you live with that, Major Oxley?

TC: No, Your Honor, and I object to it.

MJ: Well, overruled.

If you would like to proceed, you may.

DC: Okay.

In conjunction with that, General Pringle, regarding your association with the accused, were you able to formulate an opinion as to Colonel Hanson's reputation for truthfulness and integrity as an officer?

WIT: Absolutely. Going back to the situation which I described at LOwry, one of the inneundo allegations that goes on, that human beings are pretty good with, was that the Lowry procurement officer, in fact in his negotiations and his processes, was lying. Now that's a serious allegation against an officer or any person serving in the military, or anybody; it's a personal attack on your personal character. Of course, it came out clearly that the man was not a liar. There are no fibers that I could see in his character or structure that would allow him to do anything but tell the truth. That's the way he's glued together, that's the way God made him, and that's why he's been as successful as he has in the United States Air Force. You can't be a successful leader and get jobs done and being an inherent leader and last as long as he did in the United States Air Force; it won't let it happen.

Q: General Pringle, when we were talking about your testimony last night, you, in characterizing Colonel Hanson, you gave me an indication as to—in your opinion, in your learned opinion what Colonel Hanson's success would have been had he served in World War II.

A: Uh huh. Well, I guess none of us have been there, and I can only speculate because I didn't serve in World War II, either, but I think it's—

TC: Objection, Your Honor. By the witness' own admission, this is total speculation.

MJ: Oh, I'll hear it, counsel.
      Go ahead, sir.

WIT: But I think I can translate that to a period of time of combat that I did serve in.

DC: Vietnam?

WIT: Vietnam; but at any time a military person goes into combat or the military goes into combat, there are certain qualities within some people that make the military successful and it is called leadership. You search constantly in the military for those characteristics, and they don't always come out in a peacetime service. Those characteristics are very strong

165

and very natural and inherent in Colonel Hanson, and I can't think of any commander that would be forced or confronted with going into a combat situation that wouldn't want one hundred thousand Bill Hansons to step out front to lead the troops in combat.

DC: Thank you, I have no further questions.

WIT: (Nodded affirmatively)

MJ: Cross-examination?

TC: Thank you, Your Honor.

Defense Witness Pringle—Redirect

RECROSS-EXAMINATION

Questions by Trial Counsel:

Q: Sir, were you ever lied to by someone during your 32 years on active duty?

A: Huh, not that I can recall.

Q: Never?

A: Well, "never" is a big word. I'd have to say I don't know.

Q: I understand you to be saying, sir, that you never had the experience during your 32 years of active duty to have someone tell you something and later on discover that what they told you was not true.

A: Well, yeah, but I don't know that that's a lie; that might be a misapprehension and it might be a mistransmission of the proper use of words and so forth, a perception, to be said. But you know, an out and out lie is a pretty serious thing, you know, where somebody sits down and premeditatively says, "I'm going to say something else to hide something else."

Q: It certainly is, isn't it, sir, and you've never had that experi ence?

A: Not that I could recall.

TC: Thank you.

MJ: I assume there's nothing further from the defense.

DC: No, Your Honor.

MJ: General Pringle, I'm going to excuse you from the stand. We thank you for your time.

WIT: Thank you.

MJ: You're excused, sir.

(The witness withdrew from the courtroom.)

DC: Your Honor, the defense would request just a brief recess, if we could, before General Pringle leaves.

Defense Witness Pringle—Recross/Excused

MJ: Fine; we're in recess.

(The court-martial recessed at 0823 hours, 11 January 1985, and was called back to order at 0831 hours, 11 January 1985, with all parties present who were present when the court-martial recessed.)

Motions For Finding of not Guilty

DC: Your Honor, at this time the defense would make motions for findings of not guilty regarding two of the specifications, the first being Charge I, Specification 1; the second being a motion for a finding of not guilty regarding Charge II, Specification 1.

Motion For Finding of not Guilty
(Sp 1, Ch II)

I would like to briefly address Charge II, Specification 1, first dealing with the wrongful solicitation of Sergeant Boiling in that the defense's position is, in the posture of the government's evidence, the uncertainty with which Sergeant Boiling testified, the evidence did not rise to the level that the prosecution met its burden of proof as to whether there was a solicitation as they've alleged in the specification.

The defense's position on this would be, Your Honor, that the government has the burden of proof at this point to establish, to go beyond the elements of the offense, or to establish the elements of the offense, and that they *under* the circumstances would

167

have to establish that the accused wrongfully and dishonorably solicited Staff Sergeant Boiling to falsify an official record, to wit, the Weight and Balance Clearance Form F, by changing the form to reflect that two people were not on the KC-135 aircraft.

The testimony by Sergeant Boiling, or the government's evidence in this case, indicates that there was a discrepancy and that there was a need to change, to correct the Form F to reflect what had officially took place on the aircraft. The government has interpreted that to mean that there was an effort by the accused to have it changed improperly. The defense's position is that the government hasn't met that burden of proof in that changing the Form F would have been appropriate regarding the actual number of passengers aboard the aircraft anyway.

This is *the* charge the government wanted me found guilty of.

You may recall what Franz Kafka had to say about the job of the defense…

"To find a friend on the court…" General Pringle was that friend. For all practical purposes the trial was over concerning the most serious charge. I did take the stand a second time down the line. I'll leave it to you how that comes across, but it goes exactly to what General Pringle said about my dealings with him and others in the Air Force. There are some mighty fine witnesses coming up.

DC: In addition, the defense would request that His Honor consider the testimony of the witnesses regarding the communication to Sergeant Bolling and the assumptions that he would indicate that he took.

In response to several questions, he indicated that, regarding these critical issues, a lot of the information that he provided in this courtroom was something that he couldn't remember, probably happened, wasn't really sure.

Your Honor, the defense feels that the evidence presented before the court in such a fashion is legally insufficient to go beyond the government's case and, as a matter of law, ought to be dismissed as a motion for a finding of not guilty at this stage.

I would then like to...

MJ: Well now, wait a minute. Let me hear argument...

DC: Sorry.

MJ: By the prosecution as to this particular motion.

TC: The government opposes the defense's motion, Your Honor, and in brief brings to the bench's attention that the defense has mis-stated the test to sustain a motion to dismiss at this point in the trial. The question is not at this point whether or not the government has met its burden of proof to prove beyond a reasonable doubt all elements of the offense charged, especially not met the burden in the analysis of defense counsel. Rather, Your Honor, the test is has there been evidence presented on each element of the offense that, if found adversely to the accused, could result in a finding of guilty on the specification. It is the government's position that each element of Charge II, spec 1, has evidence that, if so interpreted by you, the trier of fact, could result in a finding of guilty. Therefore, we believe it's inappropriate for the motion to be granted.

MJ: Counsel, I'm going to grant the motion as to Specification 1 of Charge II, and enter a finding of not guilty as to that allegation.

Motion For Finding of not Guilty
(Sp 1, Ch I)

DC: Your Honor, the defense has a second motion it wishes to make at this time; that second motion for a finding of not guilty pertains

Motion for Finding of Not Guilty (Sp 1, Ch II)—Granted
Motion for Finding of Not Guilty (Sp 1, Ch I)—Denied R-303

DC: No further questions, Your Honor.

MJ: Very well. I assume we can release the witness.

DC: Yes, Your Honor.

TC: Yes, Your Honor.

MJ: Sergeant Gentry, I'm going to release you momentarily. I'll instruct you that you're not to discuss your testimony in the case with anyone other than these attorneys until the trial is over. Do you understand?

WIT: Yes, sir.

MJ: Thank you for your time, you're excused.

(The witness withdrew from the courtroom.)

ADC: Your Honor, at this time, the defense calls to the stand Lieutenant Colonel Joe Buttram.

(There was a considerable delay awaiting the witness.)

DC: Your Honor, maybe the witness isn't there. Would you like me to go check?

MJ: No, I don't want to lose any more people than I have to.

DC: If not, we need to call the BOQ.

MJ: We'll take a five—minute recess to allow the witness…

DC: There he is.

MJ: No, we won't.

JOE A. BUTTRAM

Called as a witness by the defense, was sworn, and testified as follows:

Questions by Trial Counsel: Would you please state your full name and rank?

A: Lieutenant Colonel Joe Anthony Buttram.

Q: Defense Witness Buttram, to what organization are you assigned, Colonel Buttram?

A: Currently the Chief of Training, 99th Air Refueling Squadron, Robins Air Force Base, Georgia.

Q: And you are a member of the United States Air Force?

A: Yes.

TC: Thank you, sir.

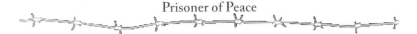

DIRECT EXAMINATION

Questions by Assistant Defense Counsel

Q: Colonel Buttram, how long have you been a member of the United States Air Force?

A: Seventeen and a half years.

And what have your duties been in the United States Air Force concerning, regarding aircraft operations?

A: Continuous flying for seventeen and a half years; currently qualified in jet aircraft.

Are you presently current and qualified in the KC—135 aircraft?

A: Yes.

Q: And how long have you been current and qualified in KC-135 aircraft?

A: Thirteen years.

Q: Have you ever served as a stan/eval or a CEVG flight examiner for KC—135 aircraft?

A: Yes, eight years total. I was a stan/eval division chief at Rickenbacker Air Force Base, Ohio. While I was stan/eval division chief there, I ran a 90-day test program to verify the current flight manual procedures that we use as far as configuring the aircraft and so forth, and then I spent five years as a MAJCOM evaluator at Barksdale with the 1st Combat Evaluation Group. At the time of the accident, I was the chief flight examiner for the Strategic Air Command.

Q: Colonel Buttram, for those of us who are not familiar with rated duties, will you explain to the court exactly what it is that a standardization and evaluation branch performs? What were your duties there?

A: Okay, the standardization branch is made up of flight examiners from all crew positions. Their job is to give annual flight checks to the other crewmembers to insure that they're up to speed on procedures and techniques for safely flying the aircraft and that they are safe in the aircraft. As a MAJCOM evaluator with headquarters, you job is to travel around the country, for SAC, approximately forty-seven bases that fly KC-135s, that includes the National Guard and the Reserves, PACAF, USAFE, and evaluate the evaluators that evaluate the crewmembers, and at the MAJCOM level you're also responsible for coordinating the procedural changes to the flight manual and the training manuals for KC-135 operations.

Q: How many hours do you have in the KC-135 aircraft, Colonel Buttram?

A: I have approximately 2,700 hours in the KC-135.

Q: And how would you characterize your knowledge based upon your thirteen-plus years as a flight examiner of the KC-135 procedures and flight manuals?

A: My knowledge of the KC-135 flight procedures?

Q: Yes, sir.

A: As knowledgeable probably as anybody that operates or works with the KC-135.

Q: Sir, while you were assigned to Barksdale Air Force Base, what was your authority concerning the flight manual? Did you have any chance to input or did you suggest, or were you just evaluating the various bases stan/eval branches?

A: As the major user of the KC-135, SAC is responsible for coordinating all of the proposed changes and recommendations to the flight manual and processing them prior to them going to the flight manual manager at Oklahoma City. In other words, the SAC folks have a great deal of it at Barksdale. I personally didn't do that, the man that worked for me did, but I personally reviewed and approved every one of the recommendations that SAC sent forward with recommendations for changes. We don't get to—we didn't get to stop-gap the proposed changes, we had to forward them up to the flight manual manager,

but we did get to put onthere whether we recommended the change or not and the reasons why we didn't want the change.

Q: So for the five years you were at Barksdale Air Force Base, you were primarily and principally concerned with the flight operations in the flight manual for the KC-135 aircraft?

A: Not—well, for the full five years I had inputs to it and reviewed the flight manual. For the last two years, I had a great deal of responsibility in that area since the man that was doing most of the research worked for me.

Q: Okay, thank you, Sir. Sir, have you had the opportunity to review the safety accident report, safety report, concerning the mishap involving a KC-135 SAC tanker and the E-3A TAC aircraft in Saudi Arabia on 9 December 1983?

A: Yes, I was aware of the accident. As a matter of fact, as the division chief of the tankers, or KC-135s, I was aware of every incident or accident that was reported for KC-135's and had to review all preliminary reports and final reports to determine if there was procedural error that, you know, where we could change the flight manual maybe to prevent such from happening, and ordinarily in an accident, I sent a flight examiner that had been to the safety school to the accident investigation board to work with them to determine what the cause of the accident was and if there was anything that we could do that might prevent future accidents.

Q: But specifically, you did have the opportunity to review the safety report...

A: Yes, I did read that report.
Colonel Buttram, were you also afforded the opportunity to review the certification of damage to the aircraft that was included in the AFR 110-14 collateral investigation?

A: Yes, I was.

Q: Colonel Buttram, did you ever have any chance to review any photographs of the KC-135 subsequent to the mishap?

A: Only since arriving here at Blytheville. I saw the photographs that you showed me of the wing and the engines.

Q: Colonel Buttram, do you believe that you have a good understanding of the nature and extent of the damage incurred by the KC-135 aircraft as a result of that accident?

A: Yes, I believe I do.

Q: Colonel Buttram, could you explain to the court the difficulties confronted by a pilot with an aircraft under those conditions?

A: Yes, I can. The flight manual that we have does not cover the procedures for recovering that aircraft under the conditions that this particular aircraft had. The training that a regular pilot or aircraft commander receives when he goes through training, when he gets his initial training and in his continuation training at the local unit, does not include the same training that an instructor pilot would get. In the condition that this aircraft was in, the instructor pilot doesn't even get training because the flight manual doesn't have all the procedures in it.

Basically, when we bought the aircraft, we bought it where it would handle—you could recover it with two major emergencies, (i.e., two engines out, your power rudder system out and one engine out, but you can't cover all situations, all emergencies when you buy an aircraft). You have to buy the aircraft so that you can handle all emergencies that will probably ever occur in it, but there's always a chance that you'll have problems that you don't have a system or have a plan for. This particular accident here, the aircraft wound up in a state with two engines out on the same side and was unable to power the powered rudder. The aircraft, in the history of it, has only been required to be recovered with two engines out on the same side approximately ten

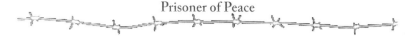

times and, to my knowledge, this was the first time it had to be landed with two engines out on the same side and no powered rudder.

Q: Colonel Buttram, what would a pilot have to do to land an aircraft with two engines out and no hydraulic system on that one side?

A: Well, first, he has to have a good understanding of—a very good understanding—of asymmetrical thrust to understand that he won't be able to use full throttle on his two good engines once he gets the aircraft in the landing configuration at a slow airspeed.

Basically, he has two problems. He has to control the aircraft to get it to a point where he can land it, and then he has to make the decision to land the aircraft, i.e., commit it to landing with no chance for a go-around, and get it to a speed at which he can put it on the runway and get it stopped. The problem is not only, with the right hydraulic system out, is not only with the rudder. You don't have the ability to increase your flap setting to get it to a slow enough speed to land it and get it safely stopped on the runway unless you commit it to land early enough.

The procedures that are taught to all instructor pilots at the Central Flight Instructor School is the two-engine-out, power-rudder-operative, and basically, we fly it with 20 degrees of flaps, when we start down the glide path we lower our landing gear, and we commit ourselves to land at 300 feet above the ground. At that point we start configuring the flaps, and sometime after that, depending on what the airspeed is doing, we pull power to idle and land, but once you start the configuration, you're committed to landing.

Q: Colonel Buttram, what specific procedures, what guidance is given to a pilot by the flight manual for operating a KC-135 aircraft under these conditions?

A: Under the conditions that I was just talking about, there is a paragraph about this long, and the techniques…

MJ: Referencing about two and a half inches.

WIT: However, that's with the power rudder operating. There is no guidance in the flight manual, procedurally or technique—wise, for landing the aircraft with the two engines out and the power rudder inoperative as this aircraft had.

ADC: And that procedure is not even instructed?

WIT: It's not instructed officially. It's talked about occasionally by some instructor pilots. As a matter of fact, I've talked with Colonel Hanson about this subject prior to the accident, probably six months or so prior to the accident, but it's not taught. It's not part of any curriculum, it's not part of the continuation training or anything.

Q: Colonel Buttram, what happens with a simulator, flight simulator trainer for KC-135 aircraft, when you program in these conditions in the simulator?

A: It rolls over and dies.

Q: What does the flight manual provide concerning the ability to go around, that is, to come in for an approach and have enough chance to make another approach under these conditions?

A: Well, there's a warning in the flight manual that says go-around with full throttle on the two good engines cannot be assured due to the extreme rudder pedal forces required to counteract the yaw, and you need close to full throttle at the weight that you're at.

Q: Colonel Buttram, from your experience as a KC-135 aircraft commander, what kind of stress would a pilot be under operating a KC-135 under these conditions?

TC: Objection, Your Honor. There's been no showing of expertise by this witness to deal with comments on stress.

MJ: Overruled.

WIT: A pilot flying an airplane under these conditions would be under a great deal of stress. Initially, to walk to a cockpit or to be sitting there when it happened and all of a sudden realize that you didn't have two engines on one side, that your right hydraulic system was gone, I believe in this case they had two fire warning lights on the right side engines also, a man would be scared to death at that point. He would think that he had better have his life insurance paid up.

ADC: Have you ever undergone a situation involving a flying emergency, your self?

WIT: Well, not to this degree. I've almost killed myself several times and realized or thought that I wouldn't survive.

Q: What kind of stress did you feel when you had those experiences?

A: I—

MJ: That's fine. I think we can move on.

ADC: All right, thank you, sir. No further questions, Your Honor.

MJ: Cross-examination?

TC: Thank you, Your Honor.

Cross-Examination

Questions by Trial Counsel

Q: Colonel Buttram, have you ever flown a KC-135 with two engines out on the same wing and it was also absent the power rudder?

A: No, not in actuality; I have simulated it in flight, however.

Q: The way I described the aircraft in my question, is that an accurate understanding of what you have of the configuration of the plane in question?

Defense Witness Buttram—Direct/Cross

A: Yes, two engines out on one side and the power rudder inoperative.

Q: And you've never flown an aircraft like that.

A: No one has ever flown a 135 like that except the crew that recovered this one. I understand. So much of what you're talking about is speculation.

A: Uh...

Q: That's a yes or no question, sir.

A: No.

Q: Upon what do you base your negative response?

A: Because I can simulate the conditions for flying the aircraft procedurally in flight without actually failed the engines, without actually having even pulled any engines back.

Q: Yes, sir, and that would be on the simulator?

A: No, that's in the aircraft in flight.

Q: You testified that if you put in the factors that were applicable to this aircraft on your simulator, what happens?

A: I believe I said it rolls over and dies. That's basically what it does; it will not fly.

Q: But we know that's not the case because we know this aircraft came back that way, right?

A: Yes, that's true.

Q: So we know that simulator isn't telling us the truth.

A: That's right.

Q: You've never flown with Lieutenant Colonel Hanson before, have you?

A: No, I haven't.

Q: Lieutenant Colonel Buttram, would you please tell me what your formal education is after high school?
Defense Witness Buttram—Cross

A: A degree in electrical engineering, Auburn University.

Q: Do you have any degrees in psychology?

A: No, but I have—I don't have a degree in psychology, but if you administer check rides for eight years, you learn a lot—

Q: I'm sure you learn a lot about life. Do you consider yourself to be an expert on stress?

A: In—maybe not all stress, but stress in the aircraft, I do.

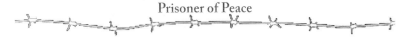
TC: Thank you.

MJ: Redirect?

DC: No, Your Honor.

MJ: Very well. I anticipate we can release the witness.

DC: Yes, Your Honor, we can.

MJ: Prosecution, do you want him held for recall?

TC: No, Your Honor, we do not wish him subject to recall.

MJ: Colonel Buttram, I'm going to release you momentarily. I will instruct you not to discuss your testimony in the case with anyone other than the attorneys until the trial is over. You're excused, and we thank you for your time.

(The witness withdrew from the courtroom.)

MJ: You have two more witnesses, Colonel Edwards and then your client?

DC: Yes, Your Honor, we do have two more, those two witnesses.

MJ: Well, let's do Colonel Edwards, and then we'll break for lunch.

Now will Colonel Edwards be lengthy?

DC: I'm sorry.

MJ: Will Colonel Edwards be a lengthy witness?

DC: I don't believe so, Your Honor.

MJ: Well, let's take him now.

Defense Witness Buttram—Cross/Excused

DC: Okay. Lieutenant Colonel Edwards, please.

MJ: I assume you'd like to take a break before your client takes the stand.

DC: Yes. MJ: A break for lunch or something?

DC: (Nodded affirmatively)

LAUREL J. EDWARDS

Called as a witness by the defense, was sworn, and testified as follows:

Questions by Trial Counsel: What is your full name and rank?

A: My name is Laurel James Edwards, I'm a lieutenant colonel.

Q: To what organization are you assigned?

A: The 405th Tactical Training Wing at Luke Air Force Base, Arizona, where I'm chief of training.

Q: And you are a member of the United States Air Force?

A: That is correct.

TC: Thank you.

DIRECT EXAMINATION

Questions by Defense Counsel: Colonel Edwards, do you know the accused in this case?

A: I do, Colonel Hanson.

DC: The proper identification.

Q: Colonel Edwards, were you stationed at Riyadh in Saudi Arabia on the 9th of December 1983?

A: Yes, I was.

Defense Witness Edwards—Direct

Q: And what was your position there?

A: At that time I was the Deputy for Operations for the U.S. Air Force section of the U.S. Military Training Mission in Saudi Arabia.

And how long were you assigned there?

A: Two years. I arrived in July, August actually, of 1982 and left in August of '84.

Q: You indicated previously that you knew Colonel Hanson. How did you come to know Colonel Hanson?

A: As previously—my initial year there, I was Chief of Current Operations and as such one of my principal additional duties was liaison between the Elf One command, both tanker and AWACS portions of that, and the Royal Saudi Air Force headquarters staff where I was the senior advisor. As a result of the need to interface, I spent a fair amount of time at Elf One. I also sat in on Elf One interface meetings with the Saudis, normally a weekly meeting, and at that time, as DO, Colonel Hanson—in my office as DO, Colonel Hanson came in and attended his initial

180

week there, I believe, and subsequently other weeks, the weekly Elf One meeting. It was the first time in my two years there, or at that time a year and a half, that I had ever seen the SAC detachment commander show the initiative and interest to attend that meeting. Normally, it was just the AWACS. I worked with him on subsequent occasions. If I may elaborate on that, I'd like to explain some of that. A major project that I was assigned right after arriving in Saudi Arabia was working out an effective interface and the procedures, letter of agreement and all that, required to enable Saudi, the Royal Saudi Air Force F-15s to refuel on Elf One tankers, and although I had some six months prior to this, in the spring of '83, had received JCS approval for this to occur, I had encountered continual obstacles in getting SAC approval.

TC: Relevancy, Your Honor. Are we going to military character here of the accused? Is that what this witness is going to speak to, or is there some other point?

MJ: I'd like an offer.

DC: It would go also to that, Your Honor, plus—the purpose of the witness' testimony is to testify concerning the stress of Colonel Hanson following the mid-air concerning Colonel Cunningham's call and…

MJ: That I agree with.

TC: Let's get to it.

MJ: Now, counsel. How is the current subject matter relevant, is all I need to know.

DC: Your Honor, the defense' position is that Colonel Hanson's efforts on behalf of the mission there with the Saudi contingency there is part and parcel as to doing what is necessary to get the job done at Riyadh, and the civilians going on the aircraft are part of that thought process that Colonel Hanson had at that time, that that was expected of him, and Colonel Edwards can provide information regarding Colonel Hanson's efforts to get that type of program operable for Riyadh Air Base.

MJ: I will allow testimony as to that. However, I think we're a little off track right now.

TC: Might I be permitted further comment, Your Honor?

MJ: Yes.

TC: Your Honor, it's the government's understanding that military character evidence is admissible in a proceeding of this type and it can come in in two forms; it can come in as opinion evidence or it can come in as reputation, but it can't come in as a specific incident.

MJ: I agree.

TC: Then how can we possibly be getting into all of these specific instances?

MJ: He is not offering this as military character evidence, as I understand it.

TC: I'm sorry, I misunderstood. Then what does it go to?

MJ: Did I misunderstand, Colonel Reed?

DC: Your Honor, the defense is offering it as part of Colonel Hanson's method of operation, why he performed his duties the way he did at Riyadh in furtherance of the Air Force, as it corresponds with his understanding concerning civilians on the aircraft; in order words, to support the...

MJ: This is going to a potential affirmative defense...

DC: Yes, Your Honor.

MJ: That being mistake of fact?

DC: Yes, Your Honor.

MJ: I'll give you wide latitude, but still, giving you wide latitude, I think you've gone too far with this witness.

DC: Colonel Edwards, I believe you indicated that you had had some contact with Colonel Hanson while you were there.

WIT: I did, numerous occasions.

Q: Okay. Did he come over to your house on the evening of 9 December 1983?

182

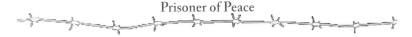

A: Yes, he did.

Q: And was he by himself?

A: No, he wasn't, three of his crewmembers were with him.

Q: And who were they?

A: The pilot, the copilot and the boom operator.

Q: Now while he was at your house, could you give us an indication as to why he was at your house? Was this an official function or anything?

A: No, it wasn't. I had been to the base on official business. The safety officer worked for me. I dispatched him right upon hearing of the accident. Shortly thereafter I went over, myself. As Deputy for Operations, I needed to go over and see if there was anything that I could do to help. In the course of that time, I stayed around, helped with witness testimony, got tape recorders and what-not for the safety officer, and at the end of all of this time, I offered Colonel Hanson and his crew an invitation to my house to come by and have a drink; figured it was something, under the circumstances, that would do them some good because they were, as we always are when we've faced death closely and starting to realize that, in a bit of an excited state.

Q: Now when they—they came over to you house that evening.

A: That is correct.

Defense Witness Edwards—Direct

Q: Do you know whether or not Colonel Hanson did have anything to drink that night?

A: Yes, he did. I offered them beer or hard liquor. The crewmen asked for the beer and Colonel Hanson requested, I believe it was, bourbon, and we had probably, over the course of the evening, three or four drinks be they beers or the bourbon.

Q: Now while they were at your house, did the crewmembers or did the crew—were they discussing anything in particular?

A: Well, they did. They were discussing their very close brush with death and things that related to that. I remember the

183

crewmembers being concerned about their families, was the news going to get back before the whole facts were out, things like this.

Q: And Colonel Hanson was partaking in that conversation with them?

A: Yes, he was. One thing I remember very clearly, though, in addition to relating to the mental state they were in, and I characterize that as physically and emotionally exhausted, but mentally very hyper, kind of an adrenaline reaction, I think, to it.

Q: Had you—and this was from your personal observations and hearing of the conversations, the manner and tone of the conversations and these things?

A: I've been there before, myself, on several occasions. I've also seen other crewmembers. I fly fighters but, you know, we also have close ones periodically.

Q: This was a couple of hours after the mishap itself, was it not?

A: Yes, it was.

Q: And so the emergency was basically over.

A: That's right, and that's when a trained crewmember is going to let down. When whatever happens in flight happens, no matter how frightening it is, you get to the task at hand and do what you need to do to fly the airplane and get it safely on the ground, and that includes putting the airplane to bed on the ground, taking care of whatever you have to there. Only when you're out of that situation and either alone, in my experiences it has been when I was alone or with someone I can relate to and would understand it, you kind of unwind and start thinking about how close you came to death

Q: What would be this after-the-fact anxiety level of the individuals who were involved in such a situation, based upon your experience?

A: Oh, very high. They've been extremely frightened, extremely anxious, but they've pretty well suppressed it, did what they needed to do, and now when you're alone or among compatriots, particularly in their case there were four of them who had gone through the same thing, there was a very evident preoccupation with their mortality and their close brush with death.

Q: What happened if—on that particular evening, during the discussions—did you have occasions where a topic would come up which was off of that subject?

A: I tried to lighten the situation a little bit, and I'd throw topics out, you know, how's your family, this kind of thing, and it was almost summarily dismissed and the topic, regardless of whether I was talking to the captain or lieutenant or Colonel Hanson, it kept coming back to the topic which was uppermost in their minds and that was the mishap and particularly the actions that were taken subsequent to it to safely get the airplane on the ground.

Q: Did you see this type of demeanor working within Colonel Hanson at that time?

A: Very much so. I would see occasional lapses into somberness, when one is self-reflecting, I would assume, and then sort of a staccato description of some of the events that took place to safely recover the airplane. I remember Colonel Hanson took the opportunity to drive an object lesson home to his men. He made the point that, he said, "This is what I've been telling you; that the time that you have alone on alerts and what-not that you spend with ACSC is fine if you've learned the dash-one first, but you have to learn your flight manual and you have to know everything about the airplane, know it completely by heart, because in times like this you don't have time to refer to the book," and from his description, and my understanding, it was corroborated by the pilot and the copilot. The general feeling among the younger crew was that if Colonel Hanson, with his experience and knowledge, had not been on the airplane, that it quite well likely may not have been safely recovered.

Q: Now during this discussion as you saw it and experienced while you were there, is it your testimony that if you sidetrack them with some social conversation, it always would come back or, take them off that train of thought, they would always come right back?

A: That is correct.

Q: Is that consistent with your experience of being involved in a midair or being involved in an aircraft emergency type situation?

A: It is. What I have seen and what I have experienced, if someone is in the situation where he can in fact start expressing his thoughts of the nearness of death and what was done to recover the aircraft safely and what-not, if someone distracts me, would distract me from that, I found it irritating, would brush it aside as quickly as possible and get back to the topic at hand.

Q: Was there any conversation among them concerning—or did they express any concerns about the investigation?

A: The ones who verbalized it, and I'm sure there was concern on everyone's part, Colonel Hanson, being more senior, having had more opportunity to witness these proceedings and I'm sure who had the more clear idea of how an investigation would proceed, but the young crewmember, and I don't remember which one it was, the pilot or the copilot, expressed concern over how long they were going to be grounded, the possibility of being in trouble, whatever, because two airplanes had contacted each other. Colonel Hanson immediately turned to his crew and said, "What I want you to do is tell it like it is." He said, "It's not hard, just answer the questions."

Q: Now let me ask you something. Was there any discussion about any civilians or passengers being on the aircraft while you were there?

A: No, there was not, but I am…

Q: Were you aware of any civilians on the aircraft…

A: No.

Q: Being on it, the KC-135?

A: Previously, I'm aware of the general's secretary having been given a ride several months prior to Colonel Hanson's arrival.

Q: Now at the time that they came over to your house, was there a phone call or anything to Colonel Hanson while you were there?

A: Yes. After, what I would guess, 45 minutes to an hour into their stay, the phone rang. The phone was in a back room. I don't recall if my wife took the call or if I answered it, but it was for Colonel Hanson. I do not recall who it was from; I had heard who it most likely was. Colonel Hanson took the call and returned shortly thereafter. He was out of hearing at that time.

DC: Nothing further, Your Honor.

MJ: Cross-examination?

TC: One moment, Your Honor.

CROSS-EXAMINATION

Questions by Trial Counsel: Lieutenant Colonel Edwards, in your experience in life, have you ever had occasion to hear someone say one thing and yet do another?

A: I have. If you're referring to this one comment, under those circumstances, I would consider it highly unlikely. It was not made off-hand.

Q: Understand; nevertheless.

A: Yes.

TC: That's all.

MJ: Redirect?

DC: No further questions, Your Honor.

MJ: Shall we hold the witness subject to recall, gentlemen?

DC: Yes, Your Honor.

MJ: Very well. You know what that means, don't you, Colonel Edwards?

WIT: No, I don't.

MJ: Well, we're going to let you leave the courthouse, but we'd like you to stay on the base and be available on 15-minute telephonic notification.

WIT: All right.

MJ: Since you're going to be here, I'll instruct you that you cannot discuss your testimony in the case with anyone other than the attorneys until the trial is over. You're excused, we thank you for you time.

DC: Your Honor..

Defense Witness Edwards—Cross/Excused

MJ: Yes.

DC: I'm sorry, I understand that Colonel Edwards needs to get back to his base, so I will not hold him subject to recall.

MJ: Very well.

WIT: I can reschedule.

DC: That's okay.

MJ: I assume the prosecution would not want him held subject to recall.

TC: We do not, Your Honor.

MJ: Colonel Edwards, you're free to go, thank you.

WIT: Thank you.

(The witness withdrew from the courtroom.)

DC: Your Honor, do you want to take a recess at this time?

MJ: Well, it's 11:30. I'm prepared to take a recess and put your client on the stand, or I'm prepared to eat lunch and then put your client on the stand, if he's going to testify.

DC: I'd like to take a recess which would include lunch and then put my client on the stand.

MJ: Okay, and reconvene at 12:30? That will give you an hour.

DC: Yes.

MJ: We're in recess.

(The court-martial recessed at 1133 hours, 11 January 1985, and was called back to order at 1229 hours, 11 January 1985, with all parties present who were present when the court—martial recessed.)

DC: Your Honor, at this time, with the permission of the court, I would like to read a stipulation of expected testimony, marked as Appellate Exhibit XII.

MJ: Colonel Hanson, do you understand that a stipulation of testimony is a substitution for the testimony of a live witness?

ACC: Yes, sir.

Advice—Stipulation/Testimony

MJ: And you have signed the document?

ACC: Yes, sir.

MJ: As have your counsel?

ACC: (No response)

MJ: And your counsel have signed it also?

DC: Yes.

ACC: Yes, sir.

MJ: So by doing this, you are consenting to the use of this stipulation in lieu of the presence of the witness personally.

ACC: Yes, sir.

MJ: And you understand that.

ACC: Yes, sir.

MJ: Fine. Proceed, counsel.

DC: "It is hereby stipulated and agreed by and between the trial counsel and defense counsel, with the express consent of the accused, that if First Lieutenant Anthony T. Kern(co-pilot on the kc-135 during collision)were called as a witness and sworn upon his oath, he would testify as follows: "I am First Lieutenant Anthony T. Kern, assigned to the 46th Air Refueling Squadron at K.I. Sawyer Air Force Base, Michigan. On 9 December 1983 I was performing TDY duties as copilot on the KC-135 aircraft which was involved in a mid—air collision in Saudi Arabia. The flight originated from Riyadh Air Base, Saudi Arabia, and was performing a refueling mission for an E-3A aircraft. During the flight the two aircraft were involved in a mid-air collision. Lieutenant Colonel William T. Hanson, the accused in this case, took control of the aircraft for the recovery procedures returning the KC—135 to Riyadh Air Base. We dialed in the Riyadh tower on the radio and reported the emergency. We requested a direct routing to Riyadh Air Base and clearance of the air space for the return. The tower proceeded to request the normal information pertaining to the nature of the emergency and aircraft condition. During these radio communications between the tower and our aircraft, the tower requested data as to the fuel condition and the number or souls, meaning persons aboard the aircraft. Lieutenant Colonel Hanson was at this time pretty much running the show and directing the recovery procedures. Respecting the report of the number of people aboard the aircraft, I know I did not provide the radio transmission identifying the number of persons aboard. I'm not sure who did, but believe that it was probably Lieutenant Colonel Hanson since he was doing all the talking on the radio at this time. As a matter of fact, he was giving them almost a play-by-play accounting of what was going on.

MJ: Give it to the court reporter.

(Appellate Exhibit XII was given to the reporter.)

MJ: Is that marked Appellate Exhibit XII?

190

REP: Yes, it is.

ADC: Your honor, prior to the accused taking the stand to testify, the defense would like to provide notice that, pursuant to Military Rule of Evidence 301(e), the accused will not be testifying concerning Charge 1, Specification 2, that specification being the charge concerning allowing a person, a passenger, not possessing an aeronautical rating, to occupy the copilot's position during takeoff and climbout. The accused will not be testifying to Charge 1, Specification 3, that specification addressing the alleged negligence in failing to insure the presence of a SOF on the ground during the launch, flight and recovery of the KC-135 aircraft, and Charge 1, Specification 5, the alleged negligence in failing to insure that his name was on the flight authorization.

MJ: Thank you, counsel.

CIV DC: Call the defendant to the stand, Your Honor.

LT. COL. WILLIAM T. HANSON, THE ACCUSED

Called as a witness by the defense, was sworn, and testified as follows:

Q: Are you the accused in this case, sir?

A: Yes, I am.

TC: Thank you.

DIRECT EXAMINATION

Questions by Civilian Defense Counsel:

Q: Colonel Hanson, how long have you been a member of the United States Air Force?

A: Twenty-one years and some months.

Q: When was your date of induction?

A: I think it was 25 August '63.

Q: Okay. What had you done by way of experience or education prior to that?

A: I graduated from the University of Maine.

Q: With a Bachelor of Arts or Science Degree?

A: Bachelor of Arts, Psychology.

Q: Upon being inducted into the Air Force, what was your initial rank?

A: I was discharged as a staff sergeant, then I went through OTS.

Q: What happened after you got out of OTS?

A: I got a commission as a second lieutenant on 20 December 1963 and became a weapons controller.

Q: And where did you serve as a weapons controller?

A: Initially, I went to Oklahoma City, schooling at Tyndall Air Force Base in Florida. I served in Oklahoma City, then I went to Newfoundland and served a remote tour in Newfoundland, then I served an airborne tour with AWACS in the EC-121 in Vietnam.

Q: What were your duties as a weapons controller?
Defense Witness Hanson—Direct

A: My duty as a weapons controller was to direct fighter aircraft to either ground and/or air targets.

Q: What did you do next in the armed forces?

A: Well, I went to—I served a short tour in Vietnam as a weapons controller, and I came back and went to pilot training.

Q: When was your tour in Vietnam?

A: The first one I think was in 1965 or '66. I'd have to check my personnel records to make it 100 percent sure.

Q: How long were you in Vietnam at that time?

A: One hundred and seventy—nine days.

Q: And what did you do there?

A: I'm not sure I'm allowed to—I flew some out-of-country missions by a special message which is referenced in my personnel records.

Q: Okay. Were you involved in combat at that time?

A: Yes, sir.

Q: Subsequent to that tour in Vietnam, where did you go?

A: I was stationed at Sacramento at McClellan Air Force Base in Sacramento, California.

Q: Okay, and what did you do there?

A: The same thing, except it was not in combat. I was a weapons director in early warning.

Q: You indicated that you went to pilot's school?

A: Yes, sir.

When did you graduate pilot's school?

A: I graduated in May of 1968.

Q: And with what—what rank were you then, at that time?

A: I think I had made captain while I was in pilot training.

Q: And what were you trained to pilot?

A: Anything we had. I could—do you mean what was my assignment after I got out of pilot training?

Q: Uh huh.

A: They assigned me to be an instructor pilot in the Air Training Command.

Q: What happened subsequent to that?

A: I went back to Vietnam again as an 0-2 pilot.

Q: And how long were you in Vietnam your second tour?

A: I had a year over there the second time.

Q: Did that involve combat once again?

A: Very much, yes.

Q: What happened subsequent to your second tour in Vietnam?

A: I came back to Randolph Air Force Base in Texas. I was still an instructor pilot in T-37s, so I was selected to be a T-39 pilot for the Air Training Command staff.

Q: And what year are we presently at?

A: Oh, we're going pretty fast.

Q: Approximately.

A: I think this is late '72.

Q: And what was your rank at that time?

A: I was a captain.

Q: Then what happened? Where did you go next?

A: After Randolph, I went into the procurement field at San Antonio, at Randolph Air Force Base. Subsequent to that I was assigned after a nine-month training program at Randolph, I was assigned as the Center procurement officer at Lowry Air Force Base, Colorado.

Q: Who did you work for at Lowry?

A: Directly, I worked for Colonel Gorman, and his boss was General Pringle, as you met this morning.

Q: General Pringle indicated this morning that, after your tour in Procurement, you decided to go back into flying.

A: Well, I had another Procurement job before that. I was selected to be the Director of Procurement for the Army-Air Force Exchange Service in Munich, Germany.

Q: After you left Procurement, where did you go?

A: I came to SAC in 1980. In October 1980, I was assigned to 135s in the Strategic Air Command.

Q: You say October of 1980?

A: Yes, sir, I believe that was right.

Q: Is that the first time in your Air Force career that you were working for SAC?

A: Yes, that's right.

Q: Have you worked for SAC since that time?

A: Continuously.

Q: What was your first SAC assignment?

A: KC-135 aircraft, or copilot at—well, I was actually checked out as an aircraft commander first at Blytheville Air Force Base.

Q: And did you stay at Blytheville?

A: Yes, sir, except for numerous TDY's.

Q: When was your first TDY to Saudi Arabia?

A: I think it was in October, and this is very close, in October of 1981.

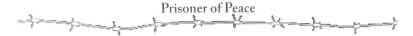

Q: You heard Colonel McCracken testify this morning?

A: Yes, sir.

Q: Were you TDY to Saudi Arabia as an aircraft commander during his tour there?

A: Yes, I was.

Q: You heard Colonel Kenney testify this morning. Were you TDY to Saudi Arabia during his tour?

A: Yes, I was.

Q: Okay. During both of those gentlemen's tours, were you there as an aircraft commander?

A: Yes, sir.

Q: Subsequent to your tour in Saudi Arabia in 1981, where did you go?

A: I came—well, I was TDY, and I came back to Blytheville.

Q: And when was the next time you went back to Saudi Arabia?

A: When I actually arrived in Saudi Arabia?

Q: Yes.

A: I think it was 8 November 1983.

Q: That was for the tour that these offenses rose out of.

A: That's correct.

Q: Between your first TDY in Saudi Arabia and what I'm assuming is your last, what were you doing?

A: I was the—let's see, in '81, I became an IP in the tanker and, in the meantime, I was a flight commander at the 97th Air Refueling Squadron, and eventually became the Ops officer, and also—

Q: Now—

A: I might add that in the meantime I had been selected to go to Offutt Air Force Base to fly the, I think it is, VC-137, the DV airplane up at Offutt.

Q: You're presently a lieutenant colonel?

A: Yes, sir.

Q: All right. How long have you been a lieutenant colonel?

A: I think the effective date is July '79.

Q: How long have you worked for the 11th Strat Group?

A: How long did I?

Q: Uh huh.

A: The only time was when I was over in Saudi Arabia.

Q: Those two times.

A: Well, yes.

Q: How long were you in Saudi Arabia the first occasion in 1981?

A: I can't remember. It was either a two-week or a three-week tour. I was thinking it was two, but they varied between two and three.

Q: And how long were you in Saudi Arabia the second time?

A: I got there on the 8th of November and left there on the twentieth of December 1983.

Q: While you were there in 1981, who was your immediate supervisor?

A: Well, it would have been either Colonel McCracken or Colonel Kenney.

Q: Were all—as I understand it, their tours shifted, went from McCracken to Kenney?

A: Yes, Colonel McCracken replaced Colonel Kenney, Major McCracken at the time.

Q: And you were there for the overlap?

A: That's correct.

Q: When you first served under Colonel McCracken, did you have any understanding from him in terms of what the SAC policy was with regard to flying civilian passengers on orientation flights on KC135s?

A: Only that we did. He put people on my airplane.

Q: Specifically, did you have a discussion with him?

A: I'm not sure we discussed it in terms of—do you mean regulations-type discussions?

Q: Well, just in terms of what the practice was in Riyadh.

A: Only the fact that they were flying them.

Q: Did he tell you why they were flying them?

A: Yeah, well, I already knew that because I—let me explain that to you, that usually the crews in Saudi Arabia, they would fly a mission, a daytime mission, a nighttime mission, and then they would usually have two or three days off. Then on my days off, I would go in to help Colonel McCracken with engine runs, taxi problems, maintenance problems, and we would discuss the whole—

Q: So in addition to your duties in '81 as an aircraft commander, you helped out administratively?

A: Yes.

Q: Okay, and based upon your helping Colonel McCracken at that time, what did you learn about the policies with regard to civilians, civilian passengers?

A: That there was a large number or groups, organizations, Northrop, Lockheed, Bendix Corporation, British Aircraft Corporation, that it was expected that those people would get rides because it was kind of a quid pro quo operation of, if you needed help or maintenance or —two reasons, basically, either to further the mission or for morale and welfare.

Q: What were the conditions at Riyadh at that time that you needed that type of quid pro quo relationship?

A: Well, I think as Colonel McCracken and Colonel Kenney explained it, it's a remote operation both in terms of distance from anyplace else and in terms of facilities. The only thing that changed, by way of example, when I was there as an aircraft commander, was the fact that they changed buildings. They used to have a trailer-type arrangement for an office and they moved us into another building with about the same size of office.

Q: That was the change you noticed between...

A: That was...

Q: Eighty-one and eighty-three?

A: Yes, sir.

Q: With regard to local custom, what was the availability to the Air Force detachment there for services that one would normally entertainment, recreation, that you would normally have in a base in, say, a Western country?

A: There wasn't any; it didn't exist.

Q: Okay. Where would the—where were the troops stationed, or where were they billeted?

A: Where they lived?

Q: Yeah.

A: They lived in a place called the Al Yamamah Hotel, and there were like about 350 people. Now I understand it's 400 with the addition of the KC-10. They just called it the compound, rather than a hotel. In 1950, it was the number one hotel and now it's probably the last.

Q: How many individuals were staying to a room?

A: Well, the crewmembers stayed four to a room and the—I think it was a max of four to a room.

Q: What was the availability of liquor, bars, movies, those types of things?

A: Technically speaking, there is no alcohol, pork, pornography, that type of thing, allowed in Saudi Arabia. As a practical matter, there are various organizations that have a diplomatic immunity, that sort of thing, and that's the people that they seemed to search out, including the United States Military Training Mission.

Q: If an officer stationed in Riyadh wished to find liquor or pork or what-have-you, where would he normally go?

A: Well, when you say an officer, they wouldn't go anywhere, because they don't—are you talking about commanders?

Q: Yeah.

A: Commanders, I can relate it to my experience, the commanders and the colonels, they were all given staff cars and they could go to a number of places. They could go to the British Aircraft Corporation, you could go to Lockheed, you could go to Northrop, you could go to the United States Military Training Mission, but the—if you're talking about just the crewmembers, they have no availability for anything like that.

Q: In terms of logistics and support for the SAC mission in Riyadh in 1981, what was it like?

A: The same as it was in '83. The maintenance facility we were allocated half a hangar for our maintenance, and we had one engine down there, as I understand it, as a spare, and a few spare parts, and that was all. Everything else you had to beg, borrow or steal.

Q: And who would you beg, borrow or steal it from?

A: Whomever; British Aircraft, from Lockheed, from Northrop, from Saudi Airlines, from whomever.

Q: What kind of support would you get from Fairford?

A: Well, the problem with the support from Fairford was the fact that, in order to get any support, they would have to send an airplane, which is seven or eight thousand miles, like that, I don't know the distance, but it's difficult to get support just because they're so far away.

Q: How long would it take you to fly to Fairford?

A: Well, you can do it in seven or eight hours, but it's not just as easy as picking up the phone and launching an airplane; it's difficult.

Q: What were telephonic communications with Fairford like?

A: Well, when the satellite was up, they were excellent; when the satellite was down, there were none.

Q: How often was the satellite down?

A: I could I don't know, sometimes.

Q: Was that the condition of communications with Fairford in '83 as well?

A: Well, in '81, I don't know what the arrangement was. In '83, all I know is that we had the satellite communications.

Q: Did you have any problems with the satellite communications in '83?

A: The satellite communications, Colonel Byrd, or somebody, could testify better on that, but the satellite was frequently down for maintenance, or whatever.

Q: Now while commander McCracken or Colonel McCracken was the SAC commander in 1981, did you fly any civilians at that time?

A: Yes, sir, I did.

Q: Okay. Do you recollect how many?

A: I can't recall. I think on a couple of flights we flew civilians.

Q: Whose idea was that?

A: Colonel McCracken, well, I don't know whose idea it was. Colonel McCracken brought them out to the airplane.

Q: Okay. Did you become involved as the aircraft commander with the manifesting of those civilians?

A: No, that's not—that wasn't my responsibility.

Q: Were you aware of whether or not those individuals were being manifested?

A: No, sir, sure wasn't.

Q: When Colonel Kenney was the commander in Riyadh in 1981, did you fly any civilians there?

A: I can't remember. Are you talking about—I knew—I flew civilians for McCracken, and I heard Kenney, or Colonel Kenney testify this morning that I did, but I don't personally remember that.

Q: You remember flying civilians during that period of time.

A: Yes, sir, I remember—I remember one or two individuals from the Bendix Corporation and, I think, one individual from some water-associated operation. I don't know who he was, though.

Q: While you were there in 1981, did you have any discussions with Colonel Kenney with regard to civil passengers

A: I'm sure we did. We talked every day, I helped him as much as I could. We talked over the whole gamut of operations.

Q: Did you have any understanding, based upon your TDY in 1981 at Riyadh as to whether or not civilian passengers could be flown?

A: I missed the first part of your question.

Q: Did you have any understanding, based upon your TDY experience in Riyadh in as to whether or not civilian passengers could be flown on SAC?

A: I assumed—

Q: KC-135s?

A: I assumed that it was okay.

Q: Had you ever heard anything to the contrary?

A: No, Sir.

Q: Were you aware of whether or not additional authority was needed to fly civilians, other than the local SAC commander?

A: No, I just assumed that they did it on their own.

Q: Now you indicated that you went back in 1983.

A: Yes, sir.

Q: Before you went back in 1983, did you receive a briefing?

A: You mean at Fairford?

Q: Yes.

A: Yes, I received a couple of briefings.

Q: Okay, and who did you receive those briefings from?

A: Well, I received a briefing from—could you hold that chart out there a second so that the judge could see that?

CIV DC: Your Honor, we're making reference to Defense Exhibit E for identification.

WIT: At that time, when I went over in, I think it was in October, to Fairford, Colonel Berringer was then the DO. I received a short briefing from Colonel Berringer, and I received a

201

short briefing from Colonel Farren, and I had a number of chats with Major Clark and Major Raul down there that worked down there for Lieutenant Colonel Bodine, and I talked to numerous maintenance personnel, including the Deputy Commander for Maintenance, whose name I don't remember.

Q: Okay. Now what you have here on this chart did you prepare this chart?

A: Yes, sorry.

Q: Could you explain it?

A: Well, it's just a wiring diagram. I wanted to show the judge that at that time Colonel Berringer was the DO, Lieutenant Colonel Bodine was the ADO, working for Colonel Berringer, and Major Clark, whom somebody made reference to yesterday or the day before, worked in another building, the DOC, the Director of well, whatever that stands for; I don't know.

Q: Now Colonel Farren, who you have at the top, of the 11th Strat Group, he's got a "CC". What does that stand for?

A: He's the commander.

Q: And Colonel Berringer...

A: He was the Director of Operations.

Q: And the ADO was the assistant?

A: Yes, sir.

Q: And that is—

A: Lieutenant Colonel Bodine. I believe he still has the same position.

Q: Okay. Is that the Colonel Bodine that was referred to this morning—

A: Yes, sir.

Q: By Colonel McCracken?

A: Yes, it is.

Q: And the DCC, you indicate you don't know exactly what that stands for?

A: You mean the letters *DOC*?

Q: Yes.

A: No, I—it just means Ops.

Q: Now you have—I take it from Major Clark through Bodine through Berringer through Farren that they are in direct line in terms of authority.

A: That's my assumption.

Q: Well, was that your understanding at the time?

A: Well, yeah, that's normally the way it's set up.

Q: Okay, and you have a direct line from Colonel Berringer to Elf One. What does that mean?

A: Well again, the DO is essentially responsible for the operations in Saudi Arabia. Obviously, the wing commander is the responsible individual.

Q: Now below this you have SAC Headquarters, Davis. What does that mean?

A: Well, just what I'm trying to explain there is that Elf One goes to the 11th Strat Group, the 11th Strap Group to 7th Air Division, 7th Air Division to Eighth Air Force, and Eighth Air Force to SAC Headquarters.

Q: Okay, and that's just basically the scale up beyond the 11th Strat Group.

A: That's correct.

Q: Now when you were at Fairford in 1983, how long were you there?

A: I think Colonel Berringer said I was there 18 days.

Q: Does that seem roughly correct?

A: I think so.

Q: What did you do during that period of time?

A: Well, first of all, I'll explain why I left early, it's because the tanker from Blytheville went to Fairford, and the 42nd Air Division people said I should go on that tanker because it would save a lot of money, which I did. When I got to Fairford, I gave some check rides, and I can't remember.

Q: What are check rides?

A: Flight checks.

Q: To whom?

A: That's just what I was trying to remember. I gave a check ride to the, I think it was, either the wing commander or the DO at Mildenhall. I gave a check ride to a captain at Mildenhall. I can't remember their names.

Q: Okay, are these—when you say check rides, are these…

A: Flight checks.

Q: Flight checks to make sure that they still know how to fly a plane?

A: That's correct, and also…

Q: Did you—

A: Do you want me to continue?

Q: Now, I was going to say that you, as an instructor pilot, is that one of your functions?

A: No, I was a flight examiner then; same thing.

Q: Now in addition to that, what else did you do while you were there?

A: Well, I went down—I got briefings from—I spent a lot of my time, most of my time, with maintenance because I was led to believe that our problems were—dealt with maintenance. We had a big "How Goes It" file, which I believe Colonel Berringer referred to the other day, and—

Q: And what is a "How Goes It" file?

A: It's just messages—there are messages that somebody referred to this morning that explain the problems, and you go through those, and then you try to go to the responsible agency, and obviously, most of the problems in Saudi Arabia dealing with the airplanes had to deal with maintenance.

Q: How long did it take you to go through the "How Goes It" file?

A: Oh, it took me two or three days, plus the briefings I was having. I talked to Chief Master Sergeant Jones, and there was a black DA, whose name I can't remember, who had previously been to Saudi Arabia, and I talked to the DCM and it took two or three days for that. I want to I must explain about the Ups people. As Colonel Berringer told you, they're responsible not only for Saudi Arabia, but they're responsible for Spain, Iceland and Germany. So, although you might think that I would have plenty of time to get briefings from all these people, when I was there a number of those people were TDY throughout the entire time I was there to one of those three locations. I think Colonel Berringer was either on leave on TDY for a week or ten days during that time period.

Q: What was the nature of the briefings that you received?

A: From?

Q: Well, from the individuals there.

A: Well, the biggest briefing I had was from the Director of Maintenance and it just had to do with—he told me I might have a personality conflict with Chief Master Sergeant Jones, which I didn't; we got along fine. We just talked about what's available and this type of thing. I got a very short briefing from Colonel Berringer and Colonel Farren before I left.

Q: Did you have any specific conversations with any of those individuals with regard to civilian passengers on KC-135s?

A: No, Sir.

Q: Did you have any general instructions from Colonel Farren with regard to how the operation was to be run in Riyadh in 1983?

A: Colonel Farren specifically told me that he had reviewed my record and thought I was well qualified to go down there and run the operation. He specifically stressed flying safety and, like somebody said this morning, they had something like 2,000 consecutive refueling sorties and they weren't too much interested in if we kept that string going or not; they would like to have, but they didn't want us to compromise flying safety to do that; and, third of all, we were a remote operation and you essentially have to do what you have to do to get the job done, and that was about the sum total of it. He did mention the F-15 program that we were going to have to develop.

Q: What was the F-15 program?

A: Well, it was when, I think Colonel Edwards this morning told you, that subsequent to refueling the AWACS, we were trying to set up a program where the Saudi F-15 pilots could come up and hit the tanker for practice to maintain their currency in air refueling.

Q: Saudi pilots?

A: Yes, sir.

Q: In the F-15s?

A: That's correct.

Q: Did that have any positive results?

A: Well, on the nineteenth of June, after refueling on the 135, they shot down an Iranian F-4.

Q: Who set up the program down there with the F-15's?

A: Colonel Edwards was the primary mover on that.

Q: Did you assist?

A: Yes, I think I was the primary mover on the SAC side. A short break is in order. When I was the University of Maine in Orono from 1960–63 I had a fraternity roommate from Iran. The sickening thought occurred to me when I heard that the Saudi F-15 pilots shot down an Iranian F-4, what if the Iranian pilot were my roommate? Hell's bells, hockey fans, here we had American AWACS, American F-15's, American KC-135s, American F-4s, and I had helped set up the procedure wherein the Iranian pilot(s?) is/are dead. All my Iranian fraternity brother wanted me to do for him was to teach him how to dance, which I did.

Q: Based upon your briefings at Fairford in 1983, and particularly your review of the "How Goes It" reports and what-have-you, did you develop any impression as to whether or not there had been a change in conditions since you had been there in '81?

A: Quite frankly, the only change I noticed was the fact that we changed buildings.

Q: Did you have a conversation with Major Raul with regard to the operation then as opposed to now?

A: Yes, Major Raul worked with Major Clark on that diagram over there, and Major, I think his name is, Raul, I'd have to ask Colonel Berringer, happened to be the night DO when I was there as an aircraft commander. In fact, he even flew back to England with us when we came back in 1981.

Q: Uh huh.

A: And he—we probably both made some assumptions. Since I was down there before, he told me things were about the same.

Q: When you assumed your duties at Riyadh in 1983, who was your predecessor?

A: Lieutenant Colonel Mills.

Q: And Colonel Mills testified, I guess two days ago, concerning the briefing that you received. Do you recollect that briefing that you received from him?

A: Well, it was very informal, you know. It wasn't a briefing exactly, it was like I said, the operation was very informal. It was kind of "watch me do it," because we only had a, I think like he said, three-day overlap. It's analogous to saying, "Watch me today, do it tomorrow, and I'll watch you do it the third day," and that's kind of how it was.

Q: Now when you assumed your duties down there as the commander in '83, in terms not so much in the physical plant, but in terms of the way the conditions were for the SAC detachment down there, had they changed since 1981?

A: No, like I said how do you mean, operationally?

Q: Yeah.

A: No, operationally, they were the same. You had an hour and twenty minute missions.

Q: How about logistics and support?

A: Still about the same.

Q: How about recreation, entertainment and morale?

A: Well, there were some changes on the Saudi base, but there wasn't any changes—the Saudis spent 90 million dollars to build a sports facility on the base, and they built it for the King Fahd Air Academy, and we tried to do some things to get people to use it, and we accomplished that.

Q: When you were in Riyadh as the commander in 1983, did you allow civilians to fly on KC-135s?

A: Yes, I did.

Defense Witness Hanson—Direct

Q: Now there's been previous testimony in this trial in terms of different individuals that were allowed to fly. Do you have any recollection of any other individuals being allowed to fly?

A: Civilians or military?

Q: Civilians.

A: No, I can't recall any.

Q: Would you just allow any civilians to fly?

A: Certainly not.

Q: Okay. What'the criteria that you used

A: Well, like I said, it was a quid pro quo operation. When it—I don't remember which flight it was when we had the people from the Saudi Sports Center, that was sort of an exchange for them, going to Major General Manaan and getting him to allow American GI's to use that sports facility.

Q: And were any of the civilian flights directly related to the sports facility?

A: Well, like I said, I don't remember what day it was on, we had the…

Q: I believe either…

A: It was the twenty-seventh of November or the 2nd of December, something like that, I can't tell you the specific date.

Q: And what were those individuals—how were they involved in the sports facility?

A: They were the directors. They were the contracted directors, American—contracted directors of the sports center.

Q: And why did you put them on the plane?

A: Because they went to great efforts to get our GIs to be able to use that facility. In fact, they let us set up our own bowling team, which all the young fellows, they started bowling every Monday night, and they let them use the rifle range.

Q: Okay. Was this open to all of the US contingent?

A: Yes, it was, if you could get there, but you have to understand that the hotel where we lived is about five miles from the base, so there is no regular scheduled bus service or any of this kind of stuff, so it was do what you can to help out other people and that was what I tried to do.

Q: And this was much improvement over the swimming pool and—

A: Oh, yes, an Olympic size swimming pool, brand new one.

Q: Now there was other testimony on the fact that on the December 9 flight you had two air traffic controllers on the plane.

A: Yes, I did.

Q: Why were they on that plane?

A: They were on that plane for two specific reasons, which I think somebody said the other day, we had some crews one crew aborted on the runway when they lost water or something like that, and it took an inordinate amount of time to get off the runway. As a result, I think two Saudi 747s had to go around and, as everybody knows, the civilian pilots don't like to go around for two reasons, one it's very expensive, and that particularly upset the Saudi folks over there at the air traffic control tower.

Second of all, they had a procedure in Saudi Arabia on the departure, when the tankers or the AWACS took off from Riyadh, they came out and made either a left or right turn and proceeded direct to the new King Khalid Airport.

Q: Was that a problem?

A: Yeah, it was a problem because the King Khalid Airport only opened, I think, on the 6th of December, okay? So don't hold me to that date, but it's a brand new airport that just opened up, and there had been no coordination as far as that departure and it flew right over the top of another airport. You can't allow that.

Q: That's a safety hazard?

A: Absolutely.

Q: Is that why you had the air traffic controllers on that flight?

A: For those two reasons, and had I had time, as you know what happened on the 9th of December, I was on the way back I was going to show them how close we actually came to that brand new airport.

Q: Trying to change the flight path?

A: Yes, sir, and can I go into the result?

Q: Sure.

A: As a result of the accident, and when I briefed Colonel Edwards and his people, they took that information that I had, took it to Prince Fahd, if you know, King Fahd is the King of Saudi Arabia, took it to Prince Fahd, and within one or two days he dispatched his own people to Geneva, Switzerland, and they took care of the problem in a couple of days.

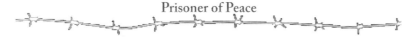

Q: Now there was further testimony, I believe, that you flew a woman with a British accent—

A: Right.

Q: In a flight suit.

A: Yes, that's right, that's Suzanne Goodchild, I believe. She and her husband worked in Saudi Arabia. He worked in the British Saudi Bank, and we met those people, not just myself, at, somebody referred to it this morning, Joyce Anderson's house, she's General Armstrong's secretary, and we were chatting back and forth, and she and her husband were the ones that suggested it. Now as I told you now, in Saudi Arabia you're not allowed to have pork and all this kind of stuff. Well, we also have a commissary in Saudi Arabia that sells all these things that we can't have, and that's not my—I don't know, that's not my problem, that's an agreement between the Saudi government and our government, but anyway, the people at the hotel don't have access to that sort of stuff. So Mister and Missus Goodchild suggested that we get some of the GI's, buy some of those hams and that bacon and that sort of stuff and bring it over to their house and they would cook it up. They lived in the U.S. Consulate area of the Saudi Arabian housing area, and that's what we did. I can't give you specific names of the people we took over there, but that was the idea.

Q: And why did you put her on the plane?

A: Well, it was sort of a, again, one of those quid pro quo operations; they were doing stuff for our people, we were doing something for them.

Q: Were there expectations of further benefits from the Goodchilds?

A: Well, they had planned a Christmas party, which we didn't get to partake of, but they were going to have a Christmas party. Joyce Armstrong, or Joyce Anderson used to throw all the big parties for all the colonels and, once again, the other four hundred GIs didn't have too much to do.

Q: Okay.

A: So it was an effort to build military morale.

Q: Why was she in a flight suit?

A: Well because, as somebody explained to you a long time ago, that, first of all, a requirement in Saudi Arabia that all women in Saudi Arabia must be covered on their necks, their arms and their legs, and she wore the required garment, it was a black, I don't know whatever you call it, and that wouldn't be acceptable on an airplane.

Q: So did you give her a flight suit?

A: I didn't give it to her, I gave it to one of the members of the US Consulate and he delivered it to her house.

Q: I believe someone also made reference to the fact that you had a Corps of Engineers individual on one of the planes.

A: That's correct.

Q: And why was he there?

A: The Corps of Engineers guys, as I explained to you earlier, had a lot of expertise, and this particular individual had a lot of expertise in the water business, and not only that, the Corps of Engineers had two C-12 aircraft which were parked across the ramp from where we were on what used to be the civilian side, and they used to take a lot of the GIs to Tabuk and Jeddah to go SCUBA diving and go to Bahrain to buy perfume and so on and so forth. So it's another one of those quid pro quo operations.

Q: Now in part of this quid pro quo operation that you described, how is the water plant related?

A: How is it related?

Q: Uh huh.

A: Well, for two years, I think somebody told you earlier, the water plant was being constructed. When I got there, the water plant was setting there, rotting away, and we used water bags, two great big water bags and a water truck to get water on the airplanes. Now as you understand, the tanker needs water, particularly on warm days, on cold days you don't use water, but on warm days you can't get that tanker off the ground, especially at 2,000 feet pressure altitude and 220 or 230,000 pounds. So it's directly related to the mission, absolutely essential.

Q: Now you say you found that water plant in a state of abandonment when you arrived?

A: Well, essentially it was just sitting there, no activity on it.

Q: Did you take efforts to get it going?

A: Yes, sir, I talked to a Major Ibraihm, the Saudi liaison officer, and he took me over to see Major General Manaan and I explained it the best way I could; that we don't mind refueling their AWACS to cover their oilfields, but we needed a little help. The point of it is they weren't aware that we needed any help, and they very soon took action and, as I understand it from somebody's testimony, it's now working.

Q: Was the Corps of Engineers helpful in that regard?

A: Helpful because he knew where to get all the parts. We needed eight or nine parts and he knew exactly where to get them.

Q: Did you ever hide or attempt to deceive anybody with regard to the fact that you were allowing civilians…

A: No, sir.

Q: To fly on the KC-135s?

A: Never did.

Q: In fact, you even flew some on the prearranged flight with Colonel Byrd.

A: That's correct.

Q: Did Colonel Byrd ever talk to you about the propriety of flying civilians?

A: Never mentioned it.

Q: Now you heard previous testimony as to a local policy at Elf One concerning approval of the Elf One commander for some passenger flights.

A: Uh huh.

Q: Did you use them with regards to civilians?

A: Use the procedures?

Q: Yes.

A: Although I don't recall ever reading a letter, I did use the procedure; yes, I did.

Q: With regards to civilians?

A: Oh, the civilians, no; the military. I was trying to say it was the military.

Q: What was your understanding of the applicability of that particular form?

A: My understanding was that it was a locally-generated form for the military.

Q: And what purpose did it serve?

A: How do you mean?

Q: Well, why did they generate the form?

A: I haven't got a clue. I don't understand your question. Who would have to—for a military individual to fly, whose authority was needed to allow him to fly?

A: The Elf One—the vice commander of Elf One.

Q: Who else?

A: And the appropriate commander, either the AWACS or the tanker.

Q: And who else?

A: Oh, let's see, on that form, I think you had the section supervisor and—I can't, I don't know all the blanks on there.

Q: Why was the section supervisor required?

A: It's part of the procedure, but it's obvious, I mean it's accountability to keep track of the people.

Q: But it's your understanding that was strictly a military form?

A: Yes, Sir. In fact, I didn't generate those forms. If a guy wanted to come fly on a tanker, wherever they got those forms, they would go get one of those forms, they would generate it, take it around and get it signed, and away they'd go.

Q: Now the time that you were there in 1983, at Riyadh as the commander, were you aware of any general SAC regulations with regard to the propriety of flying civilian passengers?

A: I wasn't aware then, but I'm really aware now.

Q: At the time, you were not aware?

A: No, sir. Can I add to that a little bit?

Q: Sure.

A: You've got to understand in the states, we don't get involved in the passenger business. In tankers, that's handled by Base Operations. We don't get in that business in a stateside operation. Our passengers are brought out to us from Base Operations or some place else.

Q: Now taking you back to the flight on December 9th, the one involving the midair—

A: Okay.

Q: How many passengers were on the plane?

A: Passengers?

Q: Uh huh.

A: Seven.

Q: Now previous testimony has indicated that there were apparently the two air traffic controllers and the Army doctor at Base Ops and they boarded the plane with the initial crew?

A: They were at my office, what you call Base Ops, that's correct.

Q: Why were you flying that day?

A: Why was I?

Q: Uh huh.

A: Because it was prearranged with the air traffic controllers. I told them, I think it was around the 7th or the 8th, I can't tell you exactly, they had called up and we had arranged, you know, talked about the flight, and I was going to go along and fly with them to show them what I wanted to show them about the departure that we had set up.

Q: Now there were apparently some Navy 0-6s added to the passengers.

A: Yes, sir, four of them.

Q: Whose idea was that?

A: That was a program, as Colonel Byrd has testified, that they had between the Elf One and the Navy.

Q: Whose request was it that the 0-6s fly?

A: Colonel Byrd, Colonel Cunningham, one of the two.

Q: They came to you, or they called you and asked you if you could get them on?

A: It was either that or it came up in a staff meeting, I don't remember how we got to it, but that's...

Q: They did not load or board with the original crew, did they?

A: No, they didn't, they boarded on the other side of the base.

Q: Why was that?

A: Because they came in, and I'm going to guess at this, like a quarter 'till 3:00 or three o'clock or something like that in the afternoon on a C-12 and they had to get planeside visas from the Saudi immigration personnel. They had some big hang—ups about that. The Saudis are not too keen on giving out planeside visas and there were some problems with that. I was monitoring the VHF radio and heard that problem, and Colonel Byrd had given us a drop dead date or a time, I'm thinking it was 3:30, I guess around 3:30 in the afternoon, if they weren't ready by then. So in order to try to accomodate them, I asked ground control located in the Saudi tower if I could taxi over there and pick them up, and I thought it would be a nice gesture because they were 0-6s.

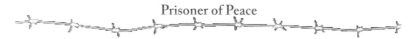

Q: When you left Ops to taxi over to the other side to pick up the 0-6s, who was in command of the plane?

A: I was.

Q: You were in the pilot's seat?

A: That's correct.
You were flying.

A: I was taxiing.

Q: Taxiing. Who was sitting next to you in the copilot's chair?

A: Lieutenant Kern.

Q: Where was the rest of the crew, do you remember?

A: I would assume the navigator was at his station and the Navy captain or Robertson was in the jump seat. I'm not sure about those.

Q: Now before you begin to taxi a plane, do you go through any set sort of procedure?

A: Sure, you have a checklist to follow.

Q: I'm showing you what's marked for purposes of identification as Defense Exhibit F. Do you recognize those?

A: These are—this is the checklist for the KC-135 starting engines, before taxi check.

Q: Was that the checklist that was applicable to the operation of the KC-135 on December 9, 1983?

A: Yes, sir.

CIV DC: At this time, I would ask for admittance of defendant's exhibit F.

MJ: Have *you* seen it, trial counsel?

TC: No. I haven't seen the graph, either, and that's already in.

MJ: Well, I really didn't think you would have any objection to that.

TC: No, Your Honor.
(A brief delay while Defense Exhibit A for identification was examined by trial counsel.)
Defense Exhibit F Offered

CIV DC: I would still move for the admittance of defendant's exhibit F.

MJ: Any objection by the prosecution?

TC: No, Your Honor.

MJ: Very well, Defense Exhibit F is received in evidence.

CIV DC: Now, could you describe what's on those three pages?

WIT: Well, it's all the things you do before you get airborne and after you get airborne.

Now particularly before you begin to taxi, before you begin to initially move the plane, what does it indicate that you have to do?

A: Well, step twelve tells you you have to do a taxi report.

Q: Okay, what is a taxi report?

A: Essentially, the copilot rings the alarm bell and the response would be, if you're ready to taxi, navigator, boom operator, "Alarm bell check, ready to taxi."

Q: Okay.

A: Then the copilot gives you his information, and when you get that, you go.

Q: Let's see, you ring the bell, you ask for a taxi report and all the crewmembers respond?

A: Either they all respond or the navigator will respond for the boom operator.

Q: Did that happen on this particular occasion…

A: Yes, sir.

Q: …before you moved across the base?

A: Yes, it did.

Q: What happened after you boarded the 0-6s?

A: When we were on the other side?

Q: Yes.

A: The 0-6s got on board. As I recall, Captain Martin, US Navy, sat in the jump seat. I don't know if it was at my invitation or Capiain Robertson's, but it really doesn't make any difference because it's a common practice, in the command at least, to put people there, and I introduced myself and chatted briefly. I did find out at that point that he used to be the commander of a U.S. Navy aircraft carrier, and I found out that he flew F-14s and F-8s, I think, or something like that.

Q: Okay. How long was it after they boarded that the plane began to move again?

A: A couple minutes, a few minutes.

Q: What did you do before you moved the plane the second time?

A: We had another taxi report.

Q: Did you make a taxi report at that time?

A: Yes, sir.

Q: And why was that?

A: Well, because we had stopped and loaded some people on.

Q: Is it always your procedure to have a taxi report each time you stop and begin to move the plane again?

A: Well, if you're going to change—if you're changing the configuration of the airplane, you've got to go back and correct the things you do, you know, like we opened up the hatch and put the ladder down and all that sort of thing.

Q: What transpired for the second taxi report?

A: The same thing as far as I know. It was documented, I think, in the 110-14 that the copilot and the boom operator and the navigator gave a taxi report.

Q: Now were you aware of where Captain Robertson was sitting at that time?

A: No, sir, I was not.

Q: When you ask for a taxi report, what are you asking for?

A: I'm just asking the crewmembers, "Is the airplane safe to taxi?"

Q: And what is their responsibility after you ask for a taxi report?

A: Well, they either tell me they're ready to taxi they tell me they're not.

Q: And if they're not ready, they should tell you?

A: They tell me whatever and I won't taxi.

Q: Did anyone tell you at that time that they were not ready for taxiing?

A: No, sir.

Q: Now you heard Captain Robertson indicate that he was in the boom operator's seat at that time.

A: Yes.

Q: Okay, and he did not have a headset on because he had given it to Captain Martin.

A: Uh huh.

Q: If he needed to communicate with you to indicate that he somehow was not ready, could he have done that?

A: Sure.

Q: How was that?

A: He can do it through contacting another crewmember or shouting out to me.

Q: Can he—can you would he be able to be heard at that time?

A: Absolutely; the engines are at idle.

Q: Even when the engines are revved up for takeoff, can he be heard from the boom's seat?

A: Sure. A number of times I've heard boom operators and navigators shout out things. They get excited or things like that and they forget to press down their mike button, and you can hear them for sure.

Q: How far is the boom operator's seat from you?

A: The number of feet?

Q: Yeah.

A: Six feet, something like that.

Q: Behind you?

A: Yes, directly behind.

Q: Okay. So you have no visual view of it.

A: Not unless I reached around and had a look.

Q: Does the person sitting in the boom's seat have a visual view of the pilot?

A: Sure. Well, he can see his head. He can see the pilot's head and his arms, things like that.

Q: Did you—you got a taxi report the second time?

A: Yes, sir.

Q: And you got affirmations from everybody that they were ready?

A: Yes, I did.

Q: Now particularly Sergeant Bolling—

A: Now wait, when you say everybody, of course, Captain Robertson doesn't have a headset, so I wouldn't get one from him.

Q: Did you notice this?

A: No, it didn't occur to me because when you—I'm not thinking of people on the airplane, I'm thinking of positions. When I heard navigator, boom operator, "Alarm bell check, ready to taxi," that clicks in my mind that we're ready to taxi.

Q: But if he needed to get hold of you, he could have.

A: Sure.

Q: Okay. Sergeant Boiling you heard testify to the fact that he indicated that all the passengers were strapped in and he was ready. Do you remember that?

A: Yes, sir.

Q: Then you moved forward, I take it. Where did you go next?

A: Well, we had to taxi east for some distance, I can't tell you exactly how far. We had to taxi east across runway 01, come back around. There was what we call the hammerhead area. We came back around to the hammerhead area and continued with our checklist.

Q: What is the next thing on the checklist?

A: It's the taxi checklist.

Q: Okay. When do you do this taxi checklist?

A: Well, you can do it while you're stopped or when you're taxiing.

Q: Okay, and I believe Lieutenant Petsch indicated you were stopped for some time less than five minutes at the hold line.

A: I can't remember how long we were stopped.

Q: Okay. Do you remember when you did the taxi checklist?

A: Sure, by the time we—from the time we left in front of the tower until we got down around, came around, across runway 01, back up around the hammerhead.

Q: What is at the end of a taxi checklist?

A: It's the takeoff report.

Q: And what is the purpose of the takeoff report?

A: Once again, it's to let you—now they've told you they're ready to taxi, now they're going to tell you they're ready to take off.

Q: And did you do a takeoff report at that time?

A: Yes, sir. I believe you'll see that in the 110-14 that Lieutenant Kern and those people said that we did.

Q: Okay. Is that identical to a taxi report?

A: Yeah, well, except that now they're telling you they're ready to take off.

Q: Okay, and did you get affirmation from everybody that they were ready?

A: Once again, I assume that I did except for, apparently, Captain Robertson who didn't have a headset.

Q: Now with regard to the fact that Sergeant Boiling, the boom operator, was apparently not in the boom's seat but was back in the back, strapped in with the passengers, is there a reason for that?

A: Sure, there's a requirement, as a matter of fact, not just a reason. In section eight of the dash-one, under crew duties, it says that either a crewmember or a person briefed,

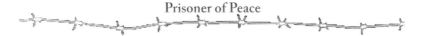

thoroughly briefed, or something like that, will be in the cargo compartment when there are personnel there anytime the airplane is airborne.

Q: Okay. Now why would the boom operator tend to be back there as opposed to anybody else?

A: Most logical choice. He's the cargo handling expert on the aircraft and he's the most logical choice.

Q: In the dash-one, is there any indication of whose duty it is within the crew to brief the passengers?

A: Yes, as a matter of fact it's part of the boom operator's checklist.

Q: So he has the responsibility to brief them.

A: Yes, Sir.

Q: Now as a practical matter for takeoff, if you have an extra pilot, would it make more sense since he's a spare to put him in the back and leave the boom in the boom's seat?

A: I don't know about more sense, the pilot knows more about the the only thing a boom operator has to do on takeoff is, prior to S-I, if he notices any problems within the airplane, S-I being the speed that we compute for stop or go, he would tell you on the interphone what your problem is and the pilot would make a decision whether to stop or go. Now nobody knows the panels better than a pilot, so in terms of safety of flight, it's no problem and it's frequently done.

Q: Would you prefer to have a third pilot or the boom sitting in the cockpit during takeoff?

A: Well, if I had used water injection, I would probably want a boom operator there, there are some tricks they can do with circuit breakers, but under normal conditions, the pilot would be equally versed. There's nothing either one of them can do. Who ever sits there, they can't do anything. We have to do all the actions.

Q: Were you using water on that particular trip?

A: No, sir.

Q: It wasn't hot enough?

A: Well, it was a temperature of seventy-eight degrees, I believe the form shows, and we had a 217 gross weight, so it wasn't required.

Q: Okay.

A: The dash-one says you don't use it unless it's required.

Q: You heard Captain Rob apparently ask about a passenger manifest and claims that you responded to him, "it's been taken care of ." Did you say that to him?

A: I recall saying nothing like that.

Q: Would you have said that to him?

A: If I had taken care of it, sure, I would, but I didn't. The point of it is that I didn't use a passenger manifest, as was brought out in one of these things, but that was—it didn't occur to me, but it occurs to me now, obviously, the reason why we're got to use passenger manifests. I didn't use passenger manifests except when the airplane was going from Riyadh to England on what we called our "deployer," and that's the only time, and once again as I've explained to you, I don't normally get into the passenger manifest business, and if I had had more experience in SAC, I'd have probably thought to do that, but I didn't use passenger manifests and it doesn't make sense that I would say that.

Q: Now you indicate that the only time that you use passenger manifests was when somebody was flying, a passenger was flying from Riyadh to somewhere else?

A: When we were going out of country, when we were sending people back to England.

Q: So that means they were off-loaded at a different location.

A: Yeah, that's right. If an airplane took off and landed at Riyadh, it didn't occur to me to use it.

Defense Witness Hanson—Direct

Q: Now with regard to passengers that were on orientation flights that would take off from and land at Riyadh, when you were the commander there, did you use any passenger manifests for them?

A: I used the—no, not passenger manifests. I did, however, for military personnel, as I explained, use that locally—generated form.

Q: So with regard to Captain Robertson's testimony, you have no recollection of saying that, and it's your indication that you would not say that?

A: If I had taken care of it, I surely would have said it, but I didn't use them, so I didn't say it.

Q: Now on the December 9th flight, there was a midair.

A: Yes.

Q: Who was flying the KC-135 at the time of the midair?

A: Well, I'll tell you who were in the seats; Captain Robertson was in the left seat, Lieutenant Kern was in the right seat.

Q: Where were you?

A: I was somewhere behind the navigator.

Q: What was your first awareness of the danger at that time?

A: What do you mean, when the airplane struck us?

Q: Well, were you aware prior to that that they were close?

A: No, when I looked out the window they were five or six hundred feet, but I don't think that's appropriate. I don't mean that offensively. I think that's for official use only, that type of information.

Q: Picking up at the time, after the mid-air...

MJ: Well, wait a minute. Colonel Hanson, I'm going to rely upon you avoid classified information.

WIT: Okay, sir.

CIV DC: After the midair—

WIT: Yes, Sir.

Q: What happened?

A: Seconds after the midair, I told Lieutenant Kern to get out of the seat, I didn't say it exactly like that, but I told him to get out of the seat and I got in.

Q: Did you assume control of the aircraft?

A: Yes, I did.

Q: What did you do?

A: Well, I just flew the airplane the way you had to fly it to get it back to Riyadh. I cut the throttles off on the two, the numbers three and four engines, I pulled the fire switches, I told Captain Robertson to depressurize the right hydraulic system, turned off the two hydraulic supplies—numbers three and four of the hydraulic supply—tripped off the number three generator. Well, it didn't make any difference because all the wires were cut and all the actions I took didn't make any difference anyway, but we ran out of fuel on the right side, and as far as the hydraulic system, I don't know about that.

Q: What was the condition of the aircraft?

A: Horrible.

Q: Specifically, what was wrong with it?

A: Well, we had a cut in the wing root area of the right wing, the number three engine was mangled, as you might see by some pictures that you had.

Q: I'm showing you what's marked as defendant's exhibit for identification G. Do you recognize that?

A: Yes, I do.

Q: What is that?

A: It's a picture of the tanker back at Riyadh.

Q: Is that a picture of the damage to the plane?

A: That's part of the damage.

Q: Okay, what does that show?

A: Well, it shows a hole in the number three fuel tank, it shows I don't know how big that hole is. It shows the wing root. It shows the number three engine had been mangled. There are some other dents and stuff in the back which you can't see in this picture.

Q: Does that picture fairly and accurately represent the appearance of the damage to that plane at the time of the midair?

A: Well, not exactly, because prior to this picture, apparently they removed part of the wing from the AWACS.

Q: Okay, but the damage that's on there.

A: Yes, but that's a better picture than the one you're got there, I think.

Q: I'm showing you what's marked for purposes of identification as defendant's exhibit number H. Do you recognize that?

A: Yes, I do.

Q: And what is that?

A: It's the same thing but a little closer up where you can see the cut in the wing root of the aircraft.

Q: And is that a fair and accurate representation of the damage to the wing at that time?

A: Yes, it is.

CIV DC: I would move for admittance of defendant's exhibits H and G at this time, Your Honor.

MJ: Any objection by the prosecution?

TC: No.

MJ: Defense Exhibits G and H are received. What about E? Do we have an E?

DC: It's the chart, Your Honor.

CIV DC: That's the chart, Your Honor, and that was just for demonstration purposes.
Defense Witness Hanson—Direct
Defense Exhibits G and H Offered/Admitted

MJ: But it's not been offered.

CIV DC: No, Your Honor.

CIV DC: Now Colonel Buttram has already testified, I believe, that you had lost two engines on one side, lost part of the wing, and had lost your hydraulics and your power rudder?

WIT: It's all connected, the power rudder and right hydraulic system are—when you turn one off, you don't have the other.

Q: Okay.

A: We also lost the ability to put the flaps down except by cranking them down.

Q: Are there any procedures in the dash-one for recovering a plane under those conditions?

A: No, you do what you have to do.

Q: Did you recover that plane?

A: Yes, sir.

Q: How were you feeling at that time?

A: I was terrified.

Q: Why?

A: Well, it's—I think it's obvious.

Q: Did you have any communication with the tower?

A: Yeah, for about thirty minutes I talked to them, I believe, every fifteen or twenty seconds.

Q: Okay, why were you doing that?

A: Well, I was doing it because at 18,000 feet I had to make a decision about the gear. After either Lieutenant Kern or Sergeant Bolling told me the condition of the wing, I know enough about aerodynamics to know that that's a real high dynamic pressure area on an airplane, and I taught aerodynamics for three years and all that stuff was clicking through my mind. So at 18,000 I had to decide—see if the gear was going to come down or not, and on that decision, you understand, that when I put that gear down, according to some experts, if that cut had been another six or seven inches the wing would have come off, and I was telling the tower all the stuff that I was doing to give them an update in case we didn't get back to the base, number one and, number two, I was talking to them just to keep my sanity.

Q: Were you the only one that talked to them at that time?

A: Yes, I was. I had all the other radios turned off.

Q: Were you giving them any information concerning the number of people on the plane?

A: I'm sure I did. I told them everything about the airplane except how many screws we had in it.

Q: Do you remember specifically telling them anything in terms of the number of people on board?

A: Yes, sir. That's a standard requirement that we do that in emergencies. The first thing I did was told the navigator to sqawk emergency, and then I called the tower and told them we were coming in, I wanted fire, crash equipment, and I told them how many souls on board.

Q: And what did you tell them?

A: I told them—I said I probably told them two or three different times.

Q: But what did you tell them?

A: I'm pretty sure I told them I had twelve souls on board.

Q: Did you break it down between passengers and crew?

A: I can't remember. I talked to them continuously. *We don't have the tape anymore, but...* [emphasis added]

Q: After you landed the plane, what did you do?

A: Well, the first thing we did was exit the airplane very rapidly and we formed up some—about three hundred feet, I think is what I told them coming in, "We're going to form up about 300 feet off the nose and to the left of the airplane to get out of the way of the fire trucks." We counted heads and then things really started rolling.

Q: After you counted heads and made sure everybody was there and after you secured the plane, what is your recollection like for the ensuing period of time?

A: Well, it's like I said, it's like Colonel Edwards explained it, you've got to do what you have to do to get it—to take care of the fire equipment. I had to tell those fire trucks what I wanted them to do because there was nobody else out there yet. Major Spathe finally arrived and I told him I wanted him to depressurize or deflate the nose gear strut because we had a CG or center of gravity—according to the dash-one, the airplane should have tipped on its tail; for whatever reason, it didn't. I'm hoping it was because of the procedures we employed on the landing, but it doesn't make any difference, it didn't tip on its tail. We had a center of gravity that was off the chart, as they say. The chart, I mean the chart or the dipstick or whatever the boom operators use goes to forty and it was past that. So it didn't tip on its tail for whatever reason. Then we stayed away from the airplane, and then I told somebody to get some ballast up in the nose. As Captain Robertson told you, we went in for a big drink of water.

Q: But after you secured the plane, what is your recollection of the time after that?

A: Well, one hour goes into the next. At some point in time, we got back to Ops and filled out our paperwork, did blood tests, made a written statement, each crewmember made a written statement.

Q: How were you feeling at that time?

A: Well, I was starting, you know—if I could use the analogy of, in 1971 or '72 over in Phu Bai, where we got a rocket attack from 122 milimeters, a 122 milimeter rocket came in, and a young sergeant, a security policeman, was guarding an ammo dump, and the rocket didn't explode. He kept doing his thing to get people out of the way, and then some hours later he went into shock. I think that's probably what I did.

Q: Do you feel that you went into shock?

A: Oh, I don't know, I was pretty spooled up.

Q: How long did that period of upset or shock, as you described it, continue?

A: A long time.

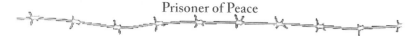
Q: Days, hours?

A: Days.

Q: Do you remember having a conversation with Colonel Cunningham concerning the number of passengers on the airplane?

A: No, sir, sure don't.

Q: Now you recollect that yesterday he testified to the fact that you initially told him on the day of the accident that there were five passengers.

A: Yes, I remember him saying that.

Q: You have no recollection of that?

A: No, sir, sure don't.

Q: Assuming that his recollection is correct, that you told him five, why would you have done that?

A: I haven't got any idea. I don't know, first of all, what the question was he asked me, and I don't know why I would respond that way. Whatever it—if I said something to him, it was completely innocuous because I had already told everybody how many people were on the airplane. I had indicated to the crewmembers, you know, to tell it like it was.

Q: Did you have any intent at that time to deceive him or anyone else with regard to the number of passengers on the plane?

A: Oh, surely not. I didn't hide the fact that I was flying people on the airplane.

Q: At that time, did you have any awareness of the fact that flying civilians on the airplane was improper?

A: No, we'd been doing it for a long, long time.

CIV DC: No further questions at this time, Your Honor.

MJ: Before inviting cross-examination, I think we'll take about a ten-minute recess to allow the court reporter to have a break. We're in recess.

It was at this time that I met the court reporter in the bathroom just down the hall from the courtroom. He said he was sorry that I had to go through so much. He further said that not everyone was against me. He concluded that one would think that the crew would at least say thanks for saving their lives. We left the rest room as Major Oxley, the lead prosecutor, came in. I said to him, "You're pretty good at what you do, and so am I."

(The court-martial recessed at 1339 hours, 11 January 1985, and was called back to order at 1402 hours, 11 January 1985, with all parties present who were present when the court-martial recessed.)

Defense Witness Hanson—Direct

(The accused had resumed his seat on the witness stand and he was reminded by the military judge that he was still under oath.)

MJ: You may proceed, counsel.

TC: Thank you, Your Honor.

CROSS-EXAMINATION

Questions by Trial Counsel: Colonel Hanson, I understand that you've been in the Air Force for twenty-one years.

A: That's twenty-one plus a few months.

Q: Do I understand that your background includes T-39 operations?

A: Yes, sir.

Q: What's the primary purpose of the T-39?

A: Well, it was then, and when I was in ATC, it was transporting VIPs.

Q: Passengers?

A: Yes, Sir.

Q: And yet you testified on direct examination that you don't have much knowledge about passenger manifests.

A: Yes, Sir.

Q: How long did you fly the T-39?

A: I'm trying to remember; it was over a year.

Q: Have you previously signed passenger manifests, sir?

A: Well, I don't think I did then because we always had a flight mechanic that took care of that.

Q: You don't recall ever signing passenger manifests?

A: You mean then, in T-39s?

Defense Witness Hanson—Cross

Q: Ever in your career, sir.

A: Oh, sure.

Q: Sir, when there's a midair collision between two aircraft in the Air Force, what can you expect is going to follow from that, not the consequences of the collision, but in the nature of administrative happenings?

A: There would be a number of investigations.

Q: Would there be investigations?

A: Oh, absolutely.

Q: Am I correct that even a second lieutenant going through pilot training school would know that?

A: I'm not sure if you're correct or not. I can't—

Q: Would a first lieutenant who's a pilot know that?

A: Probably.

TC: Might I ask for the government exhibits, Your Honor. (Prosecution Exhibits #1 through #13 were retrieved from the military judge.) Thank you.

Q: Lieutenant Colonel Hanson, I hand to you what's been admitted into evidence as Prosecution Exhibits Eight and Nine. There is an attachment to the 2 December letter. Colonel Hanson, is it your testimony that, prior to the mid-air collision, you had never seen either one of those letters?

A: I don't think I had seen the letters. I had seen the form.

Q: You in fact acknowledged that you had used the forms just like the attachment to the 2 December letter, correct?

A: Yes, Sir.

Q: I'm also correct, sir, that since this accident you've had the occasion to review these letters and read them, is that correct?

A: You mean in terms of accident reports?

Q: Possibly, possibly in preparation for this proceeding. Have you read those two letters?

A: Oh, yes, Sir.

Q: It was your testimony on direct examination that it was your understanding that the passenger form was only used for military personnel, is that correct?

A: I believe that's correct, yes, sir.

Q: Nowhere in these letters is a distinction made between military and civilian passengers, is there?

A: I don't believe so, no, sir.

Q: It just says passengers, noncrewmembers, correct?

A: Yes, Sir.

Q: After the mid-air collision, Colonel Hanson, you spoke with the copilot and, at your direction, he removed himself from the right seat and you entered the seat.

A: Yes, sir.

Q: You remained in the seat thereafter until you—until the aircraft had landed and then you exited the seat, is that correct?

A: That's correct.

Q: Colonel Hanson, is it your testimony that you were the only one talking on the tower, or on the radio to the tower during that period of time?

A: I'm not going to tell you 100 percent, but I'm 99 percent sure because I think I directed that all other radios be turned off, as I think what I said before.

MJ: Did you direct that as soon as you got in the right seat?

WIT: Sir, it was shortly after because we had a couple of conversations with the AWACS, and there were so many

234

things going on that I didn't want to have to talk to anybody except the tower.

MJ: Fine.

TC: You spoke on direct examination of your recollection of Colonel Mills' testimony.

A: (Nodded affirmatively)

Q: Do you recall his testimony to the effect that, during your overlap with him, he spoke to you about the local passenger approval procedures at Elf One? Do you recall him testifying to that?

A: I'm sorry, I don't.

Q: But it is your testimony that you do not recall having such a conversation with him.

A: Well, I don't recall the conversation and I can't remember his exact testimony, both.

Q: I see. Your memory as to testimony in this courtroom is somewhat spotty.

DC: Objection, Your Honor, argumentative.

TC: You were in the room when…

MJ: Sustained.

TC: …Colonel Mills testified? I withdraw the comment, Your Honor.

MJ: Fine.

TC: You were in the room when Colonel Mills testified?

WIT: Yes, sir.

Q: But you do not recall that aspect of his testimony.

A: I don't remember him exactly talking about—what was your question, about passengers?

Q: I understand, and I'm not attempting to use his exact words. Do you recall his testimony to the effect that he talked with you during your overlap at Elf One about the local procedures for approving passengers?

A: I remember something to that effect, but are you talking about that form?

Q: The form, the letters and the conversations that he said he had with you at the time of your arrival in 1983.
Defense Witness Hanson—Cross

A: I can't say that I remember him talking to me specifically about passengers.

Q: I understand. Now, you also don't remember the location of the boom operator at the time you took off the aircraft on 9 December.

A: No, sir, that's not correct.

Q: You do remember where he was.

A: Yes, Sir.

Q: He was not in his seat?

A: He was not in the boom operator's seat.

Q: You do remember affirmative responses from all crewmembers prior to takeoff.

A: No, Sir, I didn't say that, required crewmembers.

Q: Required crewmembers?

A: Yes, Sir.

Q: You don't remember saying to Captain Robertson, in response to his inquiry about the passenger manifest, that, "It's been taken care of."

A: No, Sir, I do not recall that.

Q: You do remember the details of you explaining to the tower how many people were on board the aircraft.

A: No, I didn't say that. I said that I talked to the tower for thirty minutes. I told them—I can't say specifically, exactly what I told them. I said I think they asked me for the number of souls on board and I told them twelve, and I think Mister Sanders asked me, did I come back later. The point is I was pretty much on the edge, if I can use that expression, and I was talking to them to maintain my own sanity. I could have told them a number of other things.

Q: Of course, but amongst the things that you do recall you responding to the tower, am I correct that it's your

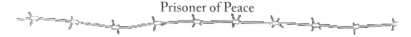

testimony you recall providing them a number as to the people on board the aircraft?

A: Yes, sir, I believe I said twelve souls on board; I think that's it.

Q: But you don't remember a conversation with Lieutenant Colonel Cunningham where he asked you how many passengers were on board.

A: No, sir, I do not.

Q: But you do remember telling the crew to "tell it like it is."

A: I don't remember that. They said I said that.

Q: Oh, it's not your memory that you said it.

A: No. I'm saying this is what the crew testified that I said.

Q: Rules change in the Air Force, don't they, colonel?

A: Yes, sir.

Q: You spoke on direct examination about your memory of conversations, briefings, the imparting of information to you while you were at Fairford prior to your trip to assume the command at Elf One as the SAC detachment commander.

A: Yes, sir.

Q: Do you recall at that time speaking with Colonel Runkle, R-u-n-k-l-e, who was with the maintenance people at Fairford?

A: I don't recall the name, but do you mean the chief of Maintenance?

Q: A full colonel...

A: Yes, Sir.

Q: ...Colonel Richard K. Runkle.

A: I think so. I remember meeting with the colonel, but I can't say that I remember his name.

Q: Did he brief you about maintenance procedures at Riyadh?

A: I can't say specifically because I had a number of briefings from a number of people. He briefed me on a number of items and I can't—it would be a lie to say specifically what he briefed me on; I can't remember exactly.

Q: Do you recall advising him that you were well versed about the procedures at Riyadh as a result of your previous tour there?

A: I may have said that.

Q: Do you recall him telling you that procedures had changed since you had been there last?

A: He may have, I don't recall him saying it; he may well have.

Q: Do you recall him providing you with a booklet which contained the various maintenance procedures—

A: Yes, Sir.

Q: There at Elf One?

A: A rather large one, yes, Sir. I'm not sure if they were procedures or problems, I can't remember; maybe they were both.

Q: Do you recall him encouraging you to take it home with you, it was a very big book, as you've just described, take the opportunity to look at it?

A: I can't remember if he said that or not. I didn't take it home with me.

Q: What did you do with it?

A: Well, I read it. I went back to Maintenance two or three times, and I can't remember exactly what I did with it.

Q: You don't recall taking it out and leaving it on his secretary's desk after you had spoken with Colonel Runkle?

A: Like I said, I can't remember; I may have.

TC: Might I see defense—ah. Has this been admitted into evidence yet, Your Honor? MJ: What is that, F?

TC: Yes, Sir.

MJ: Yes, it has.

TC: I hand to you what has been admitted into evidence as Defense Exhibit F, a checklist you talked about on direct examination. It's your recollection that you followed that

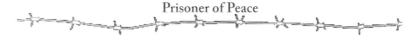
checklist prior to takeoff of the 135 flight on 9 December that was eventually involved in the midair collision.

WIT: Yes, Sir, that's my recollection.

Q: Are you in the habit of following checklists that are applicable to your duties?

A: I think so.

Q: Do you consider this a serious proceeding, Colonel Hanson?

A: You don't know how much.

Q: You do consider it to be very serious?

A: Yes, absolutely.

Q: Do you know a Second Lieutenant Booth located here at Blytheville Air Force Base?

A: Yes, I do.

Q: Do you recall having had conversations with her prior to this trial commencing?

A: Yes, I do.

Q: Do you recall having told her that this trial was going to be a full-blown circus?

A: I think that was a paraphrase.

CIV DC: I object, Your Honor.

MJ: On what grounds?

CIV DC: It's irrelevant to the proceedings, irrelevant to the charges.

MJ: Overruled.

TC: Is it correct that you testified on direct examination, Colonel Hanson, that you permitted passengers to fly on 135 aircraft out of Riyadh based solely upon your approval and not checking with anyone else?

WIT: Yes, Sir, that's correct.

Defense Witness Hanson—Cross

TC: Nothing further, Your Honor.

MJ: Redirect?

CIV DC: Excuse me a minute, Your Honor.

(A brief delay while counsel for the accused conferred.)

Nothing further, Your Honor.

MJ: Colonel Hanson, you may resume your seat at counsel's table. (The accused returned to his place at his counsel's table.) Does the defense have anything further?

DC: Yes, the only thing we don't have any additional evidence to present, Your Honor, but I would like to move at this time that Defense Exhibit A be admitted into evidence, the log book entries.

MJ: Any objection by the prosecution to the log book entries from exhibit, or were included within exhibit A being received into evidence?

TC: No, Your Honor.

MJ: Received.

DC: I believe my records are correct that all the other defense exhibits have been offered and admitted with the exception of...

MJ: I don't remember receiving *C*...

DC: That's one and...

MJ: Or *E*.

DC: C we're not going to offer.

MJ: Fine. How about *E*?

DC: No, Your Honor.

MJ: Does the defense have further evidence or do you rest?

DC: I'm sorry, Your Honor, we rest.

MJ: Thank you. Does the prosecution have a case in rebuttal?
Defense Witness Hanson—Excused
Defense Exhibit A Offered/Admitted
Defense Rested

MJ: Prior to inviting argument of counsel, I informed counsel for both sides during the recess that I intend to call Captain Johnsen back to the stand for one question.

CIV DC: Your Honor, perhaps—my understanding is that the defendant would like to retake the stand perhaps in light of that testimony. Perhaps Captain Johnsen's testimony may no longer be necessary.

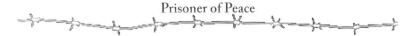

MJ: Well, if you'd like to put the accused on the stand, that's fine. Presentation of Additional Defense Matters (Not Surrebuttal)

WILLIAM T. HANSON

Recalled as a witness by the defense, was reminded he was still under oath by the military judge, and testified as follows: direct examination.

Questions by Civilian Defense Counsel:

Q: Colonel Hanson, you're retaking the stand to address to the court the question raised by the rebuttal testimony of Lieutenant Johnsen?

A: Captain Johnsen; yes, sir.

Q: I'm sorry, Captain Johnsen. You're doing this basically against the advice of your counsel.

A: Yes, sir.

Q: Why are you doing this?

A: Just ask the question.

Q: Captain Johnsen has indicated, that the second part of the log entry was entered at a later date than the first part of the log entry. Is that in fact correct?

A: That's correct. It was entered the evening of the accident based upon a call I had from Colonel Farren. He asked me who the SOF was and, as a knee-jerk reaction, I put it in the log book. I would like to state, however, nothing else in my testimony changes.

Q: You put it in after the accident?

A: Yes, sir.

Q: Now when you say nothing else in your testimony changes, does that mean that everything else that you've indicated, and everything you've indicated…

A: I'm just talking about that entry, and I'm just saying nothing changes; that's all.

Q: Is everything you've testified to here today been the truth?

A: Yes, sir.

CIV DC: No further questions.

MJ: Cross-examination?

TC: One moment, Your Honor.

MJ: Certainly.

(A brief delay while counsel for the United States conferred.)

TC: Your Honor, before making a decision concerning cross-examination or not, might I ask the bench for its position on a question?

MJ: (Nodded affirmatively)

TC: It was previously disclosed—advised that the accused would be taking the stand, but relying upon certain evidentiary rules concerning certain specifications. It would be the government's position now that that position has changed in view to the specification dealing with Supervisor of Flying operations. Is the court of the same opinion?

DC: Your Honor, the rebuttal evidence was on character evidence. I think the Military Rules of Evidence should prevail in this case.

MJ: I don't think it's changed, counsel. They haven't opened the door.

TC: Very well.

Defense Witness Hanson—Direct

CROSS-EXAMINATION

Question by Trial Counsel: Lieutenant Colonel Hanson, the entry that you just testified to was made over a year ago, correct?

A: Yes, sir, it was made on the evening of 9 December.

TC: Nothing further, Your Honor.

DC: We have nothing further, Your Honor.

MJ: Well, just a second, counsel, I may.

EXAMINATION BY THE COURT-MARTIAL

Questions by the Military Judge: Colonel Hanson, you—well, you were asked by your counsel whether you were giving this most recent testimony against his advice.

A: Yes, sir.

Q: I assume you were.

A: Yes, sir.

Q: I assume you also realize that the answer you gave me can be considered by me as it goes to your overall credibility as a witness.

A: I don't understand what you mean.

Q: I can evaluate your entire testimony based on this admission and the admission you just made could affect my evaluation of your entire testimony.

A: Yes, sir, I understand that.

Q: You know this is pretty risky, don't you?

A: Sir, it's who I am. I have to do what I have to do. I apologize.

MJ: I have no further questions. You may resume your seat at the counsel table.

TC: Cross, Major Oxley

This was a stressful event Lieutenant Colonel Hanson was under a great deal of stress; he was preoccupied by the flight itself, but he sure knew what he was doing when he made that entry in the log book after the flight. Your Honor, counsel's argument parallels quite closely the attitude of Lieutenant Colonel Hanson. Today, in his own mind, Lieutenant Colonel Hanson may actually be convinced that his actions relative to these charged offenses is excusable. No one can get inside there and know for sure. He certainly thought he could change procedures. If he didn't agree with the policies, he just didn't follow them. Well, Your Honor, the question before this court is when is an officer in the United States Air Force responsible in a court for his actions? Your Honor, by any standard that can be applied, including the standard of beyond a reasonable doubt that you will apply, that line has been crossed on every single offense. Your Honor, that's the bottom line. Thank you.

MJ: The court is closed to deliberate on findings.

(The court—martial closed at 1626 hours, 11 January 1985, and was called back to order at 1657 hours, 11 January 1985, with all parties present who were present when the court—martial closed.)

The accused and counsel will please rise for the announcement of findings.

FINDINGS

Lieutenant Colonel William T. Hanson, this court-martial finds you:

Of Specification 1, Charge I: Guilty, except the words "to obtain proper approval for orientation flights involving civilian personnel) as it was his duty to do, thereby permitting unauthorized civilian personnel to travel as passengers aboard SAC KC-135 aircraft," substituting therefor the words "to prevent unauthorized civilian personnel from traveling as passengers aboard operational SAC KC-135 aircraft, as it was his duty to do;" of the excepted words, not guilty; of the substituted words, guilty;

Of Specification 2, Charge I: Guilty;

Closing Argument by United States
Findings
Of Specification 3, Charge I: Guilty;
Of Specification 4, Charge I: Not guilty;
Of Specification 5, Charge I: Guilty; and
Of Charge I: Guilty.
Of Specification 2, Charge II: Guilty;
Of Specification 3, Charge II: Guilty; and
Of Charge II: Guilty.

An observation from the accused: It's not so much a matter of truth; it's really more about proof. What was it Tom Cruise said in the movie *A Few Good Men*? "Don't tell me about the law. I know the law. It's only about what I can prove!" Therein lies the danger in my case. When a group of colonels and generals decide to make procedural matters into crimes, we have a definite power problem. What no one will tell is that some of those same generals wanted the powers that were to have another court-martial against me after they essentially lost this one based on things they thought they knew about me. When I told my civilian attorney about this, he was flabbergasted as he said, "They wouldn't dare!" He was right. I think it was Sinclair Lewis who said that "When fascism comes to America, it will be wrapped in the flag and carrying a cross." I suppose that's why Judas Iscariot betrayed Jesus. He was disappointed in Him that He wasn't more like a general. I still love my fellow soldiers, sailors, airmen and marines, but some of our leaders bear close watching. We are not a nation of might makes right. Throughout our history people of principle have overcome armies of principals.

MJ: Have your seats, please. In view of my changing of the specification, or Specification 1 of Charge I, I had the court reporter type out my findings. Bailiff, would you distribute a copy to each counsel table? I don't think it's necessary to make these appellate exhibits, counsel. It's just for your own edification.

TC: Thank you, Your Honor.

MJ: Bailiff, take this other copy and give it to the PA representative, please.

Is the defense ready to proceed to the sentencing portion of the trial?

ADC: Your Honor, we still have not secured the presence of the defense witnesses. Presently, they are at the wing commander's call and we're having some problems getting our witnesses present to testify.

MJ: What does that mean? You have no witnesses present?

ADC: That is correct, Your Honor.

CIV DC: There are—well, actually, there are two witnesses present, Your Honor.

MJ: Colonel Hanson, what are your desires at this point? Would you rather move on with the proceedings tonight or...

ACC: I would just as soon continue, yes, Sir.

MJ: Captain Jones, have you done everything you can to secure the presence of the witnesses?

ADC: I've personally contacted one of them. I contacted another one over the brick, but he's at officers' call, and we tried to page the—we called the officers' call and they refused to page him because the wing commander is conducting officers' call.

MJ: Well, it sounds like a problem we can resolve fairly quickly.

ADC: Yes, sir.

MJ: Fine. Are we ready to proceed other than not having any witnesses here?

AX: Yes, sir.

MJ: Can I accept the first page of the charge sheet as being accurate? I realize that the pay as shown there is inaccurate. Based on the latest information I have, at lieutenant colonel, 0-5, with over twenty years for pay purposes, I believe his current pay based on the January 1 pay raise would be 3,413 dollars and forty cents per month; if counsel would like to verify that.

TC: Three-four-one-three, forty?

MJ: Yes. I would like this verified at some point because I was working from a Xeroxed copy and it was not really legible. Other than the pay, is the information shown on the first page of the charge sheet accurate?

TC: To the knowledge of the government, it is, Your Honor.

MJ: Colonel Reed, Captain Jones?

ADC: Yes, Your Honor.

MJ: It is?

ADC: It is, Your Honor.

MJ: Is the prosecution prepared to announce the accused's awards and decorations at this time?

ATC: We are, Your Honor.

MJ: Proceed.

Personal Data of Accused

ATC: The decorations and awards, Meritorious Service Medal with one device, the Air Medal with one device, Air Force Outstanding Unit Award with two devices, National Defense Service Medal, Vietnam Service Medal with two devices, Air Force Overseas Long Tour Ribbon, Air Force Longevity Service Award Ribbon with four devices, Small Arms Expert Marksmanship Ribbon, Republic of Vietnam Gallantry Cross with device, Republic of Vietnam Campaign Medal. These are the awards and decs, Your Honor.

MJ: Is that accurate, defense counsel?

ADC: Yes, Your Honor.

MJ: Before inviting the prosecution to present matters, I want to advise the accused of his rights in allocution.

ADVICE—RIGHTS OF ALLOCUTION

Colonel Hanson, you have the right to present matters in extenuation and mitigation, that is, matters about the offenses or yourself which you want this court—martial to consider in deciding an appropriate sentence. Including in your right to present evidence are the rights you have to testify under oath, to make an unsworn statement, or to remain silent. If you testify, you may be cross—examined by the trial counsel and questioned by myself on your testimony. If you decide to make an unsworn statement, you may not be cross—examined by the trial counsel or questioned by me. You may make an unsworn statement orally or in writing, personally or through your counsel, or you may use a combination of these means. If you decide to exercise your right to remain silent, this court cannot hold that against you in any way.

Do you understand what your rights are during this portion of the trial?

ACC: Yes, Sir.

MJ: Does the prosecution have any matters to present?

TC: No, Your Honor.

MJ: Does the defense have any matters to present?

CIV DC: Your Honor, I would like to call Samuel Hester. I believe he's right outside.

> Earlier, I sought out a civilian doctor because the military doctor I went to see as my stress level was at a near-breaking point told me that, under military rules, he could share with the prosecution anything I told him. Whether or not that is still the case in the military, I do not know.

MJ: What was the name again, please?

CIV DC: Hester, H-e-s-t-e-r.

MJ: Sandra Hester?

CIV DC: No, Samuel.

MJ: Samuel, okay.
Presentation Of Matters
In Extenuation And Mitigation

SAMUEL B. HESTER

Called as a witness by the defense in mitigation, was sworn, and testified as follows:

Questions by Trial Counsel: What is your full name?

A: Samuel Brown Hester.

Q: Where do you live? What is your address, Hester?

A: My home address is Rural Route Address 1 in Steele, Missouri. My office address is Blytheville Psychological Services, Blytheville, Arkansas.

Q: You are not a member of the United States Air Force, are you, Sir?

A: No, I'm not.

TC: Thank you.

DIRECT EXAMINATION

Questions by Civilian Defense Counsel: Doctor Hester…

A: Yes.

Q: What is your present occupation?

A: Clinical psychologist.

Q: Are you licensed to practice clinical psychology in any states?

A: I'm licensed in the States of Arkansas, Missouri and Tennessee.

Q: And where do you practice, Sir?

A: I practice out of my office in the Medical Plaza Building in Blytheville, Arkansas.

Q: What is your educational background?

A: I have a PhD in clinical psychology from the University of Mississippi; an internship with the National Naval Medical Center in Bethesda; currently I'm also on staff at Lakeside Hospital in Memphis, Tennessee.

Q: What is your prior experience in clinical psychology?

A: I've worked as a psychologist since graduation, four years in the military, and three years now in private practice, a total of seven years in clinical psychology.

Q: Where did you work in the military in psychology?

A: I worked two years at Bethesda, one year as an intern and one year as a department chairman in the National Naval Medical Center, two years at Millington as chief psychologist at the Naval Regional Medical Center in Millington, Tennessee.

Q: While you were working with the Navy, were you a member of the armed forces?

A: Yes, I was.

Q: And what rank did you hold?

A: I held the rank of lieutenant.

Q: You're in private practice in…

A: Blytheville.

Q: Blytheville now?

A: Right.

Q: And you've been in private practice for how long?

A: For about three years now.

Q: At some point in time, did you have cause to begin treatment and counseling for Bill Hanson?

A: Yes, I did. I saw Bill initially on June 21st, 1984, upon the military's request.

Q: You say at the military's request. Could you give me some background, reports and background as to why this request was made?

A: Bill had been seen by the mental health unit here at the base. I received a call, I believe it was from Captain Kiunder, Captain Klunder as well as Captain Astley at the time. Both would refer patients back and forth and we would be in communication frequently, and I believe it was Captain Klunder who had called and asked that I see the family. He pointed out that they had seen the colonel on the base, that they had performed some psychological testing, specifically an MMPI, Minnesota Multiphasic Personality Inventory, which showed some significant elevations that caused them some concern about his current emotional state, and felt that it would be difficult for them to provide treatment here because of the charges that were pending and asked if I would be willing to see) and his family.

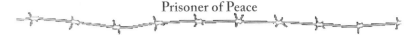

Q: Are you familiar with the MMPI?

A: Yes, I am.

Q: And what exactly is it?

A: It is a psychological inventory that is probably one of our more standardized that obtains a measurement of personality as well as current emotional state.

Q: Does it have local use, wide-spread use?

A: It has been normed on hundreds of thousands of people in various populations, and by scoring the MMPI, you're able to compare the person who is administered and has taken the test to a particular population who may have similar kinds of emotions at that particular point in time.

Q: How long has the test been around?

A: Oh, goodness, I think it's been around, probably been around for 35 years.

MJ: Counsel, if it will help you any, I am thoroughly familiar with the MMPI.

CIV DC: Thank you.

You say that there were elevated scores on his MMPI. What scores were those?

WIT: There were seven elevations out of ten, so it's essentially almost all the scores were elevated. The four, six and eight scales were all elevated, those were the highest elevations, and when you look at those in a group, it primarily suggests someone who is experiencing a great deal of confusion, anger, agitation. When you see that many elevations in one profile, it's not usually diagnostic of a particular disorder such as if you were trying to use the measurement to diagnose someone who was schizophrenic or who was manic-depressive or any particular psychiatric disorder.

They would usually have, say, two to three elevations, but to have seven elevations usually indicates someone who is in an extreme state of emotional turmoil and trauma that's brought on by situational stress, or it's like all the different emotions are coming to a head at one time.

Q: When was the MMPI done?

A: It was performed, I believe, a couple of weeks before I saw Bill the first time on the 21st.

Q: The twenty-first of what month?

A: Of June.

Q: Of this past year, '84?

A: Uh huh.

Q: How many times have you seen Bill Hanson since the initial referral?

A: I've seen Bill and his wife, Clare, a total of fourteen times.

Q: Okay. Can you tell the court in your own words what your observations were? When was the last time you saw Mister Hanson?

A: I saw Bill the last time, I believe, the first week in December.

Q: Just a little over a month ago.

A: Right.

Defense Mitigation Witness Hester—Direct

Q: Could you describe for the court in your own words what your observations were in terms of Bill Hanson during the period of time that you saw him from June to December?

A: Initially, Bill was experiencing some of what we call physical complaints. He was experiencing some sleep disturbance. He had been having some aggravated muscle spasm types of problems that we periodically see whenever there's tension and muscle tightness.

One of my main concerns was he had a great deal of manic types of racing types, high energy levels. He just really couldn't sit still, couldn't concentrate on one thing for a very long period of time, and he would tend to just sort of jump from one subject to the next. He had told me on his initial consultation that over the past eight weeks since he had— from what I understood since the original charges had been pressed, he had read something like forty-seven or forty-eight books, and that was the first time I saw him, and I know throughout the continued treatment he continued to do an awful lot of reading. The reading seemed to help him to—he would read a lot of philosophical, theoretical kinds of books in order to try to keep the whole pending court-martial in some type of a context of—sort of a larger context, thinking of things in terms of eternity and the universe, and all these types of philosophical questions would tend to allow him to take the stress of the current situation and try to minimize it and keep it in perspective. Whenever he would put down some of his defenses, when some of the intellectualization and rationalization would tend to fall away, he would tend to lapse more into a depressive type of mode in which he would have very little energy and tend to do very little, if anything, but most of the time it seemed to be more of the other extreme of the rapid types of problems.

Q: Is that type of conduct that you experienced on the part of Bill Hanson, is that typical?

A: Type of what?

Q: Conduct.

A: Conduct? Well, each person, you know, copes with their different stresses in different ways. There are a number of different defense mechanisms and intellectualization and rationalization are two. Other people can use defense mechanisms of denial in which they will just sort of pretend like nothing is going to happen and everything will be okay. We all use different defense mechanisms from time to time. The trick is to make sure that our defense mechanisms don't cause us other kinds of problems, and you know, a lot of our efforts were for me to sort of monitor Bill's defense mechanisms that he was using to try to cope with these pending stressors and make sure that he was not—that his

thinking was not going to go from the normal range of thinking to any kind of abnormal thinking, watching for a slip into a true manic episode in which there would be some psychotic thought processes.

Q: Is there anything particular about Bill Hanson's background, psychological background or whatever, that would cause this type of disturbance?

A: I believe so. In obtaining more of a history of Bill's personality development from Bill as well as from talking with Missus Hanson, Bill has what psychologists would refer to as a high external locus of control which mainly means that he puts a great deal of energy and effort in trying to attain approval by people who are around him, especially from peers, almost to the point of needing peer approval primary to working, or making sure that you have relationships with more of the nuclear family, such as with wife and children, and this type of need for extreme approval by superficial relationships with peers oftentimes sets up the conflicts within the home because it will make the more intimate relationships feel as though they're taking a back seat. Well, to me, that meant that Bill had, you know, not only spent the last twenty—some—odd years attaining a career within the military, but he also spent that time trying to nurture and cultivate and put a lot of energy into attaining approval from the Air Force and from the peers that he was surrounded with in the Air Force, and therefore when you have a personality that has that high need for approval by peers, to then have these kinds of charges pending, then it would be more devastating to that personality because the charges represent rejection by these peers then.

Q: Do you have, or did you come to any sort of diagnosis?

A: The diagnosis that I believe is accurate is what we refer to as an adjustment reaction with mixed emotional features. That primarily means that the various emotions that Bill has been experiencing, the extremes, were in response to the stressors that he has been under, which implies that once the stressors are removed, hopefully the majority of these emotional responses will subside and go away and not be truly indicative of a true psychiatric illness, even though the emotions in and of themselves would probably deserve a diagnosis such as a psychlothymic disorder in which a person has rapid mood swings from one extreme to the other. A person who truly is psychlothymic does not usually have the situational stressors pending that Bill has that would justify the mood swings. So when the stressors are pending, you tend to lean toward the adjustment reaction diagnosis. My concern was that I did not want the adjustment reaction to go from that into any kind of a true psychiatric disorder of any sort.

Q: How bad has the stress been on him since you—during the period of time that you've seen him?

A: Well, when we're making a diagnosis, the DSM-III diagnosis, we make a diagnosis as well as we have to identify the stream of the stressors of the past year the person has been under so we can see if the diagnosis is a response to the situational stressors, and I would have to say that, with Bill's personality and with the implications for the court-martial, the stressors are severe, extremely severe.

CIV DC: I have no further questions of this witness.

MJ: Cross-examination?

TC: Thank you, Your Honor.

CROSS-EXAMINATION

Questions by Trial Counsel: Doctor Hester, the elevations in the MMPI that you spoke to earlier in your direct testimony, are those elevations common for individuals who would be facing charges in a proceeding such as Colonel Hanson has been?

A: Some elevations would be common, yes.

Q: During the course of your contact with Lieutenant Colonel Hanson, you haven't had any occasion to recommend him for any kind of psychiatric medication, have you?

A: I have not recommended any medication.

Q: Doctor, isn't it not—is it a true statement that in fact since he has been experiencing these consultations with you that his condition has generally improved?

A: I think from the beginning to the end of the treatment that Bill was beginning to, perhaps through his own reading and his own work, beginning to get a better grasp on the whole thing, and I think by just being able to get him through it up to the point of the court-martial without further deterioration then, to me, that was being successful.

Q: Would you agree with the statement therefore, doctor, that his condition has generally improved?

A: Well, the last time I saw him, he did seem slightly improved over, say, the initial consultation.

Q: Doctor, you spoke about Lieutenant Colonel Hanson's need for external approval. Is it true that as most people mature the need for external approval diminishes and the need for internal approval, or one's own self-approval, becomes more important?

A: That's one of the characteristics of maturity, yes.

TC: Nothing further.

MJ: Redirect?

CIV DC: No, Your Honor.

EXAMINATION BY THE COURT-MARTIAL

Questions by the Military Judge: Doctor Hester, do you have an opinion of what effect a period of confinement might have on this person?

A: I think it would go along with my statement that just going to court-martial and having the charges pending probably have more of a devastating effect on this particular type of personality than it would on a more internally controlled personality, and by continuing with punishment to the point of incarceration, then I think it would land on a personality that would be more devastated by that than one who is more internally controlled. I couldn't make any specific prediction as to what behavior he may display.

Q: I understand. In your opinion, would he be suicidal?

A: I think it's possible.

MJ: Anything further from the defense?

CIV DC: No, Your Honor.

Defense Mitigation Witness Hester—Cross/MJ

MJ: I assume the prosecution has nothing further.

TC: No, Your Honor.

MJ: Very well, Doctor Hester, you're excused. We thank you for your time today.

WIT: Okay.

MJ: I will caution you before you leave not to discuss your testimony with anyone other than these lawyers until the trial is over.

WIT: Okay.

MJ: Thank you, you're excused.

(The witness withdrew from the courtroom.)

Do we have another witness present, counsel?

DC: We've been in here, Your Honor.

MJ: Well, would you like a short recess to see if we can't get all of the witnesses here?

DC: I believe five minutes or so, Your Honor.

MJ: We're in recess.

(The court-martial recessed at 1722 hours, 11 January 1985, and was called back to order at 1740 hours, 11 January 1985, with all parties present who were present when the court-martial recessed.)

ADC: Your Honor, at this time the defense calls to the stand Colonel Harold Kowalski.

HAROLD W. KOWALKSI, JR.

Called as a witness by the defense in mitigation, was sworn, and testified as follows:

Questions by Trial Counsel: Would you please state your full name and rank?

A: Harold W. Kowalski, Junior, full colonel.

Q: To what organization are you assigned, Colonel Kowaiski?
Defense Mitigation Witness Hester—Excused
Defense Mitigation Witness Kowalski

A: I'm assigned to the 97th Bomb Wing.

Q: And that is located here at Blytheville Air Force Base?

A: Yes, sir.

Q: And you are a member of the United States Air Force, sir?

A: I am.

TC: Thank you.

DIRECT EXAMINATION

Questions by Assistant Defense Counsel: Colonel Kowalski, do you know the accused, Lieutenant Colonel Hanson?

A: I do.

Q: If he's present in the courtroom, would you point to him and call him by name?

A: Colonel Hanson, sitting in the middle of the table.
(The witness pointed toward the accused.)

ADC: The record should reflect the proper identification by the witness.

Q: Colonel Kowalski, how long have you known Lieutenant Colonel Hanson?

A: Well, since I arrived on this base in August of '81.

Q: And what has your association with Colonel Hanson been, professional, social?

A: Professional and social in that we're both stationed at the same base. We saw each other, oh, probably two, three, four times a week.

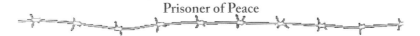

What type of professional dealings would you have with Colonel Hanson?

A: Well, during the early part of my tenure here at Blytheville, Colonel Hanson was the Operations Officer in the 97th Air Refueling Squadron. On numerous occasions I, as the Chief of Maintenance here, Colonel Hanson as the Operations Officer in the tanker squadron, would consult on various aspects of aircraft maintenance. For example, an aircraft has got a bad engine oil pump or something to that effect. I'd call Colonel Hanson, "Can we fly that airplane or can't we? Bill, tell me, if we have to fix it, we don't have much time. Tell me, can you take it or can't you?" He'd say, "No, we can't go with that, it's against the TO." I'd say, "Okay, we have to fix it, we'll be late," so on and so forth. It was a relationship where I was calling on his expertise to tell me, the guy that bends the wrenches, can we fly the airplane or can't we?

Q: Colonel Kowalski, why, out of all the aviators you have at this particular installation, at Blytheville Air Force Base, why do you single out Colonel Hanson?

A: Well, primarily because of his position, but also because I was very impressed with his enthusiasm to get the airplanes off the ground. My business is getting the airplanes fixed to get off the ground. I need that operational expertise. If you'll note, I'm a navigator, I'm not a pilot. He has to fly the airplane, I don't; I have to fix it. So I sought the expertise from him as the Operations Officer in the squadron.

Q: Colonel Kowalski, you mentioned his eagerness. What was your experience with Colonel Hanson concerning his concern for the mission of the United States Air Force?

A: I would say that in my Air Force career, which is 23 years, I've never seen anybody more enthused about doing the mission of the Air Force, of flying airplanes, and getting the mission done than Colonel Hanson.

Q: And why do you say that, colonel?

A: Well, just on my day-to-day dealings with him. He wanted the airplanes to launch on time, I wanted them to launch on time, his dealings with his crew,\his dealings with the other folks on the base here, just the aura about him that, "Hey, I'm a pilot in the United States Air Force and I want to fly these airplanes, and I want to get off and I want to pass the gas, and that's my job and I want to do it," and I appreciated that. I've never seen anybody more enthused about performing their mission than Colonel Hanson.

Q: Sir, did you ever have an occasion to observe Colonel Hanson's interaction with the younger troops in the squadron?

Defense Mitigation Witness Kowalski—Direct

A: Not on a one-to-one, but I can give you an example that impressed me as a senior officer. Nowadays, our younger folks just aren't that knowledgeable on flying airplanes. It takes years of experience. When I was a young crewmember, we had lieutenant colonels as aircraft commanders and majors as aircraft commanders, and nowadays, we've got first lieutenants and young captains as aircraft commanders. You give them an awful lot of responsibility with not a great deal of experience. I guess what impressed me about Colonel Hanson was he's the only guy I know of, aircraft commander, that ever took his crew over to the phase dock and said, "Hey, guys, I want you to see where these guys take your airplane apart and put it back together. These are the guys that are fixing your airplane that you fly." That, you know, is impressive. Nobody else did that, and we've got what, 25 crews in this wing, tanker crews, and another 20 bomber crews, and you know, that shows me the guy cares about the airplane he's flying and his younger crewmembers.

Q: Colonel Kowalski, has Colonel Hanson ever volunteered for specific assignments for you, specifically concerning...

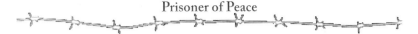

A: Well, I can…

Q: A 135 aircraft that was damaged?

A: Yes. We crashed an airplane here in January of '81, almost eight or nine months before I got to this base. When I got here, it looked like a piece of junk setting out on my ramp out there; three engines off, the nose all damaged. The aircraft was 290. Today that aircraft sets on the ramp out here completely repaired. It took us about a year, a little more than a year, well, probably six months after I got here, to get that airplane back in flying shape. A lot had been damaged on it. We had to get a lot of new parts. We bought parts from airlines. It really looked like a piece of junk sitting out on the ramp out there, but it was all put back together.

We set a target date to fly that airplane. We didn't have a whole lot of enthusiasm from our folks down in the tanker squadron to fly it, and Colonel Hanson says, "Hell, I'll fly it. You put it together and I'll fly it," and he did, and the airplane operated as advertised. You know, nobody else would step forward and say, "Hey, I'll take it, let me do it." Colonel Hanson did.

Q: Colonel Kowalski, is that instance of Colonel Hanson coming forward to take the truly difficult assignments consistent with your experience with Colonel Hanson? Defense Mitigation Witness Kowalski—Direct

A: Well, my experience with Colonel Hanson is somewhat limited, you know. He probably volunteered for difficult assignments but, you know, to me, that was the most difficult assignment I could ask for. To answer your question, I really don't know a whole lot of other difficult things, but that's because of my position and his position.

Q: Consistent with what you know of his attitude and his concern for the mission of the United States Air Force?

A: Very consistent.

Q: Colonel Kowalski...

A: The guy likes to fly airplanes, he's enthusiastic about the mission. I just was very much impressed with Colonel Hanson's attitude in my entire span here at Blytheville Air Force Base.

Q: Colonel Kowalski, I'm sure you appreciate the seriousness of these proceedings. Is there anything that I have not specifically covered with you that you would want the judge to be aware of prior to deciding on a sentence in this case?

A: Well, I guess the only other thing I could relate is that Colonel Hanson almost came to work for me. I wanted Colonel Hanson to work for me because of his enthusiasm, and I felt like he could relate to my young maintenance troops. We're talking about high school kids, we're talking about kids that are eighteen to twenty-two years old that have been sent to school for a year, then they're sent down to my flight line, and they're bending the wrenches down there trying to fix airplanes. You have to take somebody with a magnetism and a aura about him, a charismatic individual, to fire those young troops up, and Colonel Hanson had that. In fact, every crew chief on my flight line down there knows Colonel Hanson and they all liked him; "Hell of a good pilot," they would say, and he had a very good rapport with my crew chiefs.

ADC: Thank you, Sir, no further questions.

TC: No cross. You can appreciate that sentencing this particular accused is a difficult job.

A: I understand.

Q: Depending on the nature of the sentence I impose, it's possible he would return to duty here at Blytheville. Do you understand that?

A: (Nodded affirmatively)

Q: Do you have an opinion as to how well he can be integrated back into the officer corps and the base in general?

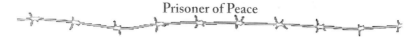

A: Oh, it would be difficult; but I would take Colonel Hanson in my organization in a heartbeat.

MJ: Anything from either side?

ADC: No, Your Honor.

TC: No, Your Honor.

MJ: Colonel, we thank you for you time, you're excused.

ADC: Your Honor, at this time the defense calls to the stand Lieutenant Colonel Charles Quinn.(Now deceased)

CHARLES D. QUINN

Called as a witness by the defense in mitigation, was sworn, and testified as follows:

Questions by Trial Counsel: Would you please state your full name and rank?

A: Charles Donald Quinn, lieutenant colonel.

Q: To what organization are you assigned, Colonel Quinn?

A: I'm presently assigned to the Site Activation Task Force, working the ALCM cruise missile activation here at Blytheville.

Q: Located here at Blytheville Air Force Base?

A: Yes, here at Blytheville.

Q: You are a member of the United States Air Force, Sir?
     Defense Mitigation Witness Kowalski—MJ Excused
     Defense Mitigation Witness Quinn

A: Yes, I am.

TC: Thank you.

DIRECT EXAMINATION

Questions by Assistant Defense Counsel: Colonel Quinn, do you know the accused in this case, Lieutenant Colonel Hanson?

A: Yes, I do, very well.

Q: If you see him present in the courtroom, will you point to him and call him by name?

A: That's Bill right there.

(The witness pointed toward the accused.)

ADC: The proper identification by the witness.

Q: Colonel Quinn, how long have you been a member of the United States Air Force?

A: Twenty-five and a half years.

Q: And what different positions have you held during your career in the United States Air Force, very briefly?

A: Well, I started off as a crewmember. During the early part of my career I worked in maintenance as an aircraft maintenance officer in F-4s in Europe; two Southeast Asia tours, one in 8-66s and B-52s. I came here to Blytheville and worked in the bomb/nav business. Since I've been here I was the Chief of Social Actions, Chief of Current Ops, Deputy Base Commander, Assistant DCM, and in the present position I'm in now.

Q: Colonel Quinn, you indicated you know Colonel Hanson. How long have you known Colonel Hanson?

A: For the three years that he's been here. I met him probably the second day he got on base.

Q: Colonel Quinn, during your three-year association with Colonel Hanson, have you had occasion to deal with him on a professional basis?

Defense Mitigation Witness Quinn—Direct

A: Yes, I have, when I was working in maintenance and he was flying in the tanker squadron.

Q: What types of dealings would you have with him on a professional basis, Sir?

A: Well, when I was working in maintenance, I was the Ops Officer or working in Training, and I considered him to be my expert in KC-135 operations.

Q: What was Colonel Hanson's level of expertise concerning KC-135 operations?

A: He was an aircraft commander and a staff officer in the squadron.

Q: Did you consider him unusually well qualified?

A: Yes, I did. That was the reason he was my main contact when I had any questions on operations when I was working in maintenance.

Q: Colonel Quinn, what was Colonel Hanson's attitude concerning accomplishing the mission?

A: His attitude as far as accomplishing the mission?

Q: Yes, Sir.

A: Colonel Hanson always accomplished the mission. If I was ever in a bind that I needed some gas, I'd like to hear his name come over the interphone.

Q: Why do you say that, Sir?

A: Because I'd get my gas.

Q: Do you know, from your association with Colonel Hanson over the three years, what motivates him? What is he concerned about? Is he concerned about himself or is he concerned about other things?

A: No, I think Colonel Hanson is as patriotic an individual as I have known since I've been in the Air Force, very dedicated to the Air Force mission, very concerned about young crewmembers, their training. It's kind of a coincidence, but I just came here from officers' call, and there was a young captain who used to almost shadow Colonel Hanson around, one that he took under his wing, and today he was awarded the Outstanding Crew of the Quarter for the tanker squadron. I think that's typical of the work that he's done.

Q: Colonel Quinn, how would you characterize your knowledge of Colonel Hanson's officership qualities?

A: Officership qualities? As far as I know, they're outstanding. I've never had any problems with it. The qualities of an officer, the requirements of being an officer are about the same as being a saint. I don't think any of us would fall in that category, we all mess up occasionally, but I certainly think he's as fine an officer as I've worked with.

Q: Colonel Quinn, would you have any hesitation to working with Colonel Hanson again?

A: I certainly would not; work for him tomorrow; be honored to work anyplace, anytime, particularly in a time of conflict. When the real warriors have to stand up, he would be one of them to do it.

Q: Colonel Quinn, is there anything that you would like to address to the bench prior to the time the military judge decides upon a sentence in this case, that you have not had the opportunity to address so far?

A: There are some areas that have bothered me. Like I said, I've been in the Air Force all of my adult life. I'm very proud of the service that I've put in and people like Colonel Hanson. I've been a bit disappointed in my company in the last year, in the time that it's taken this to be settled, the torment that he and his wife have been put through for a year; the publicity that there's been over this thing in all of Northeast Arkansas and Tennessee. They have to live in this town and I think that was a little extreme. I think the man has been tormented enough.

If you took a poll in this wing, Colonel Hanson would be flying airplanes back on the job tomorrow.

ADC: Thank you, Sir. No further questions, Your Honor.

MJ: Cross-examination?

CROSS-EXAMINATION

Questions by Trial Counsel: Sir, do you know the offenses of which Colonel Hanson now stands convicted?

Defense Mitigation Witness Quinn—Direct/Cross

A: Yes, I do.

Q: Is it your understanding that it would be fair to say that he has now been convicted of four charges of dereliction and two charges of conduct unbecoming an officer? Is that your understanding?

A: That's what I was briefed, yes.

Q: Do you also have knowledge concerning certain information that came out during the course of this trial concerning Lieutenant Colonel Hanson's actions in making an entry in a log book retroactively, thereby attempting to establish that he was somewhere when he was not?

A: I don't know what happened during the three weeks that he was over there. I know what happened when he was here and I was working with him on a professional basis here in the wing.

Q: I understand, Sir.

MJ: Counsel, I think that was a slight mis-statement also, but I understand.

TC: If I've misrepresented something, I assure you—

MJ: I don't think you misrepresented something—

TC: It was not my intention.

MJ: It was just slightly inaccurate.

TC: Colonel, you spoke about officership on direct examination. Do you believe that officership includes the concept of integrity?

WIT: Certainly, I do.

Q: You expressed the opinion on your direct testimony that, if a poll taken in this wing, you're confident that the majority of the people would want Lieutenant Colonel Hanson back in a flying organization at Blytheville Air Force Base. Is that a fair rendition of your direct testimony?

A: Yes, I consider that to be a fair estimate of this wing. I've been here nine and a half years and I think I pretty well have a feeling for the personality of this wing.

Q: Yes, sir. Do you believe that that opinion that you hold would remain the same or will remain the same once what went down in this courtroom becomes knowledgeable to all the people on this base?

A: Yes, I think it would. I think the man should be judged on his twenty years of service and not three weeks of something that went on on the other side of the world.

Q: I understand. Would you agree with the statement that the integrity of an officer is a very, very important element—

A: Yes, I would.

Q: Of the officer's worth?

A: Yes.

TC: nothing further.

MJ: I assume there's no redirect.

ADC: No, Your Honor.

MJ: Colonel Quinn, we thank you for your time this evening. You're excused and you may depart the courtroom.

WIT: Thank you.

MJ: Or, if you would like, you may stay.

WIT: Thank you.

MJ: Yes, sir. (The witness withdrew from the courtroom.)

Lt. Col. James "Red" Clevenger in his F-16. The epitome of an American fighting man and, my friend. Nearly all my military witnesses came into the courtroom wearing their Air Force Blue Dress uniforms, but with their old brass insignia on. They said they did it to make a point that my trial signified a turning point of the *Old Air Force from the New.*

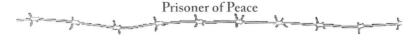

Post Flight Briefing—Sort Of

I was quite shocked when I learned from my civilian attorney that they, both defense and prosecution lawyers, often got together at the end of the day to discuss the *case*. To them it was just a job, but to me it was my life! For example, the lead prosecution attorney, one Major Oxley, told my lawyers how impressive all my character witnesses were. "It was quite a show," he told them.

"You mean to say, you guys sit around and discuss the case at the end of the day?" I asked in amazement. My civilian attorney, Dave Sanders, said, "Sure, why not? You pilots sit around and talk about your flights after you land, don'tcha?"

I was really quite naive when it came to how some things work in the real world. As one of my old fraternity (Phi Kappa Sigma) friends from the University of Maine at Orono explained: "For you it might be a revelation, but for many of us it's just a review." Boy oh boy, what an understatement that would turn out to be!

Finally, my civilian lawyer came to my house the night before the sentencing and said the judge told all the lawyers that he was not going to throw me out of the Air Force, with one small caveat. "As long as things don 't get out of hand tomorrow," he cautioned all lawyers. My civilian lawyer, Mister Sanders, said he got nervous when he interviewed Lieutenant Colonel *"Red"* Clevenger the day before he was to take the stand in my defense.

Colonel Clevenger said: "What I really want to do is bring in my F-16 squadron from Utah and napalm these bomber pukes for what they are doing to Bill Bob (one of my Air Force nicknames). Mister Sanders said, "You wouldn't really do that would ya?"

"What 'dya think I got all these medals for? This trial is a clear indication of how Air Force leadership has declined. Our commanders used to be flying the lead aircraft on missions. Now they've relegated that to some captain. We may just as well turn the Air Force back to the Army," Colonel Clevenger concluded.

"For goodness' sake," Sanders cautioned him, "don't talk like that tomorrow or the judge will throw him out of the Air Force.

The judge just wants everyone on their good behavior. Then he'll give Colonel Hanson a small fine and we'll all move on."

"Yeah," Red agreed. "We'll all move on, but what about Bill Bob? A fine?" Red asked incredulously. "What for? He just saved a twenty-five million dollar aircraft and twelve lives. They oughta be giving him a DFC(Distinguished Flying Cross). Why a fine anyway?"

"The judge said he has to do something to justify the expense of the trial," Sanders explained.

"Jesus, Mary, and Joseph!" Red said. "What an outfit. No offense," Red said knowing Sanders was Jewish.

ADC: At this time the defense calls to the stand Lieutenant Colonel James Clevenger.

Lt. Col. James "Red" Clevenger, A1-E/F-16 fighter pilot with whom I served in Vietnam. He epitomizes all that is good in the service.

JAMES O. CLEVENGER

Called as a witness by the defense in mitigation, was sworn, and testified as follows:

Questions by Trial Counsel: Would you please state your full name and rank?

A: I'm sorry.

DEFENSE MITIGATION WITNESS CLEVENGER

Q: Would you state your full name and rank?

A: Lieutenant Colonel James D. Clevenger.

Q: To what organization are you assigned, colonel?

A: I am currently the Operations Officer of the 16th Tactical Fighter Squadron at Hill Air Force Base.

Q: And you are a member of the United States Air Force.

A: Yes, sir.

TC: Thank you.

DIRECT EXAMINATION

Questions by Assistant Defense Counsel: Colonel Clevenger, do you know the accused, Lieutenant Colonel William Hanson?

A: Yes, sir, I do.

Q: If you see him in the courtroom, would you point to him and state his name?

A: Lieutenant Colonel William Hanson.

(The witness pointed toward the accused.)

ADC: The record should reflect the proper identification.

Colonel Clevenger, what is your present duty responsibilities in the United States Air Force?

A: Well, as I stated, I am the Operations Officer for the 16th Tactical Fighter Squadron at Hill.

Q: Okay, and what does that entail?

A: What I do is I supervise about thirty-five young fighter pilots in the execution of our primary mission.

Q: Are you, yourself, an F-16 pilot?

A: Yes, I am.

Defense Mitigation Witness Clevenger—Direct

Q: How long have you been a fighter pilot?

A: All my life; since April 1961 was the first time that I flew fighters.

Q: Colonel Clevenger, how long have you known Colonel Hanson?

A: I came to know Colonel Hanson in the September time frame of 1971.

Q: Could you describe to the court how you came to know Colonel Hanson in 1971?

A: In September of 1971, I was assigned to the 1st Special Operations Squadron at Na Kom Phonm, Thailand, where I flew the A-1. Our primary role there was search and rescue. Colonel Hanson at that time was stationed at NKP, an organization that I only knew as Task Force Alpha. It was an intelligence organization that was based at the same

base. Colonel Hanson at that time was what we called a FIDO, a Fighter Duty Operations Officer, and his job was to interpret the real-time intelligence that was available there through that organization, and provide that kind of information to those of us flying missions in Southeast Asia.

Q: Colonel Clevenger, as an A-1 flyer in Southeast Asia, did you ever have occasion specifically to rely on Colonel Hanson and his professional abilities during the Vietnam war?

A: Yes, I did. In March, in late March of 1972, the North Vietnamese began their final offensive while the United States was involved. They invaded through two areas, down through the DMZ, which was the border between North and South Vietnam, and through the Parrot's Beak, through a place called An Loc. I believe it was on March 30 of 1972, the day after the invasion began, a B-66, with a call sign Bat 21, was shot down. There was one survivor on board, and a search and rescue mission was launched in an attempt to recover him.

Colonel Hanson became personally involved in that thing in his role as the FIDO there at Task Force Alpha in that, through the intelligence information available to him, he discovered that the North Vietnamese were building a surface-to-air missile site near the vicinity of the survivor. The SAR was a rather protracted affair, the SAR is the search and rescue mission, lasting about ten days. It was apparent, quite obvious, that the purpose of the North Vietnamese was to install this SAM site so as to foil the search and rescue attempt. Colonel Hanson identified the location of that site and, through a very exhaustive process, was able to get the target fragged, which means an air strike was ordered against it, and it was destroyed.

Now he did that at some considerable expense of his own time and effort. As I recall, initially his request for the destruction of that target was disapproved, and a lesser man would have shrugged it off as, "Well, I tried," and not pursue the matter any farther, but he persevered, was able to convince the targeters down at Seventh Air Force in Saigon that we needed that target destroyed, and it was, and it probably saved some lives of my squadron mates.

Q: In a very personal sense, Colonel Clevenger, what have Colonel Hanson's actions meant to you as an A-1 flyer?

A: I owe him my life.

Q: Colonel Clevenger, did you ever have any other occasions to deal with Colonel Hanson?

A: Yes, I have. Our association was kind of put on the back burner for a while until September of 1982. At that time I was directed to fly an F-16 from the factory at Fort Worth to Kunsan Air Base, Korea. It's quite a lengthy trip and we don't go all the way at one time, and it requires KC-135 support.

We left the factory and started towards Honolulu, which was the first stop on our trip, and we rendezvoused with a set of three tankers west of Santa Barbara, and they took us across the water to Honolulu. As it turned out, when we rendezvoused and completed our first refueling, Colonel Hanson was the cell leader of the three tankers that was assigned for that mission.

As we progressed toward Honolulu, two of my wingmen started to develop a fairly serious problem with the fuel system. The result was that the aircraft, the fighter, would not take the fuel. It's like having the cap off your gas tank in your car; you put the fuel in and it was running out the other side. Fuel became kind of critical for not only the three F-16s but the three KC-135s, but Colonel Hanson very positively and very resolutely took charge of the situation, cycled the receivers through the right tankers so that we got not only the fighters but all the tankers to Honolulu without anybody reaching an emergency state on their fuel.

There was one other time, one other professional being that I had with Colonel Hanson, and that occurred last April. I'm not sure whether he was the base project officer for the Open House or just one of those that was helping organize it all, but he requested that I bring two F-16's down for the static display for that air show, which I did. While I was here, I had the opportunity to talk with several of the young officers at the base here about him, and it reconfirmed my suspicions about the character of Colonel Hanson. I think it was no accident that he was picked to be the Project Warrior officer for Blytheville Air Force Base. He possesses all the qualities that we need in today's modern combat warrior. He provided the inspiration, the guidance and the initiative to all the young troops. I don't know if you're familiar with the book that Tom Wolfe wrote called "The Right Stuff". There is certainly a place in that book for a character like Colonel Hanson. The bottom line is he is the type of modern day warrior that we need in the Air Force, and I feel so strongly about him that I would place my life in his hands at any time. Were I over downtown Hanoi with two minutes of fuel reserve, screaming for a tanker, he'd come get me.

Q: Colonel Clevenger, would you have any hesitation with working with Colonel Hanson again in the future?

A: Not at all.

Q: Colonel Clevenger, is there anything that you have not told this court that you feel the court should be aware of prior to the time of deciding on a sentence in this case?

A: Other than the fact that, in my opinion, he is the type of modern day combat warrior that we need, and I think that it would be a shame to destroy that.

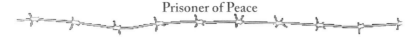

ADC: Thank you, sir.

MJ: Cross-examination?

CROSS-EXAMINATION

Question by Trial Counsel: Sir, do modern day warriors need to possess integrity?

A: I agree.

TC: Nothing further.

MJ: Colonel Clevenger, we thank you for your time, you're excused.

WIT: Thank you.

(The witness withdrew from the courtroom.)

CIV DC: Call Clare Hanson to the stand, Your Honor.

CLARE HANSON

Called as a witness by the defense in mitigation, was sworn, and testified as follows:

Questions by Trial Counsel: Would you please state your full name, ma'am?

A: Yes, my name is Clare Hanson.

Q: Where do you live?

A: I live on Rural Route 1, Steele, Missouri.

Q: And you're not a member of the United States Air Force, are you, ma'am?

A: No.

TC: Thank you.

DIRECT EXAMINATION

Questions by Civilian Defense Counsel: Missus Hanson, are you married to Lieutenant Colonel Bill Hanson?

A: I am.

Q: How long have you been married to him?

A: About eight years.

Q: Where do you folks presently reside?

A: We live on Rural Route 1, Steele, Missouri, not too many miles north of here.

Defense Mitigation Witness Hanson (Mrs)—Direct

Q: How long have you been living in this area?

A: We've been here four years. We came here in October of '80.

Q: Could you characterize for the court your husband's identification with the Air Force?

A: My husband identifies completely with the Air Force. It's his life, it means everything to him. He's very proud of his Air Force life, and he has placed his service to his country above everything else, above family, above personal gain, obligations, etc . It is the most important thing to him.

Q: When did he return from overseas after the incident at Riyadh?

A: I picked him up in Memphis on the 23rd of December, 1983.

Q: It's been now thirteen months?

A: Yes, it has been thirteen months.

Q: What was he like when you picked him up?

A: Oh, my, he was—I would be hard pressed to describe to you the state that he was in. He was so hyper and unable to do anything but just talk about it and rattle about it, what had happened, the mid-air and the ensuing investigation, and the treatment he had received upon leaving Riyadh. They kept him there a certain length of time and then they sent him to Ramstein Air Base to see somebody; I don't remember, you know, those numbers, generalish, general officer person, I think, and then he was sent on home, and he really was in a very—couldn't sleep, he couldn't eat, he couldn't—he wasn't functioning at all well.

This carried on for a long time, and we're not just talking like the day he came home, but I was, I was—when we drove back on that trip from the airport, I was really scared.

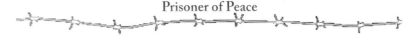

I thought, well, what's happened to him, because see, I didn't know about, you know, midair collisions and things. I was told—Colonel Croker here is the wing commander, and he telephoned me right after the—shortly—I don't know, a half a day after the accident, and he told me that Bill Bob was fine and that, at that time, it looked like he was a hero, he had brought his airplane back, and not to worry about it, and then Bill gave me a very short telephone conversation, he couldn't say anything other than just, "Don't worry about it. We're all okay, nobody got hurt. I'll be home." I, like, you know, some kind of a person that is totally out of it, kept saying, "Well, are they going to let you home by Christmas," you know, as though that were so important, and of course it wasn't. So when he got home, I was just shocked by this drastic change in his behavior.

Q: Emotionally, what has the last thirteen months been like for Bill?

A: Oh, my, he's been on an emotional roller coaster for sure. Doctor Hester told you some of that, but we had like a six months period before he was referred to Doctor Hester, and I'll tell you, this is true now, I didn't know, I travel in my job, I'm away from home sometimes, and even if I would be gone for the day, what I might be likely to find when I came home.

You see, since the Air Force is so important to him and he felt so rejected by everything, I really thought he might kill himself, and he said to me—we used to have a—we have some kind of a pistol, a .38, I think it is, because I was the first three years that we lived here, I was alone at least 50 percent of the time; he was TDY or on alert. We live way out in the country, so we have a handgun, kept in a nightstand drawer, but he began to get more suicidal, and he said to me on a couple of occasions, "You better hide that gun," and I did and it is.

Now in regard to that situation, even so, Doctor Hester told you he didn't prescribe any medication for Bill, but the flight surgeons have. They have prescribed all kinds of different things, and sometimes I think it's because they change flight surgeons here. The ones he sees now he doesn't really know, and they don't know what's happened, and they prescribe sleeping pills because he has this on-going problem of being unable to sleep. So he would have a bottle of sleeping pills and home, and also have Valium, and that was scary because I would think, when he would get on the ready down, despondent side, he could have taken those pills.

But he kept himself, he rationalized and intellectualized by reading, obsessively reading. I can't tell you how many books that he has read, marks them, has them piled all around. Everyone that comes to the house has to discuss everything. He gives people books to read. That is how he has gotten through this.

A big concern though of mine now is, you see, with it building up for so long to this trial, but now the trial is over and I don't know what will happen, but, you see, because he's identified so strongly with his Air Force life and it's ended on, you know, sort of a note where he will feel badly about it and can never look back and think it ended in any sort of a satisfactory manner, so I don't know; I'm very concerned. I think about that all the time.

Defense Mitigation Witness Hanson (Mrs)—Direct

I've been thinking about I have thought about the accident, I've thought about what we will do. It has affected every day of our lives for the past thirteen months. So what he'll do when this is over, and he may even be suicidal, I don't know, but I think it's a possibility.

Q: What kind of effect has it had on your relationship?

A: Oh, it's been strained, of course. You know, when you live with it every day as a spectator, I'm the spectator, watching this person, and the other person goes through the periods, he's way up, you know, hyper and rattling off all these things, and then he gets into the despondent part of the cycle, and he moves from the bedroom to the couch in the mornings and he lies on the couch, and he has terrible trouble with his neck and terrible trouble with his back. So I'm out working, and I come home and I see him surrounded with all this mess, and he hasn't done anything, and of course I'm crabby. You see, I don't know what will happen to us anymore, I don't know. This thing has just taken over our lives, so I'm not sure. I know that I love and respect him, and no more so than when he sat here today and told the truth about the log book because that's how he is; you know, take it, tell the truth. I didn't know about that, but I knew that when I heard that Captain Johnsen, he seemed like a very honest person, and I knew when I heard him say that, I knew that Bill I knew when I heard you say that it was against the advice of counsel, I knew he would tell the truth because that's the way he is.

Q: Is there anything else you would like to address to the court?

A: I'd like for the court to please take into consideration the fact that he has been an excellent Air Force officer for over twenty years, and that he has suffered greatly for the past thirteen months. I can look at him and see that he's aged at least ten years. Nothing is going to be the same again. I would hope that the court would take that into due consideration and please try and not be too harsh on him.

CIV DC: Thank you.

TC: No questions, Your Honor. MJ: Mrs. Hanson, you may leave the stand, you're excused.

(The witness withdrew to the spectator section at the rear of the courtroom.)

Defense Mitigation Witness Hanson (Mrs)—Direct/Excused

ADC: Your Honor, at this time the defense offers into evidence Defense Exhibit I for identification, documentary evidence consisting of character statements from retired Major General Harry Dukes, Colonel Richard Martin(Navy Captain who was on board during the mid-air collision and captain of the first nuclear powered aircraft carrier) …

MJ: I don't think you need to read all the names into the record.

ADC: All right, sir.

MJ: It will be obvious to reviewing officials.

Is there any objection to any of these statements or affidavits by the prosecution?

TC: No, Your Honor.

MJ: Defense Exhibit I is received.

ADC: At this time the defense offers into evidence Defense Exhibit J, a complete copy of Colonel Hanson's OERs.

TC: No objection.

MJ: Very well, Defense Exhibit J is received. Does the defense have anything further?

CIV DC: Only to address I would like an opportunity to address the court as to sentencing.

MJ: Well, certainly.

CIV DC: It is my preference to do this first thing in the morning.

MJ: Fine.

CIV DC: If that's convenient to the court.

MJ: I assume the prosecution has no objection to terminating for the evening and then opening with argument on sentence in the morning.

TC: No, Your Honor.

MJ: In view of the hour, I think that's reasonable. With the permission of counsel from both sides, I would like to take the documentary evidence just given to me to my room so I can review it overnight and maybe save us an hour or so in the morning. Do you have any problem with that, Mister Sanders?

Defense Exhibits I and J Offered/Admitted

CIV DC: No, Your Honor.

MJ: Major Oxley?

TC: No, Your Honor.

MJ: Fine. Anything further, gentlemen, this evening?

TC: No, Your Honor.

CIV DC: (Shook head negatively)

MJ: So basically, the defense has rested its sentencing case?

CIV DC: Yes, Your Honor.

MJ: Does the prosecution anticipate a rebuttal case?

TC: No, Your Honor.

MJ: Fine. The court's adjourned. We will reconvene at 0830.

(The court—martial adjourned at 1829 hours, 11 January 1985, and was called back to order at 0802 hours, 12 January 1985, with all parties present who were present when the court—martial adjourned on 11 January 1985.)

MJ: Before inviting argument of counsel, I don't think we've discussed what the maximum imposable punishment is. Trial counsel?

TC: The government is of the impression, Your Honor, that the maximum punishment would include dismissal, three years confinement, total forfeitures, a reprimand, and an unlimited fine.

DC: Defense agrees, Your Honor.

MJ: I concur.

Do we have any issue the defense would like to discuss regarding possible multiplicity?

DC: No, Your Honor.

MJ: Is the prosecution ready to argue?

TC: Yes, Your Honor.

MJ: Proceed.

UNITED STATES ARGUMENT ON SENTENCE

TC: Your Honor, defense counsel, there are some who haven't been in this courtroom throughout the proceedings that are of the opinion that this case has to do with a midair collision on 9 December in the air over Saudi Arabia. This court knows that none of the specifications of which Lieutenant Colonel Hanson has been found guilty relate to that occurrence.

Other people, looking at the specifications that Lieutenant Colonel Hanson has been convicted of, may hold the opinion that these specs are less than serious. As an example, so what if he didn't put his name on a flight order. It's just a piece of paper, he was clearly the commander and it was clearly appropriate for him to be on the aircraft. But that spec and others reflect that Colonel Hanson at that point in time was fast and loose with the way he attended to his responsibilities and duties, but even that is not what this case is all about. This case is about a cover-up, this case is about integrity.

Before the bench is a series of affidavits submitted by the defense which I'm confident the judge has read thoroughly. In those affidavits the words "leader" and "leadership" is repeated many times by many different individuals, and, beyond that people say the following: By Captain Gabriel, referring to Lieutenant Colonel Hanson, "He has consistently told me and other young officers that the only way of getting ahead is to do your job and be a professional." A senior master sergeant says, "If we had more Bill Hanson's to lead and follow, the U.S. Air Force would again be full of happy, dedicated and professional soldiers." A civilian, Mister Walters, says, "He, Lieutenant Colonel Hanson, was a member of the Base Community Council and did his utmost to promote an outstanding image of the Air Force in the local community." A Doctor Hess, a dentist: "I have met a large percentage of the officers stationed here," referring to Blytheville, "and only a few have impressed me as honorable as Lieutenant Colonel William Hanson."

Major Beeman: "Lieutenant Colonel Hanson is the epitome of what I tried to teach the junior officers under my command," and later in his affidavit, "He has my complete confidence as an officer and a gentleman." A Captain Carroll: "I feel that his greatest value to the squadron was his skill in developing airmanship, esprit de corps, and a professionalism among the junior officers." And lastly, Major Howell: "He's a man of honor who looks upon his commission as an oath, not a contract. I admire him for his dedication, devotion to duty, and honesty."

They don't know the Lieutenant Colonel Hanson that was revealed during the course of these proceedings. They don't know the man who made the entry in the log book retroactively, after the fact.

Now, what's significant about that log book entry? Many things, but one, if that entry was to be believed, Captain Eddie Johnsen didn't do his job. When did this information come out? The day after it had been accomplished? When it was realized that it was done under a period of emotional misgiving? No. During the numerous investigations after the mid-air collision? No. During the course of the accused's initial testimony before this court? No. only after it had been conclusively shown was the admission made. Fast and loose, and integrity, that's what this case is all about, Your Honor.

I ask the court to consider the following sentence: Concerning confinement, nominal; the government seeks nothing in excess of one month. The government seeks monetary penalties either in the nature of significant forfeitures or a large fine, and in addressing the subject of a large fine, counsel is fully aware of the judge's knowledge about the general rule of the use of fines and unjust enrichments, nevertheless, that is merely a policy or guidance and I believe that there can be exceptions to that, and this is such a case. And most importantly, and absolutely necessary, a dismissal from the United States Air Force. Officers do not jeopardize their integrity to the potential prejudice of junior officers, and

once shown to have done so, be permitted to continue to wear the Air Force uniform. That's the way it is. Thank you.

MJ: Defense.
CIV DC: Thank you, Your Honor.

DEFENSE ARGUMENT ON SENTENCE

The court has already had the opportunity to review the testimony both of the witnesses-in-chief for the defense and for the character witnesses for the defense, as well as the affidavits and Lieutenant Colonel Hanson's OER's. The only one conclusion that anyone can draw from all that information is that, with the exception of the incident at Riyadh, Lieutenant Colonel Hanson has had an exceptional career in the Air Force over the last 22 years. At least three of the witnesses, including General Pringle, in unrehearsed fashion, have indicated that it is Lieutenant Colonel Hanson that they would like to go to war with in that eventuality.

Regarding the tour at Riyadh, despite the mistakes made by him that bring us here, it should be remembered the good that he accomplished in the short period of time that he was there, a good apparently that few who preceded him were able to accomplish. I speak specifically of the water plant that Colonel Byrd indicated had been lying idle for quite some period of time, the sports facility being made available to the American troops there, renewed cooperation with the air traffic controllers, accomplishment of the F-15 refueling program for the Saudi Arabians, and also a change in the flight path to make the flights over there much safer, and yes, and finally, probably the last official act he had over there, he took control and recovered a badly damaged KC-135 when even the manufacturer thought that that would be impossible under the circumstances of the damage, not only saving a multimillion dollar aircraft, but twelve lives as well.

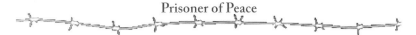
What Colonel Hanson did at Riyadh wasn't for his own benefit, it was for the benefit of the Air Force, the same type of task-oriented initiative to which he's been complimented here yesterday through the character witnesses and to which he was complimented in the OERs. As Colonel Quinn indicated, none of us are saints, whether we're officers, enlisted men or even civilians. Each of us has made mistakes and bad judgments. If we're lucky, they don't come back to haunt us the way these have Lieutenant Colonel Hanson.

Ironically, the prosecutor points out the worst mistake made by Colonel Hanson isn't anything that he was charged with, but was an entry in a log that he made some thirteen months ago halfway around the world, but it should also be remembered the physical and emotional stress that he was under at the time. Was it truly anything other than a bad decision made in circumstances of physical exhaustion and a moment of panic?

The prosecutor indicates that possibly that action should have been brought to light by Colonel Hanson sooner, but I would also like to point out to the court that, at least in my review of the previous hearings, the issue has never been raised either by the prosecution or the defense. Colonel Hanson has never testified falsely concerning that issue. He has never been asked a question under oath concerning that issue to which he has evaded.

DEFENSE ARGUMENT ON SENTENCE

I ask you to weigh these momentary bad decisions in Riyadh against the good this man has accomplished for the Air Force and for his country in the last twenty-two years. The prosecution speaks for a need for integrity in the officer corps. That's not just a military trait, that's a human trait, and it's not just based upon one incident, it develops as a trait of an individual over a period of time. What is a truer measure of the integrity of Lieutenant Colonel Hanson than a momentary failing under stress in Riyadh or the fact that, against the advice of counsel, he would get back on the stand, knowing the damage to his own case-in—chief, rather than to allow a possible interpretation that Captain Johnsen was testifying falsely to cover his own mistakes?

You don't have to be in the military to appreciate the human tragedy of this particular case, a lieutenant colonel with an exemplary career, two tours of combat, twenty-two years of service covering his entire adult life, and that career, that first love as his wife has indicated, has now been irretrievably damaged.

Despite the testimony of Colonel Kowalski and Lieutenant Colonel Quinn, conventional wisdom would dictate that Colonel Hanson's career in the military is over. It's kind of like Hurnpty-Dumpty, Your Honor, all the pieces cannot be put back together again. No matter what the sentence of this court, he's lost his first love. As Doctor Hester has indicated, that's his self-esteem, that's his self-worth, that's his social structure. He's lost everything, perhaps only saving his family.

In the past thirteen months he has suffered isolation from that social structure. He has endured stress, recounted by Doctor Hester and by his wife, extreme stress. It's been thirteen months, I believe as Doctor Hester has indicated, of hell.

Considering all these factors, and the career of Colonel Hanson, justice neither indicates confinement nor does it indicate that he should be forced to lose all the benefits he has earned over that honorable career in service of his country. To strip him of those benefits based upon a momentary failing in Riyadh would be the cruelest punishment of all. Thank you, Your Honor.

MJ: Closing by the United States?
TC: Waive.
MJ: The court is closed to deliberate on sentence.
      (The court—martial closed at 0821 hours, 12 January 1985, and was called back to order at 0845 hours, 12 January 1985, with all parties present who were present when the court-martial closed.)

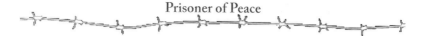
MJ: Before announcing my sentence, I have a couple of matters I'm going to put on the record, some comments for you, Colonel Hanson. I'm in my sixth year as a judge. I've sentenced a number of folks, I've sentenced a number of officers. When I came here, I knew this case was going to be a meat grinder, and it was. I can honestly say it's the hardest sentencing case I've ever considered. When we initially came to trial, I observed you to be a poised, confident, smiling, almost brash officer. In the last day and a half, I've seen you sit there in a semi-fetal position, shamed, a shell of what I saw initially, tearful, obviously concerned.

In sentencing an officer, your options are somewhat limited because you don't have available to you sentencing matters such as reduction in grade, et cetera. One of the things I had to give serious consideration to was whether or not you should be confined. After observing you throughout the trial, and hearing your wife's testimony about your shame in the community, your isolation, I determined that confinement was unnecessary. I think you've punished yourself sufficiently. The really difficult question was whether or not you should be dismissed. After reviewing all the affidavits and statements, your OERs, I determined that dismissal, in view of your record of leadership, the fact that you have taken an up-front position repeatedly, been credited for your leadership throughout your career, dismissal would be inappropriate based on your record. I also considered a reprimand, but I looked at your last OER and I determined that was reprimand enough. What I'm saying is, you've had a wonderful career. I consider your actions in Saudi Arabia to be an aberration; to be but isolated incidents. The accused counsel will please rise for the announcement of sentence.

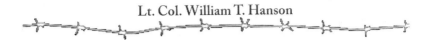

SENTENCE

MJ: Lieutenant Colonel William T. Hanson, this court-martial sentences you to forfeit five hundred dollars of your pay per month for twelve months, and to pay to the United States a fine of 2,500 dollars.

CHAPTER 21

As I left the courtroom that morning, there were numerous television reporters outside the building waiting to talk with me. I avoided them by leaving through a side door. Had they had any real interest in my case other than sensationalizing it, they would have attended the trial. I had nothing further to say to them. Had I had anything to say, I would probably have quoted one of my favorite authors, William Makepeace Thackeray from his epic novel *Vanity Fair* in which he concluded, "This has been a novel without a hero. Vanitas Vanitatum." Nobody really won. Everyone lost something. Thackeray's middle name about says it all—make peace.

Over the last twenty-six years, no one has ever asked me how I would have handled this whole tragic mess. I am confident that I would have said something like this had I been either the SAC Commander or the president of the US: "Colonel Hanson, you did one hell of a job bringing that tanker back and helping save all those lives and the aircraft. Never mind that it cost us a few bucks to have it repaired. Now get back over there and finish your job, with one small caveat—in the future try to be a little more cognizant of the rules and regulations. I have directed them to remove that last Officer Effectiveness Report and consider promoting you to full colonel. Have a nice day."—— The President of the United States. Commander in Chief of the Armed Forces of the United States of America.

That would have seemed to be the way to handle this situation rather than spending millions of tax payers' dollars just to prove the point that generals have lots of power. No medals, no hoopla, just common sense and some responsible leadership. That, I think, is the difference between now and then.

A few months after my court-martial, Lt. Gen. Campbell, along with Generals Davis (SAC commander) and Creech (TAC commander) all retired. Some folks say that General Campbell's decision to ignore the recommendations of the Article 32 President to, in effect, recommend a *no bill* finding resulted in Generals Davis and Campbell being asked to retire.. I'd like to think that their treatment of me and my family might have had something to do with their retirement. I know revenge is not a particularly Christian virtue, but it is normal sometimes. There is an old axiom that states, "Sometimes God uses the weak to confound the mighty." A former flying buddy of mine who is now a judge in Dallas, Texas told me that the government doesn't care how much trials cost nor do they particularly care whether they win or lose. Henry M. Wade, Jr. said "They'd like to win, but it's not their money, so what do they care?" It is a sad and sobering truth.

Not so long ago, my oldest daughter Michael gave me a bumper sticker which I put on the front of my guitar. The sticker reads "When words fail, the music speaks." So let's let my music speak. Several years ago, perhaps fifteen, I wrote a song called "The Day I Was Baptized." That song pretty much sums up how this sinful piece of clay was transformed into gold momentarily having gone through the fire storm that was my trial. The scariest and most bewildering part for me was, and is, what does one who has been made brand new do now?

I think that's when my bipolarity and/or PTSD kicked in. It wasn't Vietnam. I wasn't the midair collision per se. It was the enormous pressure of dealing with the awesome power unleashed against me following the crash. It was the crash landing of a rank conspiracy that set me into a tailspin that has lasted for the better part of twenty-six years. In undergraduate pilot training, we were taught how to recover from various spins. First, you neutralize the stick and rudder, then determine the direction of rotation, pull the stick full aft and hold, immediately apply full opposite rudder, one turn later abruptly push the stick full forward and hold until the nose pitches down; then recover from the ensuing dive. In civilian life there's no such procedure; well, actually there is.

Immediately after my trial ended and the verdict was announced, my civilian Jewish attorney, Dave Sanders from Livermore Falls, Maine, said, "Maybe there is such a thing as divine intervention." Please recall that I took the witness stand a second time against the advice of all three of my lawyers. Mister Sanders, the Smart New York Jew, as my cousin called him, seemed to become a believer, if only for a short while.

It was another Smart Jew who taught me how to recover from my bipolar/PTSD spin. I think he stole the idea from my departed father who used to manage the Dixfield Dixies men's baseball team. From the third base coach's box everyone could hear my father yell, "You got the green light! Keep your eyes on me at all times!" Please allow me to borrow one more Jewish phrase, the one they coined after the Holocaust: "Never again!"

Now, after having had my *real* day in court, I guess it's time to forgive them and move on with what's left of my life, but I sure as hell will never forget them and what they did to me and my family. I sure wish I could get Jesus back on the line for just a second. I'd ask him about forgiving the diabolical ones. If I was, in fact, up against a form of evil, am I obliged to forgive them? I shall end this book by sharing with you that the love shown to me from my defense witnesses was incredibly disarming to me. I was not deserving of such an outpouring of so much affection. One can usually muster up enough courage to confront one's enemies, but such unconditional love cannot be defended against. Such was the case with me during the latter portion of my trial. I could not hold all the love in. It came out of me and rolled down my face like a river. It's the same with God's love for each of us. It's a gift of grace. I am paraphrasing from a character in the movie *Saving Private Ryan* who said, *"Lord, please help me to try and become worthy of such love."* I truly loved my job in the Air Force. I truly loved the airmen with whom I served. I still love my country and it's still worth serving. I don't think my prosecutors ever really got that. I hate that I helped kill so many people and helped destroy so much territory. I am still so sad that so many of my friends were killed in Vietnam, and subsequent wars. I pray daily that we can find a way to live in peace. I so want to be a peace maker, a loving man of God. I doubt that most of my flying buddies were as naïve as I. When I think back on how much money, time and effort were spent on me and my friends to teach us to fly such awesome instruments of power and destruction, I am truly amazed. What trust the people put in us to turn us loose in the skies to defend and protect our country and the ideals we hold so dear. First among these ideals is justice. If I could reduce justice to its lowest common denominator, I would use my mother's simple interpretation, namely decency. I might add one more attribute to my dear mother's definition of what it means to be a Hanson: 1) To be honest, 2) To be hard working, 3) To have a great sense of humor, and, 4) To be a decent human being. A very close friend of mine recently informed me that the so-called *Hanson* virtues are also the virtues of most Mainers. There used to be a saying in politics that *As Maine Goes, So goes The Nation.* Maybe it can be that way again? May decency and peace kiss. I am still awestruck to think that people can take an oath with their hand on the Bible and blatantly lie. How utterly naïve I was. I hope and pray that I can stay that way. As I was leaving Blytheville AFB in Arkansas for the last time on June 30, 1985, I stopped by the wing commander's office. He was standing on the stairs in front of Wing Headquarters. I walked up to him, saluted, and then gently tugged on his uniform shirt lapel , and whispered in his ear, "Jesus forgave them because he said they didn't know what they were doing. I suppose he would insist on my forgiving you guys too, even though you knew exactly what you were doing

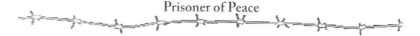

every step of the way." But I told him, "Don't ever do it again, at least not to me or my family." I think he believed me. Any further comments would be *de minimis*.

I will let my music bring this story to a close. As I said in my commissioning oath, "I swear to uphold the Constitution against all enemies, foreign and domestic, so help me God." I was, and I still am, a man of peace. My wife died in September, 2008 of an agonizing bout with cancer. During the last few months every exhalation was one of agony. She was dying in her own Garden of Gethsemane. Only moments before she died, she raised her head up using all her will and whispered in my ear: *"You're a good man, Tim."* I will accept her verdict even if the United States Air Force couldn't.

AN OLD AIR FORCE FLY BOY

(Words and music by Wm. T. Hanson)
copyright 2011

He's just and old Air Force fly boy, been flyin' too high in the jet
He's just an old Air Force fly boy and he's tryin' like hell to forget
Well, he's been to the wall in Washington and he went to the wall
    in Nam
And now he's back home where he lives all alone and sometimes
    he don't give a damn

So he went back to Texas in an old pickup truck He went back
    to Texas
He went back to Texas 'cause he was down on his luck
He looked inside his pickup on the floor And he saw his life by
    the door

He saw Budwiser beer cans, an empty pack of smokes
He saw a week old *Play Boy*; it was full of dirty jokes
He saw an empty cup of coffee; his future's in that cup
He went back to Texas, turned his radio up

(narration)

as he was drivin' out of Calais, Maine, goin' south down Route
1 he came to the Indian reservation at Pleasant Point in Perry,
Maine. He heard ninety-three-year-old Margaret Nicholas
(the oldest lady on the reservation) singin' this song…

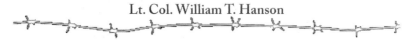

You gave us a home, no buffalo roamin',
no deer and no antelope playin'
Sometimes at night when the stars are just
right you can hear her out there prayin'

Our Father who art in heaven what's the world comin' to
Half the time she don't know what she's sayin',
and who's gonna take all the credit
Our Father who art in heaven what's the world comin' to
Half the time she don't know what she's sayin'
and who's gonna take all the blame...
Lord, who's gonna take all the blame

I Never Cared That Much For Me

(Words and music by Wm.T. Hanson)
copyright 2011

I was standin' in the bathroom, I was shavin'
Thinkin' back to when I was a kid
I remembered my shock when a girl from down the block
Shouted out the F word, that just wasn't somethin' good girls did

I tapped my razor gently on the sink
And watched the hair go spinnin' down the drain
Then I wondered where all the wrinkles came from
And the tears started fallin' just like rain

CHORUS

I've always like Elvis Pressley's songs and
"Great Balls of Fire" by Jerry Lee
I've always loved Jesus and I will till all hell freezes
But I was never really sold that much on me

16 BAR INSTRUMENTAL

I remembered what my mother tried to teach me
About how to be just an average kid
And then I went to war, can't remember what for
I guess it's just somethin' young kids did

Then I back away slowly from the mirror
After splashin' some cold water on my face
And I thought I heard Ma call me from the grave yard
She said, "son, welcome back home to this place,"

CHORUS

And I've always loved Jesus and I will till all hell freezes
No, I was never really sold that much on me
No, I was never really sold that much on me.

To hear these and other songs simply google DreamCorral.com.

"God is faithful and will not let you be tried beyond your strength; but with the trial he will also provide a way out, so that you may be able to bear it." 1 Corinthians 10:13 KJV. He did it for me. He will do it for you.